d Beyond

Contents

Carlo Carretto

The Desert and Beyond

Letters from the Desert
In Search of the Beyond
Love is for Living

Darton, Longman and Todd
London

ished in 1987 by
nd Todd Ltd
ondon SW6 1UD

ers from the Desert:
hed in Great Britain in 1972 by
arton, Longman and Todd Ltd
Originally published by
La Scuola Editrice, Brescia 1964
© 1972 Orbis Books
Maryknoll, New York 10545

In Search of the Beyond:
first published in Great Britain in 1975 by
Darton, Longman and Todd Ltd
Originally published as *Al di la delle Cose* by
Cittadella Editrice, Assisi, Italy
This translation © 1975 Darton, Longman and Todd

Love is for Living:
first published in Great Britain in 1976 by
Darton, Longman and Todd Ltd
Originally published as *Ciò che conta è amare* by
Editrice A. V. E. Rome
Translated from the Italian by Jeremy Moiser
This translation © 1976 Darton, Longman and Todd

This collected edition © 1987 Darton, Longman and Todd

The biblical quotations in *In Search of the Beyond*
and *Love is for Living* are taken from *The Jerusalem Bible*
© 1966 Darton, Longman and Todd and Doubleday & Co. Inc.

ISBN 0 232 51728 2

British Library Cataloguing in Publication Data

Caretto, Carlo
The desert and beyond.
1. Catholic Church — Prayer books and devotions
I. Title II. Caretto, Carlo [Letters dal deserto. *English*] Letters from the desert III. Caretto, Carlo [Al di la della cose. *English*] In search of the beyond IV. Caretto, Carlo [Ciò che conta è amare. *English*] Love is for living
242 BX2177

ISBN 0-232-51728-2

Printed and bound in Great Britain by
Anchor Brendon Ltd, Tiptree, Essex

The Desert an[illegible]

Publisher's Note

Since the publication in 1972 of *Letters from the Desert,* Carlo Carretto has become one of the most popular spiritual writers of today. We have chosen to make available, in one volume, three of his most important early works in order to help readers familiar with Brother Carlo's writing to assess the achievement of his early books and to provide for new readers a volume of exciting and adventurous spiritual reading.

Carlo Carretto

Letters from the Desert

Contents

Foreword

My friend Carlo Carretto has asked me to introduce him to the American and English readers of these pages, which were written originally for his European friends. I find it as embarrassing to speak about a friendship which matured in the desert as I find it presumptuous to comment on meditations as personal as these. Allow me therefore to acquit my duty of friendship by telling you how I myself met Carlo.

It was October, 1959, shortly after General Massu had taken command of Algeria. Towards noon I finally reached the market place of Tamanrassett, deep in the Sahara. I was looking for the house of the Little Brothers, the religious community established here fifty years before by Charles de Foucauld. I was unable to speak a word of Arabic, and no French word I tried elicited a reaction: not "La Fraternité" nor "Le Père de Foucauld" nor

"Eglise." So I tried again: "Le Pere *Charles* de Foucauld?" Immediately a bunch of youngsters began to shout, "Frére Carlo, Frére Carlo." They grabbed my bag, charged across the road and led me to the shoemaker's shop.

It took some time to realize who it was that earned his living by cutting up old tires and making indestructible sandals. It was Carretto. It was the same Carretto whom I had last known when he held a key post in Italian "Catholic Action," at a time when this church organization played a frequently sinister role in anti-communist politics under Pius XII.

For years I had tried not to think about Carretto, since I feared that by now he would be even more powerful as one of those lay or clerical churchmen who dominate Christian Democratic politics in Italy.

Indeed, it was Carretto, who had now become Brother Carlo to children and cripples and pilgrims at the tomb of de Foucauld.

Carlo hobbled out of his shop to lead me to the chapel in the adobe fort in which de Foucauld has been murdered: Foucauld the gourmet turned ascetic, the officer turned monk, the monk turned priest and hermit. The French nobleman had wanted to live here as poor and powerless as the least of the natives; he had died here because he had been asked to guard sixteen French rifles. On the way to the chapel Carlo stopped in front of a tombstone put up by the French Army:

Le Vicomte de Foucauld
Frére Charles de Jesus
Mort pour la France.

The words haunted me while I crouched beside Carlo in the deep sand and peace of the chapel. In Algeria, France meant empire, even at the cost of torture. In Algeria, to be a priest meant (with very few exceptions) to be chaplain to French colonials and soldiers. In Algeria, to be a Christian meant either to make the ideology of "peace" a reason for withdrawal or—for a very, very few—a reason for joining the underground. And here, in Algeria, I had to read, "He died for France." Carlo must have noticed what went on in me. When we left the chapel he pointed to the tombstone and simply said, "If you want to live like Jesus you must accept being misunderstood like him. He too dies for the people—and it was the High Priest of the Jews who said so."

I came to know Carlo: this man who was dying to the world of power, the world of good causes, the world of big words and world of political parties. I came to experience the naked simplicity in the statements of his love for the Lord. I came to marvel at his lack of embarrassment at being judged childish when he said something true: his unconcern when he was judged escapist because he refused to be militant.

I first lived as his guest in Tamanrassett. Later, he installed me in a cave below the peak of Asekrem, two days, as the donkey trots, from his shop. He had furnished the cave with a bed of stone and protected it from the icy winds which blow without cease at several thousand feet in the Ahaggar mountains.

We became friends. When he came to visit me he told me stories. Remembering them I always felt that outside the desert they would sound out of place. The immensity of the desert overwhelms both the power and weakness of men. The Muslim shepherd's song envelops the Franciscan tenderness of Italian in the austerity of unambiguous faith. The emptiness of the desert makes it possible to learn the almost impossible: the joyful acceptance of our uselessness. I fear that outside this context and not knowing Carlo in person, many readers will have to make a great effort to learn from Carlo what he taught me.

But I do hope that at least some readers of these pages in English will do so on a day of complete silence—to which they rarely treat themselves—or, more often, to which they are condemned. I hope they will open this book in an Anglo-American desert: a lonely flat in Watts or Kensington, the ward of a hospital, in an asylum or prison cell, or on a commuter train.

Ivan Illich   Cuernavaca, Mexico

Publisher's Preface

We are pleased to present Carlo Carretto to a new readership. What he has to say is at once simple and profound—simple enough to seem almost banal, profound enough to involve the labor of a lifetime if one were to follow Brother Carlo into the desert, not, of course, 'the desert' as a geophysical fact but as a part of the landscape of the spirit.

Letters From the Desert was written, in the form of a diary-epistle, to the many friends whom Carlo Carretto had made during his twenty years as a leader of both Italian youth movements and Catholic Action in the tense years before and after the Second World War.

The book was an immediate success upon its publication in Italy, and is now in its eighteenth printing. But so much has happened in the Church in the eight years between the initial appearance of *Lettere dal Deserto* and this English-language edition that we were at first tempted to request the author to "update" and modify what he had written in solitude less than a decade before.

After much consideration, we did not make that request. We had come to believe that the type of spirituality Carlo Carretto lives and writes about is perhaps more relevant, more needed now than it was in the seemingly serene pre-Conciliar Church.

Some readers may well regard this type of spirituality as 'old fashioned.' Others, more discerning perhaps, will see in *Letters From the Desert* a man who presents in himself the deceptively simple and timeless message of the Gospels.

Introduction

God's call is mysterious; it comes in the darkness of faith. It is so fine, so subtle, that it is only with the deepest silence within us that we can hear it.

And yet nothing is so decisive and overpowering for a man on this earth, nothing surer or stronger.

This call is uninterrupted: God is always calling us! But there are distinctive moments in this call of his, moments which leave a permanent mark on us—moments which we never forget.

Three times in my life I have been aware of this call.

The first one brought about my conversion when I was eighteen years old. I was a schoolteacher in a country village.

In Lent a mission came to the town. I attended it but what I remember most of all was how boring and outdated the sermons were. It certainly wasn't the words which shook my state of apathy and sin. But when I knelt before an old missionary—I remember how direct his look was and how simple—I was aware that God was moving in the silence of my soul.

From that day on I knew I was a Christian, and was aware that a completely new life had been opened up for me.

The second time, when I was twenty-three, I was thinking of getting married. It never occurred to me that I should do anything else.

I met a doctor who spoke to me of the Church and of the beauty of serving her with one's whole being, while remaining in the world. I do not know what happened at that time nor how it happened; the fact is that I was praying in an empty church where I had gone to escape from my state of inner confusion. I heard the same voice that I had heard during my confession with the old missionary. "Marriage is not for you. You will offer your life to me. I shall be your Lover for ever."

I had no difficulty in giving up the idea of getting married and consecrating myself to God because everything within me was changed. It would have seemed incongruous to me, falling in love with a girl, for God engaged my whole life.

Those years were full of work, of aspirations, of meeting different people, and of wild dreams. Even the mistakes—and there were many—were caused by the fact that so much within me was still unpurified.

Many years passed; and many times I was amazed to find myself praying to hear once more the sound of that voice which had had so great an importance for me.

Then, when I was forty-four years old, there occurred the most serious call of my life: the call to the contemplative life. I experienced it deeply—in the depth which only faith can provide and where darkness is absolute—where human strength can no longer help.

This time I had to say 'yes' without understanding a thing. "Leave everything and come with me into the desert. It is not your acts and deeds that I want; I want your prayer, your love."

Some people, seeing me leave for Africa, thought that I must have had some personal crisis, some disappointment. Nothing is further from the truth. By nature I am optimistic, my orientation is one of hope; and I don't know the meaning of discouragement and it would never occur to me to 'give up the fight' in this way.

No, it was the decisive call. And I never understood it so deeply as on that evening at the Vespers of St. Charles in 1954, when I said 'yes' to the voice.

"Come with me into the desert." There is something much greater than human action: prayer; and it has a power much stronger than the words of men: love.

And I went into the desert.

Without having read the constitutions of the Little Brothers of Jesus I entered their congregation. Without knowing Charles de Foucauld I began to follow him.

For me it was enough to have heard the voice say to me, "This is the way for you."

Wandering among the desert tracks with the Little Brothers I discovered how real that way was. By following Charles de Foucauld, I was convinced that it was the way for me.

God had already told me that in faith.

When I reached El Abiod Sidi Seik for the novitiate, my novice master told me with the perfect calm of a man who had lived twenty years in the desert: *"It faut faire une coupure, Carlo."* I knew what kind of cutting he was talking about and decided to make the wrench, even if it were painful.

In my bag I had kept a thick notebook, containing the addresses of my old friends: there were thousands of them. In his goodness God had never left me without the joys of friendship.

If there was one thing I really regretted when I left for Africa, it was not being able to speak to each one of them, to explain the reason for my abandoning them, to say that I was obeying a call from God and that, even if in a different way, I would continue to fight on with them to work for the Kingdom.

But it was necessary to make the "cut" and it demanded courage and great faith in God.

I took the address book, which for me was the last tie with the past, and burnt it behind a dune during a day's retreat.

I can still see the black ashes of the notebook being swept away into the distance by the wind of the Sahara.

But burning an address is not the same thing as destroying a friendship, for that I never intended to do; on the contrary, I have never loved nor prayed so much for my old friends as in the solitude of the desert. I saw their faces, I felt their problems, their sufferings, sharpened by the distance between us.

For me they had become a flock which would always belong to me and which I must lead daily to the fountains of prayer.

Sometimes I almost felt their physical presence when, for example, I entered the Arab-style church at El-Abiod or, later, the famous hermitage constructed by Fr. Charles de Foucauld himself at Tamanrasset.

Prayer had become the most important thing. But it was still the hardest part of my daily life. Through my vocation to prayer I learned what is meant by "carrying other people" in our prayer.

So, after many years I can say that I have remained true to my vocation, and at the same time I am completely convinced that one never wastes one's time by praying; there is no more helpful way of helping those we love.

The address book is mine no longer, but this is of no importance because there are other ways of reaching one's friends.

And so I'd like to make an appointment with you in one of the many wonderful corners of the Sahara towards evening at sunset.

Here there would be no need for torches, for the sky is so clear with stars.

We'd sit down on the sand and through the night we'd tell each other the story of these past years of our lives, of the stages we'd reached, and the trials we'd undergone. I think that the morning star would find us still talking.

For my part, in these "Letters from the Desert," I've tried to jot down the things I should say if such an opportunity were given me, and which of course represent part of myself.

Nothing systematic, nothing important. A few ideas matured in solitude and taking shape around an activity which has been, without any doubt, the greatest gift that the Sahara has given me: prayer.

Carlo Carretto

1.

Under the great rock

The track, white in the sun, unwound ahead of me in a vague outline. The furrows in the sand made by the wheels of the great oil trucks forced me to keep alert every second, if I was to keep the jeep on the move.

The sun was high in the sky, and I felt tired. Only the wind blowing on the hood of the car allowed the jeep to continue, although the temperature was like hell-fire and the water was boiling in the radiator. Every now and then I fixed my gaze on the horizon. I knew that in the area there were great blocks of granite embedded in the sand: they provided highly desirable sources of shade under which to pitch camp and wait the evening before proceeding with the journey.

In fact, towards mid-day, I found what I was looking for. Great rocks appeared on the left of the track. I approached, in the hope that I would find a little shade. I was not disappointed. On the north wall of the thirty foot high slab of stone, a knife of shade was thrown on to the red sand. I pulled the jeep against the wind to cool the engine and unloaded the *ghess,* the necessary equipment for pitching camp: a bag of food, two blankets, and a tripod for the fire.

But approaching the rock I realised that in the shade there were some guests already there: two snakes were curled up in the warm sand, watching me motionlessly. I leapt backwards and retreated to the jeep without taking my eyes off the two serpents. I took the gun, an old contraption lent me by a native who used it to get rid of the jackals which, urged on by hunger and thirst, used to attack his flocks.

I loaded the gun, drew back a bit and took aim in order to try to hit the two snakes together, so as not to waste another bullet.

I fired, and saw the two beasts leap into the air in a cloud of sand. When I was cleaning up the blood and the remains of the snakes I saw, coming out of the mangled entrials of one of them, a bird he hadn't had time to digest. I spread out the mat. In the desert it is everything: chapel, dining-room, bedroom, drawing-room. It was the hour of Sext. I sat down, took out my breviary, and recited a few Psalms, but I had to force myself because I was so tired. Besides, every now and then the wind blew fragments of the two vipers I had killed onto the verses I was reading. Warm sultry air was coming from the south and my head ached. I got up. I calculated how much water I had to last me until I reached the well of Tit, and decided to sacrifice a little. From the goatskin gourd I drew a basinful of two pints and poured it on my head. The water soaked into my turban, ran down my neck and on to my clothes. The wind did the rest. From 115° the temperature descended in a few minutes to 80°. With that sense of refreshment I stretched out on the sand to sleep; in the desert you take your siesta before your meal.

In order to lie more comfortably I looked for a blanket to put under my head. I had two. One remained by my side unused, and as I looked at it I could not feel at ease.

But to understand you must hear my story.

The evening before I had passed through Irafog, a small village of Negroes, ex-slaves of the Tuareg. As usual when one reaches a village the people ran out to crowd round the jeep, either from curiosity, or to obtain the various things which desert-travellers bring with them: they may bring a little tea, distribute medicines or hand over letters.

That evening I had seen old Kada trembling

with cold. It seems strange to speak of cold in the desert, but it is so; in fact the Sahara is often called 'a cold country where it is very hot in the sun.' The sun had gone down, and Kada was shivering. I had the idea of giving him one of the blankets I had with me, an essential part of my *ghess;* but I put the thought out of my mind. I thought of the night and I knew that I, too, would shiver. The little charity that was in me made me think again, though reasoning that my skin wasn't worth more than his and that I had best give him one of the blankets. Even if I shivered a little that was the least a Little Brother could do.

When I left the village the blankets were still on the jeep; and now they were giving me a bad conscience.

I tried to get to sleep with my feet resting on the great rock, but I couldn't manage it. I remembered that a month ago a Tuareg in the middle of his siesta had been crushed by a falling slab. I got up to make sure how stable the boulder was; I saw that it was a little off-balance, but not enough to be dangerous.

I lay down again on the sand. If I see to tell you what I dreamed of you would find it strange. The funny thing is that I dreamed that I was asleep under the great boulder and that at a given moment—it didn't seem to be a dream at all: I saw the rock moving, and I felt the boulder fall on top of me. What a nightmare! I felt my bones grating and I found myself dead. No, alive, but with my body crushed under the stone. I was amazed that not a bone hurt; but I could not move. I opened my eyes and saw Kada shivering in front of me at Irafog. I didn't hesitate for a minute to give him the blanket, especially as it was lying unused behind me, a yard away. I tried to stretch out my hand to offer it to him; but the stone made even the smallest movement impossible. I understood what purgatory was and that the suffering of the soul was "no longer to have the possibility of doing what before one could and should have done." Who knows for how many years afterwards I would be haunted by seeing that blanket near me as a witness to my selfishness and to the fact that I was too immature to enter the Kingdom of Love.

I tried to think of how long I was to remain under the rock. The reply was given me by the catechism: "Until you are capable of an act of perfect love." At that moment I felt quite incapable.

The perfect act of love is Jesus going up to Calvary to die for us all. As a member of his Mystical Body I was being asked to show if I was close enough to that perfect love to follow my master to Calvary for the salvation of my brethren. The presence of the blanket denied to Kada the evening before told me that I had still a long way to go. If I were capable of passing by a brother who was shivering with cold, how should I be capable of dying for him in imitation of Jesus who died for us all? In this way I understood that I was lost, and that if somebody had not come to my aid, I should have lain there, aeon after aeon, without being able to move.

I looked away and realised that all those great rocks in the desert were nothing more than the tombs of other men. They too, judged according to their ability to love and found cold, were there to await him who once said, "I shall raise you up on the last day."

2.

You will be judged by love

Even now I could not tell you if the episode of the great rock were a dream, let alone what kind of dream. Its influence upon me has been so strong, my attitude towards things so changed by it, that I have never been able to describe it as what we commonly have in mind when we say upon waking, 'I have had a dream.'

No, for me that tract of desert between Tit and Silet is still the place of my purgatory, where I was forced to meditate seriously about the ways of God and where I shall probably ask to go after death to continue my expiation, if in life I have not been capable of performing an act of perfect love.

There is the great stone under the blinding sun of the Sahara, the slit of shade on the warm sand, the land up to the horizon furrowed with the marks of the oil trucks and the geologists' jeeps.

'You will be judged according to your ability to love' this place reminds me insistently. And my eyes, burnt by the sun, gaze up into the cloudless sky.

I don't want to deceive myself any more; indeed I am not able to. The truth is that I did not give my blanket to Kada, for fear of the cold night. And that means that I love my own skin more than my brother's, while God's commandment tells me: 'Love the life of others as you love your own.'

And even that belongs to the Old Testament, to God's first revelation to man: 'Love God above all things, and your neighbour as yourself' (Leviticus 19:18).

It's when we come to the New Testament and the revelation of Jesus that things get more complicated. 'Love one another. Just as I have loved you, you must also love one another' (John 13:34).

As I have loved you. This is not only to give up the blanket, but life itself. The perfect act of love consists in being ready to do what Jesus did: he died for Kada, for me, for everybody. Seen in this way, heaven is that place where everyone must be so mature in love as to offer his life for all others. It is love which is universal, and lies at the heart of things; where every vestige of hate, resentment and selfishness has been destroyed by this love and cast into its fire.

And so, after the vision of the great rock,

I expect my purgatory to be long, terribly long, perhaps as long as the geological eras. This sand which I am touching with my hands and which is running through my fingers, belongs to the 'first era.' Any geologist will tell me that it is 350 million years old.The great reptiles that inhabited these regions, whose remains I have seen in Sahara ditches, belong to the second era: 130 million years ago. Those camels which carry the salt of the Niger and are passing in front of me in long well-ordered caravans have their ancestors in the distant third period: 70 million years ago. And man, at once so tiny and so great, how slowly he advances upon the remains of the animals which have preceded him. He is of the fourth era, of yesterday: 500,000 years ago.

God does not hurry over things; time is his, not mine. And I, little creature, man, have been called to be transformed into God by sharing his life. And what transforms me is the charity which he pours into my heart.

Love transforms me slowly into God.

But sin is still there, resisting this transformation, knowing how to, and actually saying 'no' to love.

Living in our selfishness means stopping at human limits and preventing our transformation into Divine Love. And until I am transformed, sharing the life of God, through love, I shall be of 'this earth' and not of 'that heaven.' Baptism has raised me to the supernatural state, but we must grow in this state, and the purpose of life is precisely that growth. And charity, or rather God's love, is what transforms us.

To have resisted love, not to have been capable of accepting the demand of this love which said to me, 'Give the blanket to your brother,' is so serious that it creates an obstacle between me and God and this is my purgatory.

What's the use of saying the Divine Office well, of sharing the Eucharist, if one is not impelled by love?

What's the use of giving up everything and coming here to the desert and the heat, if only to resist love?

What's the good of defending the truth, fighting over dogmas with the theologians, getting shocked at those who haven't the same faith and then living purgatory for geological epochs?

'You will be judged according to your ability to love,' says the great stone under which I spent my purgatory waiting for perfect love to grow within myself, that which Jesus brought to earth for me, and gave me at the price of his blood, shot through with the great cry of hope, 'I shall raise you up at the last day' (John 6:40).

May that day be not far off.

3.
You are nothing

The great joy of the Saharan novitiate is the solitude, and the joy of solitude—silence, true silence, which penetrates everywhere and invades one's whole being, speaking to the soul with wonderful new strength unknown to men to whom this silence means nothing.

Here, living in perpetual silence, one learns to distinguish its different shades: silence of the church, silence in one's cell, silence at work, interior silence, silence of the soul, God's silence.

To learn to live these silences, the novice-master lets us go away for a few days' 'desert.'

A hamper of bread, a few dates, some water, the Bible. A day's march: a cave.

A priest celebrates Mass; then goes away, leaving in the cave, on an altar of stones, the

Eucharist. Thus, for a week one remains alone with the Eucharist exposed day and night. Silence in the desert, silence in the cave, silence in the Eucharist. No prayer is so difficult as the adoration of the Eucharist. One's whole natural strength rebels against it.

One would prefer to carry stones in the sun. The senses, memory, imagination, all are repressed. Faith alone triumphs, and faith is hard, dark, stark.

To place oneself before what seems to be bread and to say, 'Christ is there living and true,' is pure faith.

But nothing is more nourishing than pure faith, and prayer in faith is real prayer.

"There's no pleasure in adoring the Eucharist," one novice used to say to me. But it is precisely this renunciation of all desire to satisfy the senses that makes prayer strong and real. One meets God beyond the senses, beyond the imagination, beyond nature.

This is crucial: as long as we pray only when and how we want to, our life of prayer is bound to be unreal. It will run in fits and starts. The slightest upset—even a toothache—will be enough to destroy the whole edifice of our prayer-life.

"You must strip your prayers," the novice-master told me. You must simplify, deintellectualise. Put yourself in front of Jesus as a poor man: not with any big ideas, but with living faith. Remain motionless in an act of love before the Father. Don't try to reach God with your understanding; that is impossible. Reach him in love; that is possible.

The struggle is not easy, because nature will try to get back her own, get her dose of enjoyment; but union with Christ Crucified is something quite different.

After some hours—or some days—of this exercise, the body relaxes. As the will refuses to let it have its own way it gives up the struggle. It becomes passive. The senses go to sleep. Or rather, as St. John of the Cross says, the night of senses is beginning. Then prayer becomes something serious, even if it is painful and dry. So serious that one can no longer do without it. The soul begins to share the redemptive work of Jesus.

Kneeling down on the sand before the simple monstrance which contained Jesus, I used to think of the evils of the world: hate, violence, depravity, impurity, egoism, betrayal, idolatry. Around me the cave had become as large as the world, and inwardly I contemplated Jesus oppressed under the weight of so much wickedness.

Is not the Host in its own form like bread

crushed, pounded, baked? And does it not contain the Man of Sorrows, Christ the Victim, the Lamb slain for our sins?

And what was my relationship to him?

For many years I had thought I was 'somebody' in the Church. I had even imagined this sacred living structure of the Church as a temple sustained by many columns, large and small, each one with the shoulder of a Christian under it.

My own shoulder too I thought of as supporting a column, however small.

Through repeating that God needed men and the Church needed activists, we believed it.

The structure was a burden on our shoulders.

After creating the world, God went away to rest; with the Church founded, Christ had disappeared into heaven. All the work remained for us, the Church. We, above all those in Catholic Action, were the real workers, who bore the weight of the day.

With this mentality I was no longer capable to taking a holiday; even during the night I felt I was "in action." There was never enough time to get everything done. One raced continually from one project to another, from one meeting to another, from one city to another. Prayer was hurried, conversations frenzied, and one's heart in a turmoil.

As everything depended on us, and everything was going so badly, we were quite right to be worried.

But who noticed that? So convinced were we that the path of action was right, was true.

Even from childhood we began with the motto: "Be first in everything for the honour of Christ the King"; then, as teenagers "You must show the way"; and when we were adults, "You are a person of responsibility, a leader, an apostle." The soul always had to be 'something'; the words of Jesus: "You are unprofitable servants, without me you can do nothing," "Whichever of you want to be first shall be last," seemed to have been said to other people, people of another age. They flowed over our heads without leaving much impression on us; they flowed over the heart without affecting it in any way, without bathing it, softening it.

My first master had told me, "The beginning of everything should be the honour of Christ the King;" the last, Charles de Foucauld, had advised me: "The end of everything is the love of Jesus Crucified."

And yet perhaps both of them were right, and the guilty one was I, for not understanding the lesson properly.

In any case, now I was here, keeling on the sand of the cave, which had taken on the dimensions of the Church itself; on my shoulders I could feel the small column of the activist. Perhaps this was the moment of truth.

I drew back suddenly, as though to free myself from this weight. What had happened? Everything remained in its place, motionless. Not a movement, not a sound. After twenty-five years I had realised that nothing was burdening my shoulders and that the column was my own creation—sham, unreal, the product of my imagination and my vanity.

I had walked, run, spoken, orgainsed worked, in the belief that I was supporting something; and in reality I had been holding up absolutely nothing.

The weight of the world was all on Christ Crucified. I was nothing, absolutely nothing.

It had taken some effort to believe the words of Jesus who had said to me two thousand years earlier: "When you have done everything that is commanded you to do, say, 'We are unprofitable servants, because we have only done our duty' " (Luke 17:10).

Unprofitable servants!

4.

Who guides the world?

My first feeling after this was one of freedom; new, vast, real, joyful freedom.

The discovery that I was nothing, that I was responsible for no one, that I was a man of no importance, gave me the joy of a boy on holiday.

Night came, and I could not sleep. I left the cave, and walked under the stars above the vast desert.

"My God, I love you. My God, I love you," I shouted to the heavens through the strange silence of the night.

Tired of walking, I stretched out on a sand dune and gazed at the starry vault above. How dear they were to me, those stars; how close to them the desert had brought me. Through spending my nights in the open, I had come to know them by their names, then to study them, and to get to know them one by one. Now I could distinguish their colour, their size, their position, their beauty. I knew my way around them, and from them I could calculate the time without a watch. The constellation of the Swan seemed to be in conversation with Altair which was as clear as a diamond. Confined by their smallness, Sagitta and the Dolphin seemed to be listening. Pegasus was rising in the East with his entourage of stars, while the Pearl was disappearing into the West.

I cast my eyes back to Andromeda. The night was so clear that I could just discern the nebula that bears the name of the constellation. It is the celestial body which is farthest from the Earth yet visible to the naked eye: 800 thousand light years away. Between them and the Earth is Proxina, the four light-years of which would appear to me in two months' time in the constellation of Centaurus. Such is the space occupied by this mass of forty million stars in which is gathered the galaxy to which we belong—on a tiny grain of sand called Earth.

Beyond the nebula Andromeda are other millions of nebulae, and thousands and thousands of stars which my eyes cannot see, but which God has created.

It is true that Jesus said, "Go, and make disciples of all nations." But he also added,

"Without me you can do nothing." It is true that Saint Ignatius said, "Act as though everything depended upon you." But he added, "But pray as though everything depended upon God." God is the creator of the physical cosmos as well as of the human cosmos. He rules the stars as he rules the Church. And if, in his love, he has wished to make men his collaborators in the work of salvation, the limit of their power is very small and clearly defined. It is the limit of the wire compared with the electric current.

We are the wire, God is the current. Our only power is to let the current pass through us. Of course, we have the power to interrupt it and say 'no.' But nothing more.

Not, then, the image of the column acting as a support, but that of the wire allowing the current to pass through it.

But the wire is one thing, the current is another. They are quite different, and there is certainly no reason for the wire to become self-satisfied, even one which transmits at high tension.

The thought that the affairs of the world, like those of the stars, are in God's hands—and therefore in good hands—apart from being actually true, is something that should give great satisfaction to anyone who looks to the future with hope. It should be the source of faith, joyful hope, and, above all, of deep peace. What have I to fear if everything is guided and sustained by God? Why get so worried, as if the world were in the hand of me and my fellow men?

And yet it is so difficult to have genuine faith in God's action in the affairs of the world. To refuse to believe it is one of the gravest temptations to which we are subjected on this earth.

The whole Bible is there to testify to this fact. And basically the story of the chosen people is nothing more than that of a handful of men of whom God asks, time and time again:

> Do you believe in me? I am the God of Abraham and of Isaac and Jacob. I am the God who with a strong arm has brought you out of the slavery of Egypt, and guided you into a parched land, I have nourished you with bread from Heaven and I have given you to drink water gushing out of the rock. For you I have stricken the first-born of Egypt, for you I have struck down many kings. And what have you done to pay me for all these wonders, for this continual help? You have constructed for yourselves idols of wood and silver, and have abandoned me, your God.
>
> Instead of worshipping Him who has created you and saved you a thousand times from your

> enemies, on the hill-tops and in sacred woods, you have burnt incense to strange gods; gods who can do nothing and know nothing; who have hands and cannot touch, feet and cannot walk, and no sound comes from their mouths.

This is true of all time, of the history of Israel and of our history. We too believe in God. But then we put our trust in men of power, believe their advice, and in the end think that the affairs of this world are safe in their hands, and that it is to them we must make our petitions. We too believe in God and we pray to him. But then we convince ourselves that it is the great preachers who convert souls. And if we have this in mind when we pray for the growth of the Kingdom our prayer will be futile; like making a request which will almost certainly be ignored.

And so, under a strange sky, the poor life of our soul goes on, in the light of unreal faith and sentimentalism. Halfway between God and the world there is a confusion of aspirations, contradictions and compromises.

Only God is, only God knows, only God can do anything. This is the truth, and with the help of my faith I discover this more deeply every day.

God alone rules the cosmos, only God knows

when I shall die, only God can convert China.

Why try to take on responsibilities that are not ours, why be amazed if Islam has not yet discovered Christ, or if millions of our brethren adhere to Buddhism, and are spiritually satisfied? The hour will come, but that in no way depends on me.

Does God have a plan for the world, a sacred history for all peoples? Is there an advance in time towards some goal?

Abraham did not know Christ, except in the hope of the promise. But this was no reason for him to be lost, or forgotten by the Father. The moment for the Incarnation had not come; and if Jesus came when he came and not before, it was certainly all part of the Divine Wisdom. God's plans count. Human plans count only in so far as they synchronise with God's.

God comes first, not man. Mary herself could have died without seeing Christ, had God not decided that the moment for the Incarnation had come.

The men of Galilee would have gone on fishing in the lake and attending the synagogue of Capernaeum if he hadn't been there to say 'Come.' That is the truth we must learn through faith: to wait on God. And this attitude of mind is not easy. This 'waiting,' this 'not making plans,' this 'searching the heavens,' this 'being silent' is one of the most important things we have to learn.

The moment will then follow when we are called, when we must speak out, when our hands will have grown tired from baptizing: the moment of the harvest. But even then we will be blind if we think of ourselves as the sole agents in bringing it about. The extraordinary thing is that God uses us, who are so insignificant and unworthy.

I didn't want to reach this point, because there is a question I am loathe to tackle. Even to ask the question seems impertinent, and lacking in faith.

"Pray or act? Stay or opt out? Go out into the world or use the Church as a refuge?" And there we are at the beginning again, where man persists in posing irrelevant questions. His hankering curiosity is so much stronger than his desire to obey the word of God.

But now I'm tired of arguing. I don't want to go on disputing any more. My belief in the ability to convince by words alone has gone.

I am silent under these African stars, and I prefer to worship my God and Saviour.

But I must react in some way to the insistence of the young people who have written to me here; they do put their finger on an important point, and what is more they have suffered. I can reply only that in the world everything is problematic except one thing: charity, love. Love alone is not a problem for him who lives it.

I can only say, "Live love, let love invade you. It will never fail to teach you what you must do."

Charity, which is God in us, will point to the way ahead. It will say to you "Now kneel," or "Now leave."

It is love which gives things their value. It makes sense of the difficulty of spending hours and hours on one's knees praying while so many men need looking after in the world; and in the context of love we must view our inability to change the world, to wipe out evil and suffering.

It is love which must determine man's actions, love which must give unity to what is divided.

Love is the synthesis of contemplation and action, the meeting-point between heaven and earth, between God and man.

I have known the satisfaction of unrestrained action, and the joy of the contemplative life in the dazzling peace of the desert, and I repeat again St. Augustine's words: 'Love and do as you will.' Don't worry about what you ought to do. Worry about loving. Don't interrogate heaven repeatedly and uselessly saying, "What course of action should I pursue?" Concentrate on loving instead.

And by loving you will find out what is for you. Loving, you will listen to the Voice. Loving, you will find peace.

Love is the fulfillment of the law and should be everyone's rule of life; in the end it's the solution to every problem, the motive for all good.

"Love and do as you will."

This is the crux. When I love I can no longer do as I will.

When I love I am love's prisoner; and love is tremendous in its demands when it has God as its object; especially a crucified God. I can no longer do my own will. I *must* do the will of Jesus, which is the will of the Father.

And when I have learned to do his will, I shall have fully realised my vocation on earth and I shall have achieved the highest stage a man can reach.

The will of God. That's what rules the world and moves the stars, what converts the nations, what brings to life and brings triumph out of death.

The will of God raised up Abraham, our

father in faith; it called Moses, inspired David, prepared Mary, sustained Joseph, made Christ incarnate and demanded his sacrifice; this it was that founded the Church. And it is God's will still to continue the work of redemption until the end of time.

It will call people to enter one by one into the visible body of the Church when the time is ripe after having belonged to his invisible soul through their good intentions and good will. Whether you are on the sand worshipping, or at the teacher's desk in a classroom, what does it matter as long as you are doing the will of God?

And if the will of God urges you to seek out the poor, to give up all you possess, or to leave for distant lands, what does the rest matter? Or if it calls you to found a family, or take on a job in a city, why should you have any doubts?

"His will is our peace," says Dante. And perhaps that is the expression which best brings into focus our deep dependence on God.

5.

Purification of the heart

It is clear we are made to love. The difficulty is to establish what to love and how.

I don't think it is mistaken or contrary to our aims to 'love a creature.' And it is certainly according to our aims to 'love Christ.' Therefore we must love both creature and creator. But why in the Christian tradition are these two loves often placed in mutual opposition, almost as though love of the one made love of the other impossible? The reason must be found in ourselves. It is our heart which is no longer capable of loving. It is like a rusty machine that won't work properly.

The heart, with all its potential, loses its balance too easily when it loves a creature.

It throws itself upon the creature loved and wants to possess it; and possessiveness kills. It holds on to the creature so passionately that it loses sight of the creator.

Moreover it ruins the object of its love by its obsession with it. It ruins it, makes it a slave. Characteristic in this sense, because it is more violent, is the love of sex for its own sake, withall the jealousy and selfishness that entails. Equally characteristic is the so-called blind devotion in which the human heart attaches itself exclusively to another, losing its peace, its serenity, its balanced vision of things, and in the worst cases its purity.

What should we say then of the love of money? Of the slavery in which man is held by the love of riches?

Even love of work may become dangerous, especially if it is hidden behind a facade of virtue. There are so many country-people who are no longer capable of taking a rest on Sundays! Their obsession with goods and profit drives them into the fields.

And how many business men make a hell out of their lives, sucked in by the machine of their "obligations."

The higher one rises the worse it is. Even the love of study can make people unbelievably selfish; the passion for research can make men as mad and blind as termites in their dark tunnel. In situations such as these, it is clear that the love of creatures is an obstacle to the love of God.

The love of God is by nature pure, balanced and holy. Whoever is dominated by it lives in deep peace, has an ordered view of things and knows the meaning of true freedom. But the love of God, too, passing into man's heart, must be worked at, cultivated, pruned, fertilised. And the most uncompromising farmer is God Himself.

Above all such love must be purified.

What does it mean, to purify love?

It means releasing love from the fetters of the senses and from the pursuit of pleasure. In other words, making it free to grow in our hearts.

Freeing the gift of love! What a difficult undertaking for creatures like ourselves, willingly trapped as we are by sin, shut in by our selfishness.

We often fail to realise the depth of evil, terrifying as it is. I am not speaking only of the selfishness of the wealthy, heaping up riches for themselves, or of those who sacrifice to achieve their self-selected goals. Or of the dictator who breathes in the incense due only to God.

I am speaking of the selfishness of good people, devout people, those who have succeeded through spiritual exercises and self-denial in being able to make the proud profession before the altar of the Most High, "Lord, I am not like the rest of men." Yes, we have had the audacity at certain times of our lives to believe we are different from other men. And here is the deepest form of self-deception, dictated by self-centredness at its worst: spiritual egotism. This most insidious form of egotism even uses piety and prayer for its own gain.

This becomes a form of insult to the altar itself. It is when the very desire for holiness itself is turned upside down. It is not love and imitation of Christ Crucified, it is the desire for glory. It is not charity, it is egotism.

I believe very strongly that a large proportion of the good intentions which drive us on to seek God are ruined in this way. One can reach the point of consecrating oneself to God for egotistic motives, becoming a religious for that reason, building hospitals, doing all kinds of good works.

There is no limit to such self-deception. And the path, once entered upon, is so slippery that God has to treat us harshly to bring us back to our senses.

But there is no other way of opening our eyes. It has to be painful.

Butoften it isn't enough. Disaster, illness, disappointment hover like birds of prey over the poor carcass that had the temerity to say, "Lord, I am not like the rest of men."

How can we possibly entertain the idea that we are different from other men, when we shout, cry, feel afraid, lack determination, and behave atrociously just like everybody else?

> Yahweh my God, I call for help all day,
> I weep to you all night;
> for my soul is all troubled,
> my life is on the brink of Sheol;
> I am numbered among those who go
> down to the pit,
> a man bereft of strength:
> You have plunged me to the bottom of the pit,
> to its darkest, deepest place,
> weighed down by your anger,
> drowned beneath your waves. (Ps. 87)

It is the purification of love, the refining fire which exposes our nakedness.

And God himself, who is love, is not powerless.

On the contrary, because he is love, he acts with greater determination.

If the soul does not free itself by way of the cross it can never be free. It is the tremendous surgical operation which the Father himself carries out on the flesh of his son in order to save him. And it is a dogma of faith that without the cross "there is no forgiveness." A mystery, but it is so. Pain purifies love. It makes it true, real, pure. And in addition it gets rid of what is not really love. It frees love from pleasure which falsifies it like a mask. It makes it a gift freely given.

When the flood of pain has passed over the soul, what remains alive can be considered genuine. Certainly not much remains. Often it is reduced to a thin shrub. But on this the dove of the Holy Spirit may rest to pour out his grace. It is reduced to a 'yes' murmured among tears and anguish, but echoed by the all-powerful 'yes' of the dying Jesus; it is reduced to a child who has ceased to argue with God and men, but is helped on by the kiss of the Father.

In this state the soul is capable of a love which is freely given. It can no longer bear any other kind of love. It feels nausea when faced with sentiment. It loathes calculated love. It has finally entered into the logic of God, so often illogical to men of this earth.

Let us consider the logic of the most famous parable on the nature of true love:

> The kingdom of Heaven is like a householder who went out early in the morning to hire

laborers for his vineyard. After agreeing with the laborers for a denarius a day, he sent them into his vineyard. And going out about the third hour he saw others standing idle in the market place; and to them he said, 'You go into the vineyard too, and whatever is right I will give you.' So they went. Going out again about the sixth hour and the ninth hour he did the same. And about the eleventh hour he went out and found others standing; and he said to them, 'Why do you stand here idle all day?' They said to him, 'Because no one has hired us.' He said to them, 'You go into the vineyard too.' And when evening came the owner said to his steward, 'Call the laborers and pay them their wages, beginning with the last, up to the first.' And when those hired about the eleventh hour came, each of them received a denarius. Now when the first came, they thought they would receive more; but each of them alsoreceived a denarius. And on receiving it they grumbled at the householder, saying, 'These last worked only one hour, and you have made them equal to us who have borne the burden of the day and the scorching heat.' But he replied to one of them, 'Friend, I am doing you no wrong; did you not agree with me for a denarius? Take what belongs to you and go; I chose to give to this last as I give to you. Am I not allowed to do what I choose with what belongs to me? Or is your eye evil because I am good?' (Matthew 20:1-16)

Understanding this parable for us who have an 'evil eye' is not easy. Anyone who understands it just a little before he dies is blessed. For it means that now his eye sees straight and thus he can enter into the kingdom of freedom which is the kingdom of a love which is real and unqualified.

6.
Toward prayer

I have come into the desert to pray, to learn to pray. It has been the Sahara's great gift to me, and I should like to share it with all my friends. It is immeasurable and contains every other gift within itself. It is the *sine qua non* of life, the treasure buried in the field, the pearl of great price discovered in the market.

Prayer is the sum of our relationship with God.

We are what we pray.

The degree of our faith is the degree of our prayer. The strength of our hope is the strength of our prayer. The warmth of our charity is the warmth of our prayer. No more nor less.

Our prayer has had a beginning because we have had a beginning. But it will have no end. It will accompany us into eternity and will be completed in our contemplation of God, when we join in the harmony of heaven and are "filled with the flood of God's delights."

The story of our earthly-heavenly life will be the story of our prayer. Thus, above all it is a personal story.

Just as no flower is exactly like another flower, and no star exactly like another star, so no man is exactly like another man. And since prayer is the relationship between one particular man and God, it is different for every man. So no prayer is exactly like another.

Prayer is a word of infinite variety, were it repeated into infinity with the same syllables and in the same tone of voice.

What varies is the Spirit of the Lord which gives it life, and this is always new.

St. Bernadette Soubirous, who couldn't say anything but 'Ave Maria' and the mystic who can only repeat one monosyllable, 'God,' have both the most variable and personal prayer imaginable.

Under the veil of the single word passes alone and entire the Spirit of Jesus, which is the Spirit of the Father.

Understanding prayer well means understanding that one is speaking with God.

Thus there are two poles. One very, very tiny and very, very weak: my soul. One immense and powerful: God.

But here is the first paradox, the first surprise: that he who is so great should have wanted to speak to me, tiny as I am.

It is not I who wanted prayer. It is he who wanted it. It is not I who have looked for him. It is he who has looked for me first. My seeking him would have been in vain if before all time he had not sought me.

The hope on which my prayer rests is in the fact that it is he who wants it. And if I go to keep the appointment it is because he is already there waiting for me.

If he had remained in his silence and isolation, I'd not have been able to break mine. Nobody has ever concentrated for long on talking to a wall or a tree or a star. He'd have given it up very soon if he didn't get a reply.

I've been speaking with God all my life; and I've only just begun!

There's another thing to say about prayer. It doesn't come from earth but from heaven. The cry which fills my breast and makes me exclaim, "God, I love you!"; the force which makes Farragi, the blind Moslem, repeat as he walks on the track at my side, "How great God is!"; the cry of David, "Have mercy!"; the exaltation of Mary, "Magnificat!"; the tear sparkling in the penitent's eye, "Jesus have mercy on me!"; the sudden ecstatic gasp of the scientist before the wonders of the universe, all these are the words of the Holy Spirit.

It is the Holy Spirit who fills the world and makes us cry 'Father,' and inspires the current of prayer within us. We should respond quickly with our lips and our hearts, full of awareness of the passage of God's current. We should repeat again and again what the Spirit of Jesus has prompted us and given us the strength to say. Certainly we can resist him, as we do most of the time. We can close our lips and be silent. If we were attentive to the call we should be in continual prayer.

To be precise, we must add there's a prayer we can call ours, that is, born on earth in the heart of man. But there's nothing special about this prayer. Often it's a bit of spiritual pettiness: asking for things which aren't for our real good and which would be bad for us if they were granted to us, filling our mouths with pious words of fear, of loneliness or pain. Jesus had already warned us of this: "When you pray, do not do as the heathen do . . ." If we wish for a comparison between the value of this prayer (let's call it 'not inspired') and the other true one dictated in us by the Spirit of the Lord, let's say that the difference between the two is like the difference between what philosophers have said about God, and what the Bible and the Church have said about him. After endless argument and deliberation the philosophers hardly succeeded in agreeing on the existence of God. The Church has a warm, living, spiritual knowledge of God even if it is obscure and hidden in the 'darkness' of faith.

In any case there's no point in concerning ourselves with "our" prayer. We know it well.

How often we have been found with our mouths full of it, far from the Spirit of God! How often we've taken refuge in it precisely to escape the Spirit of God and his Will!

We have gone into choir to recite our breviary, while our duty was to go into the parlour to receive some tedious, grumpy bore. We have said the rosary while going to keep an appointment which could only cause harm to our soul. We have lit a candle and asked for money. We have bent our heads in adoration while our hearts were full of impure love.

This prayer comes from earth, not heaven. And on earth it remains, rich only in its uselessness, its deceit.

The Prophet will say of it, "I shall put clouds to stop it."

But I don't think even clouds are necessary, because it goes no further than the hearts of our blind obstinacy.

Yes, blind obstinacy that can last years. It

creates in us a deep-seated hypocrisy which dominates every aspect of our daily lives. A man can go to Mass daily and proceed to exploit the poor; a man who is basically selfish can have his head crammed with ideas for reforming the Church.

Basically the answer is simple, very simple. We need only to listen to what Jesus has told us. It's enough to listen to the Gospel and put into practice what it tells us.

In short, it's the will that counts, not words.

God's inspiration searches out our will. The spirit of Jesus settles where the will desires it, because it is love. And two are needed to make love.

When I bow before his love he is not slow to come; rather he has already come, for he loves me much more than I, poor creature, can ever love him.

And love shows itself in action, as for the Prodigal Son.

Rising up is a fact, leaving the pigs is a fact.

The soul must say with sincerity, "Now I will arise and go to my Father."

7.
The stages of prayer

Prayer is words, poetry, song.

Turn your ear, O Lord, and give answer
For I am poor and needy.
Show me, Lord, your way,
so that I may walk in thy truth
Guide my heart to fear your name. (Ps. 85)

Often it contains a shout, a cry,
a groan of anguish.

Lord my God, I call for help by day;
I cry at night before you.
Let my prayer come into your presence.
O turn your ear to my cry.

For my soul is filled with evils;
my life is on the brink of the grave.
I am reckoned as one in the tomb:
I have reached the end of my strength,

like one alone among the dead;
like the slain lying in their graves;
like those you remember no more,
cut off, as they are, from your hand. (Ps. 87)

And sometimes an explosion of joy:

I love you, Lord, my strength,
My rock, my fortress, my saviour.
My God is the rock where I take refuge. (Ps. 17)

Or ecstatic admiration of God's works:

The heavens proclaim the glory of God
And the firmament shows forth
the work of his hands. (Ps. 18)

Or the impassioned praise of His providence:

The Lord is my shepherd;
There is nothing I shall want.
Fresh and green are the pastures
Where He gives me repose

He guides me along the right path;
He is true to his name.
If I should walk in the valley of darkness
no evil would I fear.

You are there with your crook
and your staff;
And with these you give me comfort. (Ps. 22)

This way of speaking to God is for men of all ages and cultures. Man will express himself in those ways from the beginning of his spiritual life until the end. With words he will express his feelings to his creator.

But here too, it is the same as with love. Words pour out to begin with. Then they get rarer and deeper. In the end they are reduced to some monosyllable which none the less contains everything. Mostly a soul speaks a great deal at the time of its conversion, during the period of its novitiate, that is, the first years of its discovery of God. It is the easiest time for the soul. Prayer has a certain novelty, it seizes the imagination. And God, for his part, encourages the soul; everything pours out as in the beginning of a happy marriage.

My heart is ready, O God;
I will sing, sing your praise.
Awake, my soul;
awake, lyre and harp.
I will awake the dawn.

I will thank you, Lord among the peoples,
Praise you among the nations;
for your love reaches to the heavens
and your truth to the skies. (Ps. 107)

Another stage of prayer is meditation. Sometimes it naturally follows the use of words. Especially when the soul is mature, the two become blended and fused. Sometimes meditation comes later.

We are now at the stage when we need to know what others have said about God; the stage of deep reflection, and of theological study; it is very, very rewarding.

If the world knew the joy a Christian feels at this time, the peace which reigns in his heart, and the sense of balance which dominates his whole being, he would be intrigued, fascinated.

I have known this and I have had the good fortune to share it with hundreds, thousands of other young people. God, the Church, souls, were the only enthusiasms we had. It seemed everyday we had a new world to forge. We moved against error like David against Goliath. A number of us met together to pray and speak of God. What did they matter, those sleepless nights, those long train journeys on wooden benches, those treks across the countryside by bicycle to spread our movement; the economic sacrifices and the holidays we gave up so that once a year we could make a retreat? These are among the dearest memories of my life and I always recall them with joy and peace.

There are a thousand ways of meditating,

and everyone must find what suits him best. We will realise, as we go on, which way is the most suitable for us. Here I would like to mention two things which I have learned from my great master, John of the Cross—one on the method of meditation, and the other on the book to choose.

The Method: Saint John divides it into three parts, and up to this point there's nothing new.

1. Imaginative reflection on the mystery which one wishes to meditate.

2. Intellectual consideration of the mysteries represented. (Here too there's nothing new).

3. (And this is important) Loving and attentative respose in God, to make sure we are fully prepared for that moment when the intelligence opens itself up to God's illumination.

This exercise of love, which is deeply human, results in a serene and devout repose before God. It must be meditation clearly directed towards simplicity and interior silence.

The Book to Chose: Above all other books, choose the Bible. If you like, read as many books of meditation as possible, but that isn't essential. It is essential to read and meditate on the Scriptures. Christianity without the Bible is a contradiction in terms. Preaching not anchored in the Scriptures is equally impossible. There is no true religious formation which is not based on the Gospel. The Bible is the letter which God himself wrote to men in the thousands of years of their history. It is the long drawn out sigh for Christ (Old Testament) and the account of his coming among us (New Testament).

When the temple of Jerusalem was burning, the Jews abandoned all its treasures to the flames but saved the Bible. Paul knew the Bible by heart, and Augustine said, "Ignorance of Scripture is ignorance of Christ."

The Bible is the word of God, the Word made flesh is the Eucharist. I put both of them on the altar and kneel down before them.

There's an awakening of interest in the Bible at the present time. Let us thank God for it; but we are still a long way from fully realising the importance of the Bible in and to our lives.

I said earlier that prayer is like love. Words pour at first. Then we are more silent and can communicate in monosyllables. In difficulties a gesture is enough, a word, or nothing at all—love is enough. Thus the time comes when words are superfluous and meditation is difficult, almost impossible.

That is the time for the prayer of simplicity. The soul converses with God with a single loving glance, although this may often be accompanied by dryness and suffering.

In this period the so-called litanical prayer thrives; that is, repetitions of identical expressions, poor words, but very rich in content.

Hail Mary . . . Hail Mary . . . Jesus I love you . . . .Lord have mercy on me . . . My God and my all.

And it is strange how in these ejaculations, monotonous and simple, the soul finds itself at ease, almost cradled in God's arms. It is also a time for the rosary, lived and loved as one of the highest and most inspired prayers.

Often in my life as a European I have taken part in animated discussions on the pros and cons of the rosary. But in the end I was never fully satisfied. I was not in a fit condition to really understand this way of praying.

"It's a meditative prayer," some would say. Well, then, the young people are right to complain of the distractions which this useless repetition of ten Hail Marys bring to the meditation. Announce the mystery and leave me to my thoughts.

"No, it's a prayer of praise," others would say. "And one must think of what one is saying word by word."

But it's impossible! Who's capable of saying fifty Hail Marys distracted by the pictures of five mysteries without losing the thread?

I must confess that never in my life, although I have made the effort, have I succeeded in saying a single rosary without getting distracted.

It was in the desert that I came to realise that those who discuss the rosary—as I discussed it in that way—have not yet understood the soul of this prayer.

The rosary belongs to that type of prayer which precedes or accompanies the contemplative prayer of the spirit. Whether you meditate it or not, whether or not you get distracted, if you love the rosary deeply and can't let a day go by without saying it, you are already a person of prayer.

The rosary is like the echo of a wave breaking on the shore, God's shore: 'Hail Mary. . . Hail Mary . . . Hail Mary . . . ' It is like your mother's hand on your childhood cradle.

The rosary is a point of arrival, not of departure. For Bernadette the point of arrival came very soon, because she was destined to see Our Lady on this earth. But normally it is a prayer of spiritual maturity. If a young man doesn't like saying the rosary, and says he gets bored, don't force him. Reading a text from scripture is best for him, or maybe some more intellectual kind of prayer. But if you meet a child in the remote countryside, or a peaceful old man or a simple old woman who tells you they love the rosary without knowing why, rejoice and be glad, because the Holy Spirit prays in their hearts. The rosary is an incomprehensible prayer for the 'commonsense' man, just as it is incomprehensible to repeat "I love you" a thousand times a day to a God one cannot see. But for the pure of heart it is understandable; the person rooted in the Kingdom and living the beatitudes understands the rosary.

The orthodox, who are highly contemplative, have developed a litanical prayer similar to our rosary; they call it "the Jesus prayer."

It is said by repeating slowly, again and again, with one's soul peacefully disposed, the Kyrie Eleison:

Lord have mercy on me
I am a sinful man
Christ have mercy on me
I am a sinful man

In this prayer they keep time with their breathing, or even their heartbeat.

As prayer becomes richer in content and uses fewer words, meditation grows difficult and distasteful. What before was a source of intellectual pleasure, now becomes dry and painful. One gets the impression of reaching a crossroad in the spiritual life. Sometimes one thinks he is going backward instead of making progress.

The heavens have lost their bright colours, the soul feels 'grey' in mood.

At this stage of spiritual life the person who has a good guide is fortunate, especially if he has the humility to let himself be led.

It is not easy. We all think we know how to get along alone and only failure puts things in the right perspective.

What is this dryness in meditation which I am describing; this refusal to fix our thoughts on spiritual things? Clearly it may depend on some fault in ourselves. It may depend on some unhealthy attachment in our hearts, lack of vigilance, or the thorns in which we have let the good seed be choked. Difficulty in meditation is not always the sign of an advance of the soul towards God, or the progress to a higher type of prayer.

But it may, thank God, be a sign of that. How can one know the difference?

Again John of the Cross tells us.

There are three signs which indicate the movement from discursive to contemplative prayer:

1. We lack the desire to use the imagination.

2. The imagination and the senses no longer have the will to think about specific things. The things of the earth offer no consolation.

3. The soul wants to remain still, directed

towards God alone. It desires inner peace, quiet and repose; it no longer feels the need to use the human faculties.

This third condition is good. If it is present in the soul it justifies the other two. If I have difficulty in meditating on God, if I no longer succeed in fixing my attention on one mystery or another in the life of Jesus, on one truth or another, but I am craving to remain alone and motionless and silent at the feet of God, empty of thought but in an act of love, . . . it means something great. It is one of the most beautiful secrets of the spiritual life.

8.

Contemplative prayer

We are now approaching the essence of prayer. At this point we shall see the true penetration of God's revelation, the depth of God's mystery. We shall plumb the depths of our own being as Christians.

Jesus, on the night he was betrayed, said: "If you love me you will keep my commandments." (John 14:15)

Then he added: "Anybody who receives my commandments and keeps them will be one who loves me; and anybody who loves me will be loved by my Father and I shall love him and show myself to him." (John 14:21)

And he concluded: "If anyone loves me he will keep my word, and my Father will love him, and we shall come to him and make our home with him." (John 14:23)

God offers himself in three ways: his Spirit,

his presence and his revelation of himself. And for these three offers he asks but one thing: 'If a man loves me.'

The man who offers God his love becomes 'paradise on earth,' the Trinity is a reality within him; he is an instrument of the Spirit and of God's will.

These three ways of God offering himself to us are possible because of the death and resurrection of Christ, and are a reality because of him.

It is through prayer that we absorb this reality, for prayer establishes us in the deepest possible relationship with God. By our prayer we share the life of God.

The Trinity becomes a reality in us as the guest of the soul. Earth becomes heaven. Why go on searching for God beyond the stars when he is so close to us, within us. Heaven, this hidden place, is not some lofty vaulting construction, studded with stars. It is a land of intimate closeness, so near that we can speak to God, stay with him, worship him anywhere.

His Holy Spirit is in us.

He is the skilled craftsman who unites us with God. It is he who incorporates us in Christ Jesus, who teaches us what we must say to the Father. He creates a new spirit in us. He carries our prayer to the Most High and gives our feeble, childish yearnings value in the sight of God. How can I still say to myself, 'Who will teach me to pray?' when I have a master like that at the center of my being? Why doubt the power of my prayer when, even if pathetic and stammering, its passage is sustained by the same Creator-Spirit?

No, I shall no longer try to pray by myself or rely on my own efforts, since in faith I have discovered that the Spirit of God is there in my heart.

But this is not enough. The promise of Jesus speaks of his presence, an activity of his Spirit, and of a revelation. 'I shall make myself known to you.'

Making themselves known to one another is the task of lovers; a task never finished, never complete. There always remains something mysterious to discover, an element of the unknown.

Think of God; in him everything is to be discovered. But in the case of God one thing must be made very clear. God is unknowable to man directly. We can know him only through figures, symbols and signs. But they themselves are not God. Only God knows himself, and knowledge of him remains a mystery for us. But in his love God has decided to make himself known to man, to reveal himself to him. And that happens in a supernatural manner, in a language untranslatable on earth. A man who grasps this revelation can say nothing. He cannot repeat it.

Whoever wants to learn to pray must know this.

I have lost too much through knowing this truth too late. And yet it was clear in the Gospel.

I thought that in prayer everything depended on me and my efforts, on the books passing through my hands, and the beauty of the words which I was able to introduce into my conversations with God.

What is worse, I thought the knowledge of God I was acquiring through study and reasoning was the real and only one. I hadn't yet understood that it was only an image, a covering, an introduction to God's true and authentic revelation, which is supernatural and eternal.

God is unknowable, and only he can reveal himself to me through ways which are wholly his, unrepeatable in words and in concepts beyond our understanding.

So true prayer demands that we be more passive than active; it requires more silence than words, more adoration than study, more concentration than rushing about, more faith than reason. We must understand thoroughly that true prayer is a gift from heaven to earth, the Father to his child; from the Bridegroom to the bride, from he who has to him who has not, from Everything to nothing.

And the nearer this Everything comes to nothing, the more the unknowing becomes unlimited.

Of the man coming down from the mountain after having spoken at length with God, you ask: 'Talk to us about Him.' And he will repeat with Angela of Foligno, one of the great Italian mystics:

> Before God the soul is wrapped in his shadows and in them becomes acquainted with him more than I should ever have imagined it could; and with such splendour, such certainty and such depth that there is no human heart which can in any way understand or conceive such a thing.
>
> The soul can say absolutely nothing, because it has no words to express itself with. In fact, there is neither thought nor intelligence that can reach that far, so greatly does it surpass everything; the ways of God cannot be explained.
>
> When I again returned to myself, I knew for certain that those who feel God most deeply can say least about him. Precisely because they feel something of that infinite and unspeakable goodness, they can say less about it.

Of course it is pleasing to heaven that when you go to preach, you should understand. For if not, you would not be able to say anything at all about God. And so you would have to be silent! Then someone would come up to you and say: "Brother, speak to me a little about God," and you would not be able to say anything or think anything about God. His infinite goodness would overcome you.

But on the contrary the soul does not lose consciousness, the body does not lose any of its faculties. In fact, we are fully conscious.

But you would say to the people: 'Go with God's blessing, because I can say nothing!' All the things that are said in the Scriptures and by the saints from the beginning of the world until now, seem to me to express hardly anything of the love of God; their words are like a speck of dust compared to the universe.

As it was for Angela of Foligno, so it is for all of us. We feel the knowledge of God becoming greater in us little by little as our love for him becomes greater. And of this knowledge we are unable to say anything. We know that it is a rich, mysterious, dark, personal knowledge of him; but we are not able to utter a syllable about what we know.

"I shall make myself known to you."

This revelation of himself which God makes to man is the core, the fruit, the breath of contemplative prayer and it is a real sharing of eternal life. In John we find the definition of it: 'Now this is everlasting life, that they may know thee, the only true God, and him whom thou hast sent, Jesus Christ' (John 17:3).

O Lord, my heart is not proud
nor haughty my eyes.
I have not gone after things too great
nor marvels beyond me.

Truly I have set my soul
In silence and peace.
A weaned child on its mother's breast,
even so is my soul. (Ps. 130)

This is the psalm of contemplative prayer. Man on the way to the roots of his being, towards his end, his creator, after having passed the first degrees of prayer, after having been purified by the suffering dryness of human pleasure and selfishness, finds himself at the doorway of eternity. His own strength can do nothing, meditation itself becomes impossible, and words, once so effortless, can only repeat some monosyllable of love and lament.

No image sums all this up so exactly as that of a child that has been weaned in its mother's arms. And it is still Jesus who tells us, "Unless you turn and become like little children, you will not enter into the Kingdom of Heaven"

(Matthew 18:3). But by now the soul has made itself small and has understood that it must receive everything and that its only power is that of loving.

No, there is still the other power, that of knowing. But what use is that in such moments!

The anonymous medieval author of *The Cloud of Unknowing* says:

> But since all reasonable creatures, angels and men, have in them, each one by himself, one principal working power, the which is called a knowing power, and another principal working power, the which is called a loving power. Of the which two powers, to the first, the which is a knowing power, God who is the maker of them is evermore incomprehensible; but to the second, the which is the loving power, He is in every man diversely, all comprehensible to the full.
>
> One loving soul alone in itself, by virtue of love, may comprehend in itself Him who is sufficient to the full. And this is the endless marvelous miracle of love, the working of which shall never have end; for ever shall He do it, and never shall He cease for to do it.

It would seem strange at first sight. But nothing gives the sense of God's universality and his justice more than this truth. If God were attainable with the intelligence, how unjust it would be!

It would have made easy the task of the wise and the great of this world, and would have made knowledge of God all but impossible for the little ones, the poor, and the ignorant. But God himself has found the way to be equally accessible to everybody. His revelation comes in love, in that faculty which we can all share.

He loves equally queen and peasant, wise and ignorant.

'I bless you, Father, Lord of heaven and of earth, for hiding these things from the learned and the clever and revealing them to mere children.'

But what becomes of concepts? They are not stifled. That would be contrary to the nature of our intelligence. The concepts are always there but are silent, and sleep like the apostles on the mountain.

That is what is known as infused contemplation or mystical knowledge. It feeds upon silence. It becomes negative in a new and absolute sense.

Hadewijch the Beguine says: "The single and naked truth abolished every kind of reasoning. It holds me in this emptiness and fits me for the simple life of eternity. All speech finishes here. He who has never understood the word of God would vainly explain what I have found without means, without a veil, above every reasoning."

He who believes that he can speak of what is in the depths of his own soul betrays his own inexperience. My God, what an adventure it is, not to understand any longer, nor be able to see. If earlier we possessed 'something,' love has now reduced us to nothing.

Yes, love has reduced us to nothing. It has taken from us all presumption of knowing or being. It has reduced us to true spiritual childhood.

> I have held my soul
> In peace and in silence
> As a child
> In its mother's arms.

This is the highest state of prayer: to be children in God's arms, silent, loving, rejoicing.

And if, through this desire of ours to say something, or do something, you feel that you must open your mouth, then do this: choose one word or a little phrase which well expresses your love for him; and then go on repeating it in peace, without trying to form thoughts, motionless in love before God who *is* love.

And with this word or this phrase transformed into an arrow of steel, a symbol of your love, beat again and again against God's thick cloud of unknowing.

Don't become distracted, whatever happens.

Chase away even the good thoughts; they serve no purpose now.

The highest degree of contemplation one can attain in this life lies entirely in this darkness, this cloud of unknowing. With an impulse of love and a blind glance one is carried to the naked being of God himself and God alone.

A blind impulse of love, fixed on God himself, which presses secretly on the cloud of unknowing is nobler and more profitable for your soul, than any other spiritual exercise.

This is my wish, a synthesis of all the gifts which the desert has made me.

9.

Purification of the Spirit

There is a slogan known all over the world which runs, "If the money spent on slimming treatments and medicines for curing the after-effects of overeating in the well-to-do continents of Europe and America were put together, there would be enough money to give bread to the needy, undernourished peoples of Africa and Asia."

Which means that greed is one of the besetting sins of man, including intelligent, cultured, refined, and—all too often—religious people.

On this subject Jesus would say to us, "You have not managed to be faithful in little things. Who will entrust you with great things?" If we have demonstrated such greed at the table of the body, imagine how we would have behaved at the table of spiritual things, if we had felt ourselves attracted by it.

It is unnecessary to repeat it: we are sick, unbalanced, sensual, evil. And let there be no mistake: 'we' means every one of us.

Jesus, in a true judgement of us summed up, "You who are all evil" (Matt. 7:11).

And he completed his judgement on the cross, "Father forgive them, for they do not know what they are doing" (Luke 23:34).

Evil and insane. This is true of us in little things and in great: we have indigestion from overeating, yet let our neighbour starve, and this spreads over into our prayer and spiritual life.

But in order to hinder our spiritual indigestion God offers something radical: bare faith, simple hope, love without sentiment. The man who after his first steps in the spiritual life, throws himself into the struggle of prayer and union with God, is astounded at the dryness of the road.

The more he advances, the more the darkness thickens around him. The more he goes on, the more bitter and insipid everything becomes. He derives little comfort from the recollection of times past when God seemed to make his spiritual path easier.

Sometimes he is even tempted to shout, "But Lord, if you helped a little more, more people would follow you."

But God does not listen to such entreaty; rather, instead of consolation he sends boredom, and instead of light, darkness. Right there, halfway along our road, we don't know whether we are going backwards or forwards.

But only then the real battle begins and becomes serious. We are beginning to discover what we are worth: nothing, or little. At earlier stages we thought we were generous; we now discover that we are egoists. We thought, under the false light of religious aestheticism, that we knew how to pray; now we find that we no longer know how to say "Father." We were convinced that we were humble, charitable, obedient; now we find that pride has invaded our whole being, down to the deepest roots. Prayer, human relationships, working to spread the Gospel, all these seem thwarted.

But we must render our accounts, and these are very poor. With the exception of those privileged souls who understood right from the beginning what the problem really was, and who immediately set out upon the true, rough road of humility and spiritual childhood, the greater part of mankind is called upon to undergo a hard and painful experience.

This normally occurs around the age of forty: a great liturgical period in one's life, a Biblical period, a period of the noonday devil, the period of one's second youth, a crucial period for man: "For forty years that generation repelled me, until I said: 'How unreliable these people who refuse to grasp my ways!' "(Psalm 94:10).

This is the time when God has decided to take the man who until now has escaped behind a smokescreen of halfheartedness, and make him put his back to the wall.

Disaster, boredom, depression, all these but especially the experience of sin make man discover what he really is: a poor, fragile, weak thing; a mixture of pride and wickedness; inconstant, lazy, illogical.

There is no limit to this misery in man. And God lets him drink the bitter cup to the dregs.

Even for those who in this situation do not sin because they are helped by grace, there opens up the vision of things as they really are: God, man, sin.

The soul becomes aware that it is walking on a tightrope. And beneath it can see the hell which it has merited a hundred times, and a hundred times escaped, by God's mercy.

There is no sin which it has not committed, or which it does not feel truly capable of committing. But this is not enough.

In the depths lodges the most crucial fault, greater than any other even though it is hidden.

It rarely, or perhaps never, breaks out in single concrete actions pushing towards the surface of the world. But from the depths, from the inmost layers of our being, it soaks in a poison which causes extreme damage. It is a fault which appears more in general attitudes than in individual actions, but it is this, rather than the actions themselves, which determine the real quality of the human heart. Because it is hidden, or rather camouflaged, we can barely catch sight of it, and often only after a long time; but it is alive enough in our consciousness to be able to contaminate us and it weighs us down considerably more than the things which we habitually confess. These attitudes envelop our whole life like an atmosphere and are present, as it were, in every action or omission. They are hidden and general sins we cannot rid ourselves of; laziness and cowardice, a falsehood and vanity, from which not even our prayer can be entirely free. They burden our whole existence and damage it. The time for playing games at spirituality, for "Let's pretend," is over. One has got as far as knowing one's ignorance. He stands on the edge of the abyss which separates the creature from the Creator.

There one can live but on alms, and on the grace that can be neither known nor grasped.

Every means has proved powerless, every

path too short. God's impenetrable night wraps round us. Terrible loneliness accompanies us, but his is necessary and inevitable.

Every word of consolation seems like a lie. One believes one has been abandoned by God.

In this deeply painful state, prayer becomes true and strong even though it may be as dry as dust.

The soul speaks to its God out of its poverty and pain; still more out of its impotence and abjection.

Words become even fewer and barer. One is reduced to silence, but this is a step forward in prayer! It is limitless, whereas every word has a limit. And spiritual greed?

Oh, that's always there! It hides under the ashes, but it is less violent, more prudent.

God now again intervenes with his consolation, since it would be impossible to live in that state of abandonment. He returns to encourage the soul with the touch of his gentleness. The soul accepts that touch with gratitude. But it has become so timid through the blows it has received that it dare not ask anything more.

Deep down the soul has understood that it must let itself be carried, that it must abandon itself to its Saviour, that alone it can do nothing, that God can do everything.

And if it remains still and motionless, as though bound in the faithfulness of God, it will quickly realise that things have changed, and that its progress, though still painful, is in the right direction.

It is the direction of love! This realisation will come like light after darkness, the midday sun after the dawn.

What matters is to let God get on with it.

10.

Contemplation in the streets

At this point, my friend, I am sure there is a question in your mind, accompanied by a slight smile.

"Well, then! Is there no value in action, duty to our fellow-men, plunging oneself like leaven into this secular city? Must we all go into the desert? Is that possible? The desert is far away, I shall never be able . . . "

I know that's what you were thinking, and I must explain myself quite clearly, because something really crucial is at stake.

Charles de Foucauld said one day: "If the contemplative life were possible only behind convent walls or in the silence of the desert we should, in fairness, give a little convent to every mother of a family, and a track of desert to every person working hard in a bustling city to earn his living."

The vision of the reality in which the majority of poor men live determined the central crisis of his life; the crisis which was to carry him far from his first understanding of the religious life.

As you may know, Charles de Foucauld was a Trappist, and had chosen the poorest Trappist monastery in existence, that of Akbès in Syria. One day his superior sent him to watch by the corpse of a Christian Arab who had died in a poor house.

When Brother Charles was in the dead man's hovel he saw real poverty around him: hungry children and a weak, defenceless widow without assurance of the next day's bread. It was this spiritual crisis which was to make him leave La Trappe and go in search of a religious life very different from the earlier one.

"We, who have chosen the imitation of Jesus and Jesus Crucified, are very far from the trials, the pains, the insecurity and the poverty to which these people are subjected.

"I no longer want a monastery which is too secure. I want a small monastery, like the house of a poor workman who is not sure if tomorrow he will find work and bread, who with all his being shares the suffering of the world."

"Oh, Jesus, a monastery like your house at Nazareth, in which to live hidden as you did when you came among us."

When he came out of La Trappe Foucauld founded his first fraternity at Beni-Abbès in the Sahara; later he built his hermitage at Tamanrasset where he died, murdered by the Tuareg.

The fraternity was to resemble the house of Nazareth, a house just like one of the many houses one sees along the many streets of the world.

Had he renounced contemplation then? Had his fervid spirit of prayer weakened? No, he had taken a step forward. He had decided to live the contemplative life along the streets, in a situation similar to that of any ordinary man.

That step is much harder!

It is a step that God wants mankind to make.

The life of Charles de Foucauld opens up a new understanding of the spiritual life in which many will force themselves to make the fusion between contemplation and action—really living and obeying the first commandment of the Lord, "Love God above all things and your neighbour as yourself."

'Contemplation in the streets.' This is tomorrow's task not only for the Little Brothers, but for all the poor.

Let us begin to analyse this element of 'desert' which must be present, especially today, in the carrying out of such a demanding program.

When one speaks of the soul's desert, and says that the desert must be present in your life, you must not think only of the Sahara or the desert of Judea, or into the High Valley of the Nile.

Certainly it is not everyone who can have the advantage of being able to carry out in practice this detachment from daily life. The Lord conducted me into the real desert because I was so thick-skinned. For *me*, it was necessary. But all that sand was not enough to erase the dirt from my soul, even the fire was not enough to remove the rust from Ezekiel's pot.

But the same way is not for everybody. And if you cannot go into the desert, you must nonetheless "make some desert" in you life. Every now and then leaving men and looking for solitude to restore, in prolonged silence and prayer, the stuff of your soul. This is the meaning of 'desert' in your spiritual life.

One hour a day, one day a month, eight days a year, for longer if necessary, you must leave everything and everybody and retire, alone with God. If you don't look for this solitude, if you don't love it, you won't achieve real contemplative prayer. If you are able to do so but nevertheless do not withdraw in order to enjoy intimacy with God, the fundamental element of the relationship with the All-Powerful is lacking: love. And without love no revelation is possible.

But the desert is not the final stopping place. It is a stage on the journey. Because, as I told you, our vocation is contemplation in the streets.

For me, this is quite costly. The desire to continue living here in the Sahara for ever is so strong that I am already suffering in anticipation of the order that will certainly come from my superiors: "Brother Charles, leave for Marseilles, leave for Morocco, leave for Venezuela, leave for Detroit.

"You must go back among men, mix with them, live your intimacy with God in the noise of their cities. It will be difficult but you must do it. And for this the grace of God will not fail you.

"Every morning, after Mass and meditation, you will make your way to work in a store or shipyard. And when you get back in the evening, tired, like all poor men forced to earn their living, you will enter the little chapel of the brotherhood and remain for a long time in adoration; bringing to your prayer all that world of suffering, of darkness, and often of sin, in the midst of which you have livedfor eight hours taking your share of pain and toil."

Contemplation in the streets. A good phrase, but very demanding.

Certainly it would be easier and more pleasant to stay here in the desert. But God doesn't seem to want that.

The voice of the Church makes itself heard more and more. It points out to Christians the reality of the mystical body and the People of God. It calls men to the life of love. It invites everybody to a life of action which, couched in contemplation, is a witness and presence among me.

Convent walls are becoming thinner and the ceilings ever lower. The laity are becoming conscious of their mission and are searching for a genuine spirituality. It is truly the dawn of a new world to which it would not seem unworthy to give as an aim 'contemplation in the streets' and to offer the means of achieving it.

But there is another basic element of the contemplative life, above all as it is lived in the world: poverty.

Poverty is not a question of having or not having money. Poverty is not material. It is a beatitude. "Blessed are the poor in spirit." It is a way of being, thinking and loving. It is a gift of the Spirit. Poverty is detachment, and freedom and, above all, truth.

Go into almost any middle-class home, even a Christian one, and you will see the lack of this beatitude of poverty. The furniture, the drapes, the whole atmosphere are sterotyped, determined by fashion and luxury, not by necessity and truth.

This lack of liberty, or rather this slavery to fashion, is one of the idols which attracts a great number of Christians. How much money is sacrificed upon its altar!—without taking into account that so much good could otherwise be done with it. Being poor in spirit means, above all, being unrestrained by what is called fashion; it means freedom.

I don't buy a blanket because it is fashion. I buy it because I need it. Without a blanket my child shivers in bed. Bread, a blanket, a table, fire, are things necessary in themselves. To use them is to carry out God's plan. "All the rest comes from the evil one," to paraphrase an expression of Jesus' about truth. And this 'rest' is fashion, habit, luxury, over-indulgence, greed—slavery to the world.

One seeks not what is true, but what is pleasing to others. We seem to need this mask. We seem incapable of living without it.

Things get really serious when 'styles' come

into the picture and prices become astronomical. ''This is a Louis XIV—this is genuine crystal—this is etc. etc.''

It is more serious still when 'styles' enter the homes of churchmen, called by God to preach the Gospel to the poor.

There was a period during which churchly opulence might possibly have been justified.

From the Renaissance to the eighteenth century, the triumphant posture of the Church and the need felt by the masses to give worthy honour to God and the things of God, were expressed with extraordinary luxury and pomp.

The poor then were not scandalised; indeed they seemed pleased with all that glitter and magnificence.

Even more recently I remember my mother who, although poor, spoke with 'Christian' pride and satisfaction of the beauty of the Bishop's house, and the length of the prelates' cars parked under the window.

But things have changed. If that same bishop today knew of, or rather heard, the curses hurled at his long, elegant car, he would quickly change it for an economy model or better still, he'd use a bicycle.

We speak increasingly of the Church of the Poor, and I don't think it's a merely rhetorical phrase

It's necessary, however, to understand the meaning of the words. When one speaks of poverty in the Church one must not identify it with the beatitude of poverty. This, the beatitude, is an interior virtue, and I cannot, and must not judge my brother by it. Even the wealthy man, or the pontiff covered with a golden cope, can and must possess the beatitude of poverty. Nobody can judge another in this respect.

But when one speaks of poverty in the Church, one means social poverty, care for the poor, help for the poor, preaching the Gospel to the poor.

When one speaks of poverty in the Church, one means the kind of life Christians live, and this it is which scandalises the poor, as Paul was scandalised by the behaviour of the Christians of Corinth.

> The point is, when you hold these meetings, it is not the Lord's Supper that you are eating, since when the time comes to eat, everyone is in such a hurry to start his own supper that one person goes hungry while another is getting drunk. Surely you have homes for eating and drinking in? Surely you have enough respect for the community of God not to make poor people embarrassed? (1 Cor. 11: 20)

> And don't we perhaps put the poor man to shame when we pass by with our power and riches while he cannot afford to pay the rent? How can we preach the Gospel to him, while enjoying economic security when he doesn't know whether tomorrow he will have work and bread?

But poverty as a beatitude is not only truth, freedom and justice. It is and always will be love, and its limits become infinite, as infinite as the love of God.

Poverty is love for the poor Jesus, and voluntary self-denial. Jesus could have been rich. He did not have to live the kind of life he lived. No, he wanted to be poor in order to share the restrictions of real poverty, to put up with the lack of comfort, to suffer in his body the hard reality which weighs down the man searching for bread, to experience the abiding instability of one who possesses nothing.

This authentic poverty, borne for the sake of love, is the true beatitude of which the Gospel speaks.

It is easy to speak of spiritual poverty, to fill one's mouth with pious words, and yet not lack anything, not really feel the pinch, have a secure house, a well-stocked larder and the security of a bank account.

Let us not deceive ourselves and let us not dilute the most precious things Jesus said.

Poverty is poverty and always will be poverty; and it is not enough to make a vow of poverty in order to be "poor in spirit."

Today the poor are a real cause for scandal; to be rid of this scandal it would be better to spend less time arguing about the nature of chastity and put more emphasis on this beatitude which is in danger of being forgotten by those who are trying to 'live as Christians.' If it is true, as it is, that the perfection of the law is love, then it must fully control my desire for possessions and riches. Otherwise I shall not know what the beatitude really means.

If I love, if I really love, how can I tolerate the fact that a third of humanity is menaced with starvation while I enjoy the security of economic stability? If I act in that way I shall perhaps be a good Christian, but I shall certainly not be a saint; and today there are far too many good Christians when the world needs saints. We must learn to accept instability, put ourselves every now and then in the condition of having to say, 'Give us this day our daily bread,' with real anxiety because the larder is empty; have the courage, for love of God and one's neighbour, to give until it hurts and, above all, keep open in the wall of the soul the great window of living faith in the Providence of an all-powerful God.

I know that what I have said about poverty is challenging, and I also know that when in the world I did not really put it into practice. It is I who have lived for years behind the mask of 'pleasing others'; it is I who have spent money, and not only my own, on things which are 'not real.'

And yet, in spite of this, I cannot remain silent; and to my freinds I must say: beware of the temptation of riches. It is much more serious than it may appear today to well-intentioned Christians, and it sows destruction primarily because we underestimate its danger.

Riches are a slow poison, which strikes almost imperceptibly, paralysing the soul at the moment when it seems healthiest. They are thorns which grow with the grain and suffocate it right at the moment when the corn is beginning to shoot up. What a number of men and women, religious people, let themselves get caught up in their later lives by the spirit of middle-class tastes.

Now that solitude and prayer have helped me to see things more clearly, I understand why contemplation and poverty are inseparable. It is impossible to have a deep relationship with Jesus in Bethlehem, with Jesus in exile, with Jesus the workman of Nazareth, with Jesus the apostle who has nowhere to lay his head, with the crucified Jesus, without having achieved within ourselves that detachment from things, proclaimed with such authority and lived by him.

One will not reach this high state of poverty at once. Indeed, life itself will not be long enough to achieve it fully. But we must think about it, reflect and, above all, pray.

Jesus, God of the impossible, will help us. He will work, if need be, the miracle of making the parable of the camel pass though the narrow rusty eye of our poor sick soul.

11.
Sectarianism

This evening Abdaraman is accompanying me to the hermitage for adoration. We walk the two hundred yards together, hand in hand and chatting.

Abdaraman is a Moslem boy of perhaps eight years old. I say 'perhaps' because no Registry of Births exists among his people; a child's birth is simply not recorded. So few people know their exact age.

Abdaraman does not go to school, even though there is one beyond the river, attended by the Europeans and some "Mosabites," the sons of local tradesmen. He doesn't go to school because his father Aleck won't let him go.

"Aleck," I asked him, "why don't you send your sons to school?" Aleck looked at me deeply. "Brother Charles, I don't send my sons to school because they become bad. Look at the boys who go to school. They don't pray, they no longer obey, and they care about nothing but the way they dress."

Abdaraman is quite naked. He looks like a beautiful dark-grey statue, the result of infinite crossings between black Africans brought here as slaves, and white Africans from Northern tribes: Arabs, Berbers, and Tuareg.

Abdaraman, like all the sons of Ishmael, is circumcised and of the strict observance. His father Aleck is a good man, with strong faith and many sons. When the month of Ramadan comes around he fasts from dawn to dusk though continuing to work in his field along the banks of the river at Tamanrasset. Aleck is very devout and every year he remembers the sacrifice of Abraham by the killing of a sheep; then he buys a pale cotton dress for each of his little ones. His faith in God is absolute, and, poor as he is, he does not steal, but lives from his work. This consists in digging a canal, called a *seghia*, for months at a time in the sands of the river bank, and for the other months cultivating his little field, which needs water at least three times a week.

Once a detachment of the Foreign Legion arrived and pitched camp along the *seghia* which carries water to Aleck's corn. Soon the water ran short and Aleck's corn began to wither.

"Aleck," I said to him, "if it goes on like this your corn will dry up. Go and tell the captain the *seghia* is yours, and to pitch his camp elsewhere."

Aleck answered, "Allah is great and will provide for my children." And he let the corn die while the legionnaires washed their vehicles and threw water at one another in fun.

Abdaraman is accompanying me this evening tothe hermitage. The sun has set and the air has freshened. It's good to walk. We always have many things to talk about because we are really fond of one another. Every morning I find him outside my cell waiting for me to finish my meditation. Often we have tea together and he tells me how much he likes the bread I make. Abdaraman is always hungry. But he never asks me for anything; it's always I who have to guess that he wants food.

This evening he is serious, and answers my questions with difficulty. I realize that he has something important to say to me and hesitates to do so.

But I know it won't be long before he speaks, because there are no secrets between him and me.

"What's the matter, Abdaraman?"

Silence.

"Are you hungry?"

Silence.

"Did Daddy spank you?"

Silence.

"Has your bird escaped from its cage?"

Silence.

"Speak to me, Abdaraman. You know I am your friend."

Abdaraman bursts into tears, his naked body shaking. Tears stream down his face and then continue down onto his chest and abdomen.

Now it's my turn to be silent. I must await the stilling of the storm. I squeeze his hands harder as a sign of affection.

"Well, then, Abdaraman, what's making you cry?"

"Brother Charles, I am crying because you don't become a Moslem!"

"Oh," I exclaim, "and why should I become a Moslem? Abdaraman, I am a Christian, and believe in Jesus. I believe in the God who created heaven and earth, just as you do, and our prayers go to the same heaven, because there's only one God. It is he who has created us, who feeds us and loves us. If you do your duty, don't rob, don't kill, don't tell lies, and follow the voice of your conscience, then you'll go to heaven, and it'll be the same heaven as mine, if I too have done what God commanded me. Don't cry any more."

"No, no," Abdaraman cries. "If you don't become a Moslem you'll go to hell like all Christians!"

"Oh, what a thought, Abdaraman! Who told you I would go to hell if I didn't become a Moslem?"

"A man in the village told me that all Christians go to hell. And I don't want you to go to hell."

We have almost reached the hermitage, and Abdaraman stops. He has never come any further than this. He has always stopped ten steps away from that building, and he would not enter for all the gold in the world, as though inside there were some mysterious deviltry forbidden to little Moslems. His love for me, and it is great, has always been injured by this wall which divides us and which this evening is taking on such an absolutely terrible name—hell.

I tell him, "No, Abdaraman. God is good and will save both of us. He will save your father, too, and we shall all go to heaven. Don't believe that just because I am a Christian I shall go to hell, as I don't believe you'll go there just because you're a Moslem. God is so good! Perhaps you didn't understand really what the man meant. Perhaps he said that bad

Christians go to hell. Cheer up! Go home and say your prayers while I say mine. And before you finish, say this to God and I'll say it too: 'Lord, let all men be saved!' Go on. . . " And sadly I entered the hermitage, this little mud building, constructed by the same Charles de Foucauld who wanted to be called the Little Brother of all men and who was murdered, through ignorance and fanaticism, by sons of the same tribe as Aleck and Abdaraman.

But this evening it is difficult for me to pray. What a tumult of thoughts my little friend has aroused in me!

Poor little Abdaraman! You, too, are a victim of fanaticism, the stormy zeal of religious people, the so-called 'men of God,' who would send half the human race to hell, just because they are not 'one of us.' How can the thread of love which links me to a brother be broken by an alleged purity of faith, or that religion, instead of being a bridge of union, should become a trench of death, or at least of unconfessed hate? We're best off without it, this religion which divided us. Best to fumble around in the dark, than to possess a light like that!

After an hour's effort to face my poor soul with the silence of the Eucharist, I realised that tears were staining my white robe. I was the one to weep now.

While examining my conscience in order to

cleanse *my* soul, not Abdaraman's, from sectarianism, a scene from my childhood rose again to my mind. I was eight years old then, the same age as Adbaraman. I lived in a village in the shade of an ancient church tower. The townspeople were not very religious, but they were excessively narrow-minded in their "purity of faith."

One day a man came to sell books, going from house to house. I didn't understand much then, but it was the first time I understood the word Bible.

An unusual commotion seized the village. First the women, then everybody. Some out of zeal, some out of human respect. The excitement quickly reached the children.

The hysterical cry of a woman shouting from a window: "Rascal! You rascal! We don't need your religion. Go away!"

The man was walking in the middle of the street. His books were in a big, heavy bag.

A woman from behind him threw a book she had bought a rew minutes before. Without turning around, the man bent down to pick it up. A stone from a boy hit him in the back. The man quickened his pace, followed at some distance by the boys, each carrying a stone. I was among them. That evening at May Devotions the parish priest praised us for defending the parish citadel.

At a distance of forty years, and particularly this evening, that event acquired a new meaning for me.

I had never confessed to throwing a stone at an undefended man, out of religious zeal at that. The episode is recorded in a world which used to accept things of that kind, without seeing all their heinousness.

Nearly half a century things have changed. There is something new in the air. A breath from the Spirit is animating the whole universe. An old world is dying, and a new one is being born. New concerns, new needs, new forces. We are at the dawn of an epoch marked by a great desire, at least, for love and peace among men and nations. Truth and charity are again striving to meet one another; respect for the individual is increasingly championed among all peoples.

An ecumenical spirit is loosening the most complicated knots, and the desire to know one another is far greater than the temptation to remain closed in the old citadel of our presumed truth.

Man, perhaps for the first time, is going into the field undefended, hopeful of fruitful encounters, of making friends of strangers.

Abdaraman, my dear little Abdaraman, have no fear: we shall love one another again, and we shall meet one another—and not only in heaven.

12.
Nazareth

Charles de Foucauld, born in Strasbourg September 15, 1858, was a nobleman. In his veins ran the blood of proud people accustomed to giving commands. He himself had attended the military academy of Saint Cyr, become an officer in the French army, and at the age of twenty-five had embarked on what was then a most dangerous undertaking—the exploration of Morocco.

Yet this man, soldier, adventurer—and apostate since his schooldays at Nancy—suddenly, in 1886, fell in love with Christ with the strength of a Saint Francis.

Very rarely does one find a man more passionately dedicated to discovering the details of the life of Jesus. He searched in the Gospels for clues to Jesus' personality, character, and life, so that he might imitate the Lord's attitude, gestures, and innermost intentions; and in his loving search for faithful and living material for imitation, Charles de Foucauld was above all impressed by the fact that Jesus was poor and a workman. Astonishing! The Son of God—who, more than anyone else, was free to choose whathe would—chose not only a mother and a people, but also a social position. And he wanted to be a wage earner.

That Jesus had *voluntarily* lost himself in an obscure Middle Eastern village; annihilated himself in the daily monotony of thirty years' rough, miserable work; separated himself from the society that "counts"; and died in total anonymity—all this confused the noble convert. (We must realize that the words "Laborer," "worker," and "wage earner" have a quite different ring in the ears of a nobleman than they have in the average person's. Therefore it seemed to Charles de Foucauld that choosing to become a worker meant abasement, annihilation of oneself.) Why hadn't Jesus become a scribe, he wondered? Why hadn't he wished to be born into one of those families destined for command, responsibility, social and political influence?

Not too long after de Foucauld began the passionate search for the intentions which had guided the Divine Master in the choice of his life, his whole life, he made the discovery that was to remain, basically, the ascetical guide of the life of this great Moroccan explorer and Saharan mystic: "Jesus has so diligently searched for the lowest place that it would be very difficult for anyone to tear it from him."

Nazareth was the lowest place: the place of the poor, the unknown, of those who didn't count, of the mass of workers, of men subjected to work's grim demands just for a scrap of bread.

But there is more. Jesus is the 'Holy One of God.' But the Holy One of God realised his sanctity not in an extraordinary life, but one impregnated with ordinary things: work, family and social life, obscure human activities, simple things shared by all men.

The perfection of God is cast in a material which men almost despise, which they don't consider worth searching for because of its simplicity, its lack of interest, because it is common to all men.

Once he had discovered the spiritual reality of Nazareth, Charles de Foucauld tried to imitate it as faithfully as possible.

He tried to found a community in a small home like the one at Nazareth; he tried to lose himself in the silence of an unknown village; he imitated Jesus by working manually, and he wanted his Little Brothers to be always searching for the last place, there where the poor are, where the climate is roughest, the wages the most meagre, the toil hardest. Nazareth symbolised all this, and more.

The imitation of Nazareth is no small thing. When I think that a door, a wooden partition, was all that divided a holy family like that of Jesus from that of a neighbour, I am convinced of the immense interior richness of the Gospel message. The same actions, if carried out under God's light, radically transformed the life of man, family and society.

Joy or sadness, war or peace, love or hate, purity or impurity, charity or greed, all are tremendous realities which are the hinges of a man's interior life. Everyday things, relationships with our fellow-men, daily work, love of our family—all these may breed saints.

Jesus at Nazareth taught us to live every hour of the day as saints. Every hour of the day is useful and may lead to divine inspiration, the will of the Father, the prayer of contemplation—holiness. Every hour of the day is holy. What matters is to live it as Jesus taught us.

And for this one does not have to shut oneself

in a monastery or fix strange and inhumane regimes for one's life. It is enough to accept the realities of life. Work is one of these realities; motherhood, the rearing of children, family life with all its obligations are others.

These realities must be sanctified; we must not think that a person is holy just because he has made vows. One with this outlook thinks of the hour of spiritual reading or prayer as the only time for the spiritual life and ignores the longer time dedicated to work and everyday living. The result is at best an anaemic and unreliable religious personality.

The whole man must be transformed by the Gospel message. Nothing he does can be indifferent. All his actions must be determined by the Gospel.

Nazareth is the life of a man, of a family, fully engaged in human activity.

Few men have summed up the sanctity of common things so well as did Gandhi in his writings:

> If when we plunge our hand
> into a bowl of water,
> Or stir up the fire with the bellows
> Or tabulate interminable columns of figures
> on our book-keeping table,
> Or, burnt by the sun, we are plunged in

the mud of the rice-field,
Or standing by the smelter's furnace
We do not fulfill the same religious life
as if in prayer in a monastery,
the world will never be saved.

But there's another aspect of Nazareth which is important above all for those who think it is impossible to carry out the Gospel message without tools, means or money.

Jesus was himself the carrier of the message; he was at the same time the Supreme Intelligence, capable of devising the best way of making himself understood, and of carrying out the divine plans.

Well, what did he do? He did not open hospitals or found orphanages. He became flesh, lived among people and he embodied the Gospel message in its entirety, *Coepit facere*. He began to act.

He *lived* his message before he *spoke* of it. He preached it by his life before explaining it in words. This was Jesus' method and we too easily forget it.

In many cases catechesis is reduced to words rather than to 'life,' to discussions rather than to the pursuit of Christian living.

And here, perhaps, is the reason for the poor

results, and still more, the reason for so much of the apathy and indifference among Christians today. Teaching is ineffective because it is not life-centred; there is no life because there is no example; there is no example because empty words have taken the place of faith and charity.

"I want to preach the Gospel with my life," Charles de Foucauld often said. He was convinced that the most effective method of preaching the Gospel was to live it. Especially today, people no longer want to listen to sermons. They want to see the Gospel in action.

Nazareth is the long period of separation, prayer and sacrifice. It is a time of silence, of intimate life with God; the time of long solitude, purification, understanding men, and knowing the value of detachment: the things that matter to a Christian.

From Nazareth we will learn how to live the Gospel, to be apostles. What does it mean to be an apostle?

The word is one of the most misunderstood today. It is a term used both correctly and incorrectly. Everybody has become an apostle, and even moving a chair counts as apostolic activity.

Perhaps we have gotten into the habit of using big words to enhance parochial or diocesan life;

but things don't change and words remain words.

All I should like to say on the subject is that having meditated for a long time on Nazareth, I have learned from the depths of this mystery a deeper appreciation of the life of the layman and the life of the priest, of the apostolate of the laity and the apostolate of the priest.

My generation has lived through an extraordinary and in many ways chaotic period and many things must be justified either by reason of our childish incompetence and lack of preparation, or attributed to special historical circumstances.

After all, when a house is on fire, even a woman may do the fireman's job, and a layman gives orders to a bishop.

But normally these things should not be. It is not for the layman to undertake the curate's duties, nor for the priest to be the parish bookkeeper. As for me, in the middle of the desert, as the termites eat up the books in my cell, it is enough to think of Nazareth. To me the greatest inspiration for the spirituality of the laity is in the life of Jesus, Mary and Joseph.

The spirituality of the laity shouldn't be a copy, good or bad, of that of priests, but something else: authentic and genuine in its own right, true before God and men. The activity of a priest is one thing, the activity of a politician another; the activity of a pastor is one thing, that of a workman or the father of a family another.

If it is true that by spirituality we mean the way of thinking, living and sanctifying the acts of our lives, then the way in which a priest lives and sanctifies the acts of his life is something profoundly different from the way in which a worker, a married man or a civil servant does.

The layman is not to be a quasi-priest. He must sanctify his work, his marriage, his varied relationships as a layman.

Saint Peter, in his first epistle (2:4) says to the laity:

"You, too, must be a holy priesthood to offer up the spiritual sacrifice which Jesus Christ has made acceptable to God, living stones making a spiritual house."

There is no question then that a real and authentic priesthood exists for baptised Christians. It is very different, naturally, from the priesthood conferred by the sacrament of Holy Orders, but it is a real priesthood which the layman must live and develop in its own right.

This is extremely important, and the layman

who does not respond to it has either betrayed or failed to understand his vocation.

The workman is a priest in his work; the father of a family is a priest for his wife and children; the head of a community is a priest before its members; the peasant is a priest for his farm, animals, fields and flowers.

The royal priesthood of which Peter spoke and the meaning of the "offering of spiritual sacrifices which Jesus Christ has made acceptable to God" have been emphasised too little. This has created the dryness apparent in so much discussion on the apostolate of the laity, and, what is more, of the position of the layman in the Church.

How can we speak of the spirituality of the laity if we omit this fundamental prerogative of the priest of created things, voice of nature, consecrator of the goods of the earth, saint of the earthly city?

If this is not expounded the layman who wished to become 'good' will end up by copying the parish priest, whom he feels to be spiritually ahead of him, and he will become half layman and half priest. This may be to the edification of the good parishioners, but perhaps of no influence on those outside, especially the "lapsed."

These latter—rightly—cannot bear the scent of religious hybrids and they continue to think that Christianity has no answer to the world's problems.

There is still a long way to go, but some progress has been made.

Priests and laymen have begun to realise their respective roles in the Church.

That's what I hope for, because I would like those who enter this arena of apostolic activity today to avoid the false assumptions of my time, whereby priests were dragged in as canvassers, and the laity expected to give advice to the bishops on the Church government.

13.

The last place

I became a Little Brother of Jesus because God called me. I never doubted the call. Equally, if God hadn't called me I couldn't have survived for long!

Sleeping in the open, living in rough climates, associating with really poor tribes and putting up with the stench: all this is small compared with the revolution in one's personality, the breaking off with the past, the living among civilisations and peoples so different from one's own.

As you know, the Little Brother may not have a life apart. He must choose a village, a slum, a nomadic town, settle in it and live as all the others live, especially as the poorest live.

This is quite contrary to the behaviour of Europeans who had previously come here. The

European arrived as a soldier, missionary, technician or official, built himself a European house and lived as a European among the natives. His standard of living was not the local one, but that of his country of origin.

His task was to spread the Gospel, educate, help, organise, support; but always in the European way, with Europeanculture, methods and aims. These men preached their faith by what they gave.

And that's no small thing! Miracles of love and heroism were written in the earth of Africa and Asia: churches, hospitals, dispensaries, schools, social institutions were created in order to cure disease, avert death and hasten the progress of people in underdeveloped countries.

It was the great missionary moment of the Church; it coincided with the growth of colonisation and empire-building.

It represented the infiltration of the white race into the coloured ones, the movement of the rich towards the poor, Christians towards "pagan." Things didn't always go smoothly; a missionary wasn't always synonymous with a man of God, nor an official with generosity and justice.

It's a long story. If we went on with it we

should end by bringing the past to trial, and our only interest is the way in which in a few years everything has begun to change.

The African churches are becoming aware of their own identity and no longer wish to be copies of the English, the Italian or the Dutch churches. Not only do coloured people no longer tolerate colonialism; through reaction, they are closing their hearts to the white man, they no longer have the trust they once had, and often they despise or hate everything which comes from the "master race" of former times.

As is natural in such cases, this reaction can be excessive and result in injustice and intolerance if one sees only what was bad in the past.

It is more true than ever that we must review past position, reconsider all the attitudes.

In this light, and in view of the new attitudes to mission work in the Church today, the work of Charles de Foucauld can be seen as prophetic.

This man of God, never truly aware of the problems but driven on by the strength and light of the Spirit, went to Africa in the period of full colonisation. At that time, there was not the slightest indication of the way in which events would turn in Africa. Caring only about carrying the Gospel to the Berbers or the Tuareg, he understood what other men did not, and worked as though the process of decolonisation had already begun.

He did not arrive with gifts, hospitals, dispensaries, schools and money.

He arrived alone, defenceless, poor. He had understood that the power of the European, even if expressed in hospitals and schools, had hardly anything to say to the African on the spiritual level and was no longer the witness it had once been.

He understood that the native, however poor and ill-educated, was no longer willing to accept as from on high a message which seemed to him entirely bound to a particular people and a particular civilisation.

Someone had to show a new way; in a sense it was not a new way, for it was there in the Gospel. But it had to be lived with a new purity and strength: It is the way of poverty, sacrifice, humility, and silent witness. It is arguable that this is the way not only for poor countries; people everywhere are afraid of power. The powerful, rich, dominating Church of today makes men afraid.

Man's eye, terrorised by the possibility it sees in science, rests joyfully upon what is little, undefended, weak. People are even afraid of an orator who shouts too loudly.

Here is the secret of the wide acceptance

of Charles de Foucauld. He arrived, undefended, among savage tribesmen like the Tuareg. He came to the Arab world dressed as an Arab. He lived among those who were the servants of the Europeans as though they were his masters. He built his hermitages, not on Roman or Gothic lines, but on the simplicity and poverty of the Saharan mosques.

Being poor, dressing like "them," accepting their language and customs, he immediately knocked down the barriers and lived in dialogue with them. Real dialogue: between equals.

I shall never forget a scene which, in its simplicity, expresses concretely the degree of love in this new "going towards them who do not yet know Christ."

I was traveling by camel along the track between Geriville and El Abiod, heading for a desert area to spend some days in solitude.

At a certain point along the track I came to a work detail. About fifty natives, under the direction of a minor official of the Engineer Corps, were toiling to repair the road, ruined by the winter rain.

No machines, no technology under the Saharan sun; only the toil of wielding the shovel and pick all day in the heat and the dust. I passed up the line of workmen scattered on the track, replying to their greetings and offering the litres of water in my *gherba* for their thirst.

At a certain point, among the mouths approaching the *gherba* to drink, I saw a smile break out which I shall never forget.

Poor, ragged, sweating, dirty: it was Brother Paul, a Little Brother who had chosen that detail in which to live out his Calvary, to be a kind of leaven there.

Nobody would have detected the European underneath those clothes, that beard and that turban, yellow from the dust and the sun.

I knew Brother Paul well, because we had been novices together.

A Parisian engineer, he had been working on the Reganna atomic bomb when he heard the Lord's call.

He left everything, and became a Little Brother. Now he was there. Nobody knew he was an engineer. He was a poor man like the others.

I remember his mother when she came to the novitiate on the occasion of him making his vows.

"Brother Charles," she had said, "help me understand my son's vocation! I have made him an engineer; you have made him a manual labourer. Why? You might at least have used my son for what he is worth! Wouldn't it be more advantageous, more useful for the Church to have him work as an intellectual?!"

"There are things," I replied, "we cannot understand by mere intellect and common sense. Only faith can enlighten us. Why did Jesus wish to be poor? Why did he wish to hide his divinity and power and live among us as the least of us? Why the defeat of the cross, the scandal of Calvary, the ignominy of death for him who was life? No, the Church doesn't need one more engineer; she needs a grain of wheat to die in her furrows."

So many things cannot be understood on this earth. Isn't everything around us a mystery?

I can understand why Paul had to give up everything—his way of life, his career—for love of God and love of his brethren. But I also understood the reactions of his mother. Indeed, many would say: "What a pity! Such an intelligent person going to work in the Sahara! He could have built a printing press for making available good literature. He could have . . . " And they would be right too.

It's difficult to fathom the mystery of man, which is part of the great mystery of God. There are those who dream of a powerful Church, rich in resources and potential, and there are those who want her poor and weak. There are those who devote their lives to study in order to enrich Christian thought, and those who renounce study for love of God and their neighbour.

That is the mystery of faith!

Paul was not interested in having influence upon men. He was content to pray, to disappear. Others will search other paths and achieve holiness in other ways.

Can I doubt the faith of my mother, who would have desired all riches to be in the hands of the Church, to be used for more effective missions?

And I, her son, quite the opposite: dreaming of a simpler faith, a more deeply-felt poverty, and above all, a vocation founded on the lack of riches. Wasn't I right in a way, too?

It's so difficult to judge! So difficult that Jesus besought us not to try to answer these questions.

But to one truth we must always cling desperately—to love!

It's love which justifies our actions; love must initiate all we do. Love is the fulfillment of the law.

If, out of love, Brother Paul has chosen to die on a desert track, by this he is justified.

If, out of love, Don Bosco and Mother Seton built schools and hospitals, by this they were justified.

If, out of love, Thomas Aquinas spent his life among books, by this he was justified.

The only problem is to put into their right perspective these different kinds of 'love-in-action.' And here Jesus himself teaches us in an uncompromising way:

"The greatest among you must be as the least, the leader be as one who is a servant."

And again: "A man can have no greater love that to lay down his life for his friends."

14.

Oh, you who pass by

The track to Taifet is simply horrible.

In fact, I avoid it whenever possible. I prefer to go a few miles out of my way through Ideles and Irafok, rather than through those impassable gorges. One had to make one's way with pick and shovel through rocky tracks, and afterwards sink into the soft sand of the endlessly winding *oued*.

But this time I had no choice and as I set out I mustered all the courage I had, which wasn't much, after a week of warm southerly wind and the fatigue caused by the extreme changes of temperature between day and night.

As usual, the sky was cloudless, and the sun relentless from eight o'clock in the morning on. But I didn't notice. My only concern was the engine of the jeep which seemed on the verge of giving up and no longer wanted to cooperate when the car sunk into the sand.

And yet I had to go on. Who would have come to my aid on that track?

The previous evening, at the well of Tazrouk, I had taken on all the water possible, but what would happen when that was gone?

What would I do if I were stranded in the desert, the very image of death and perpetual silence?

All my hope lay in that engine, whose throb was so familiar to me and which had never let me down before. But now? Would I succeed in crossing the fourteen miles of the ravine of Taifet, with its soft burning sands, its dry, arid gorges?

Nine o'clock, ten, eleven—after three breaks to let the engine cool down I finally reached sight of Taifet, a tiny village of ex-slaves on the edge of the ravine.

I hurled the jeep forward over the track, hoping in this way to avoid having to try to get the wheels to grip the soft sand. The heat was suffocating, and the water was boiling in the radiator.

Then, in a last attempt to keep up the pace, the engine gave one last groan and stopped. The jeep sank down into the sand. I got out of the car, although I was afraid of sunstroke. I didn't have the energy to take the shovel to free the car from the sand. I looked for a little shade. In the *oued*, here and there, were etel bushes, I sought the nearest one and threw myself on the ground in its shade.

I don't know why but at that moment I remembered the prophet Jonah, sitting under the ivy which protected him from the sun while Ninevah burned.

But I had little time for such Biblical reflections because I went to sleep almost at once.

I awoke slowly to the sound of people talking in low voices interspersed with bursts of laughter. I was bathed in sweat and my head ached. I opened my eyes and saw around me men from Taifet, looking at me and smiling. How white their teeth were, how their dark skin glowed! There were a score of them, and they had interrupted their work on my arrival. Under the etel they had already prepared the fire for tea. The warmth of the beverage restored me.

They invited me to eat with them, and I offered them everything I had on the jeep. The tobacco, particularly, made them talkative. A pleasant interlude followed, but it was so short! They had to get on with their work. And what work!

They had dug in the ravine a subterranean canal called a *fogara*, which would collect the water in which the sand was soaked like a sponge, and conduct it to the nearby fields.

There the grain which had been sown was by now fully grown and very thirsty. The usual unpredictable sandstorm had destroyed the old *fogara* and they had to make another without delay. If they were late, even by a week, it could be enough to ruin the harvest, which would mean hunger for the rest of the year.

I offered to work with them for a few days, although I knew my help was not worth very much.

And so I lived for a week with one of the poorest human groups on earth. Work began at dawn, and lasted until sunset.

With primitive tools we dug the tunnel which ran about three yards beneath the surface of the *oued*.

The man working in the tunnel had the advantage of suffering less from the heat, but it was nevertheless an uncomfortable position to work in; working outside one suffered backache less, but the heat was suffocating. In either case it was very arduous and one longed for the evening, for food and rest.

In the evening we ate around the fires and if any dieticians had been present, they could easily have calculated that the calories consumed were well below the vital minimum. It was a small compensation, however, to be able to eat things which were rare for the European taste and palate.

The first evening we were served a little *couscous* with a dish of roasted grasshoppers. The next day came sand mice called *gerboise;* at another time a big firefly called *dobb;* this was very tasty and contained—according to the Tuareg—forty precious medicaments.

At night, wrapped up in a blanket near the huts, I used to gaze at the sky before going to sleep.

What connection could there possibly be between that glittering mass of stars and the misery among which I had fallen; between that infinity of space in the cosmos, and the needs of these mortal men?

This was the mystery of evil, of suffering. The mystery of men who die of starvation, who live, robbed of human dignity, condemned to a life in which the perpetual anguish of trying to find a little bread poisons the joy of the daily sunrise.

But I was too tired to think of why God didn't intervene since he is so powerful and so good. I sought a scapegoat in the "gods" of the earth, the men who could so easily have helped.

What would it cost to write a letter to my friends in Italy? They might immediately have sent me a bulldozer to dig out the trench in a few days. At least they could send me great cement tubes to make the trench stable and secure, and stop it caving in when water first ran into it. And there I was, just sitting motionless and looking at the stars!

Was I justified, just lying there and reflecting in this way?

What use could my poor hands possibly be with so much work to be done?

Wouldn't it be better to look elsewhere for help? This is a question I have often asked myself: so often, in fact, that it has even forced me to question the basis of my vocation.

And yet, faith must be the guide and not common sense.

The common sense of Brother Paul's mother, who could not understand her son's 'useless' sacrifice on the Saharan tracks; my own common sense which made me try to convince myself that I would be more use to the people of Taifet if I went away in search of materials for their trench; the common sense of men who believe that one can solve everything with money and that to share people's suffering is simply a waste.

But is the Gospel common sense? Or is it mystery?

When Jesus came on this earth, he, the All-

Powerful, he who was love, could he not perhaps have healed all the sick, fed all the hungry, healed all the wounded, raised all the dead?

He raised Lazarus and Jairus' daughter and the son of the widow of Nain, it is true, but only in order to prove that he did not intend to raise all the others—and there were many of them.

This is why, for him who suffers, theology is not enough. Something more is necessary.

When I left for Africa to become a Little Brother of Jesus I lived for some time in Algiers, as the guest of an old friend.

I was very unsettled in those days, and the world appeared to me under quite a new light. It had something to do with that intuition born in the heart of him whom I now wanted to follow along the desert tracks, Charles de Foucauld.

The perspective of a European, materially and culturally endowed, desirous of giving and doing something for others, had turned somersault in me. I would have liked to hide, without money in my pocket, dressed as an Arab, among the anonymous crowd of poor Moslems seething in the alleys of Kasbah.

I remember that around midday I noticed a long string of men in rags lining up near the convent, whose walls were as solid as a fortress.

Each man had a tin can. I saw a door open and a nun in a white habit appear; nearby was an enormous smoking pot. It was time for the daily distribution of alms, and each man received his share along with a loaf of bread and warm soup.

I stared at that procession as though in a dream; as I watched those men and women branded with misery, tears ran down my cheeks, so that I could no longer see the bright sky above the African city.

I tried to find a place for myself. I had left my native land, urged on by the desire to give up everything in order to give myself to God among all this poverty; to search out among the poor the crucified face of Jesus, to do something for my wretched and despised brethren, so that, by loving them, I might deepen my union with God.

What was I to do then? Was I to open dispensaries and give bread, medicine and education to these poor people. What was my place in the great evangelising work of the Church?

I tried to learn from him who had drawn me to Africa, Charles de Foucauld. Quite small, quite humble, tin can in hand, I found him in my imagination, at the end of the queue. He was smiling faintly, as if he wanted to ask pardon for adding himself to the number of the deprived and underpriviledged.

Undoubtedly, at that moment, in spite of my fear of suffering, my reluctance to bear the burdens of others, my fear of taking up the cross, I understood that my place, too, was there, amid the ragged poor, mixing in the mob.

Others in the Church would have the task of evangelising, building, feeding, preaching. The Lord asked me to be a poor man among poor men, a worker among workers.

Yes, above all, worker among workers, since the world of today was no longer in search of alms as in the time of Francis of Assisi, but a world in search of work, justice and peace.

The world towards which I was journeying was the world in which real poverty is experienced. For people in that world, work is their sackcloth, but they have not chosen it; moreover it is painful, dirty, and poorly paid.

After a week spent at Taifet I left again for Tamanrasset. I felt that I could not bear that wretchedness and poverty any longer. In this I was poorer than those poor men, for I had been unable to bear what they had always borne.

I needed prayer. I longed to find myself alone in my hermitage where Jesus was exposed day and night, in order to unburden myself to him, beseech him, lose myself in him.

Above all I wanted to ask him to make me smaller, emptier, more transparent—and to enable me to return to Taifet.

Yes, return to Taifet to live the last years of my life. Have a little hut 'like them,' no possessions but a mat and a blanket, 'like them,' on the shore of that *oued;* drag a little water from it with those *fogaras* which were continually breaking down as though laughing at our labour!

But also to have Jesus in the Host, hidden in the hut; to adore him, pray to him, love him, and obtain from him the strength not to rebel, not to curse, but to accept lovingly what the day would bring.

And so I pray for the day when on the shore of that *oued* a little etel cross will rise like a sentinel to watch over the solitude of those men as they wait, wait for others to come and love them and help them to love.

15.

The revolt of the good

The fact that my vocation leads me to seek the lowest place mans absolutely nothing. What counts is forcing myself to stay in that place every day of my life. And that is terribly difficult.

At the bottom of the human heart there is an ulcer which grows with the years. It is the ulcer of resentment at being exploited by others. Nobody escapes it; it takes time for the soul to locate it and, if and when God wills, to root it out.

Take a family situation. The burden of work is often ill-distributed; one member of the family bears most of the burden. Most often it is the mother.

As the shoulders of one person carry most of the weight, the rest of the family gets away lightly.

But under those shoulders there's a heart; and in that heart, little by little, an ulcer of resentment develops, and grows.

One day, one terrible day, because of some particular incident, serious or trivial, the ulcer bursts and spreads its poison throughout the body.

"I'm putting my foot down! I've had enough! I've been your servant up to now and you haven't even realised. I've sacrificed my life while you enjoyed yourselves," etc., etc.

The same thing can happen in a religious community and then the storm is much greater. Often the very foundations of the community seem in danger of collapse. The poison which is diffused among the members is so strong that it has the power of paralysing love itself.

And yet that mother is right. She has sacrificed herself for her family. The others have allowed themselves plenty of freedom. She has had no share of it. She has worked, saved, given up every moment of her day.

But there's something more serious, something which is the real cause of suffering. She hasn't been understood. They have taken her for granted; they haven't, for example, noticed her crying in silence.

Each one of us at this point can tell his own story, and, strangely, each one feels himself in exactly the position of that mother: each one of us feels himself the victim of someone or something. Someone has had a childhood without affection, another is badly paid at the office, another feels his abilities have not been fully used; someone else hasn't had the promotion he thinks he deserves, another hasn't been understood by his bishop, another has been forced to resign as chairman of his company, and another has been sent to work in the kitchen instead of being appointed superior of the convent!

But strangest of all is that each of us is right to a certain extent.

Of course, in our lives we receive insults and abuse from others, but we rather tend to enjoy being the victim. We like to think that the pain is unbearable, the more so because it seems to affect the roots of our being, our relationship with God and with our neighbour.

How can I love, really love my brother who sees me working day after day and repays me with indifference, and even with derision? How can I feel at ease in a convent where my brethren haven't really taken my personality into account and haven't understood my abilities? Why should I still work with enthusiasm when someone has been promoted who doesn't really deserve it.

In fact, I no longer love; I am unable to. But this inability to love is quite crucial because it leaves me with an enormous feeling of indifference.

Whether I like it or not, love is the aim of my life, the reason for my existence, the only thing that really satisfies me. In fact, since I ceased to love I have known no peace.

During my sleepless nights I feel sapped of energy, tormented by the wanderings of my spirit. I try to pray, but even my prayer has become bitter and senseless to me.

It seems that heaven is no longer interested in me. My cry for justice seems to go unheard. It is as though something has changed in heaven and the canons which governed the old system seem no longer to hold with God.

Until the Incarnation it was exactly like that. But the rule of justice alone was not enough. It was good, it was true, but it wasn't complete. Above all, it didn't express God's dynamism, God's infinity. To man in his blind alley of sin, the canons of justice and truth were unable to offer salvation. Something else was necessary.

Then Jesus came. And his own received him not. Not only that, but they sent him out into the desert like a scapegoat and rejected him.

All humanity surged round him to strike, spit and revile.

And Jesus, the only truly innocent man, bent his head under the blows. He did not invoke justice, and with his flesh and spirit he paid for the sins of the world.

From that moment was established for once and for all the law of forgiveness, mercy and love, which goes far beyond the bounds of justice.

After Calvary, peace was no longer to operate on the thin blade of truth or in the court of law, but in the torn heart of a God who had become man for us in Jesus Christ.

The era of victimisation had ended and with Jesus the reign of the victim was to begin.

The true victim, silent and lamb-like, the victim who accepts to be a victim and destroys the thorns of injustice in the fire of his love.

"The Lord loves a happy giver," Paul was to say. And the victim is the happy giver.

God will be the happy giver in his Christ. His gift of himself is unconditional. He will pardon all sins for ever. He will give life again to the tired bones of the sinner, he will transform a prostitute into a Mary Magdalene and an ordinary pleasure-seeker into a Saint Francis.

Life will triumph over death, and spring will find strength and beauty in the dung of the earth itself.

"I have overcome the world," Christ will shout in his sacrifice, and joy will flow again in our anguished heart.

Yes, I too must go beyond justice. To triumph over the sickness of victimisation I must go beyond it. Like Jesus and in imitation of him, I must wearily climb again the slope of my pain, and throw myself courageously in the descent towards my brothers, above all towards those whom the short-sightedness of my sick eyes sees asthe cause of my evils.

There is no other solution. There is no true peace and union with Jesus without it. As long as I waste time defending myself I get nothing done and I am not truly Christian; I do not know the depths of the heart of Jesus.

To forgive, really forgive, means convincing ourselves deep down that we merited the wrong done to us. What is more, it is good to suffer in silence. Jesus taught that the beatitude is reserved for those who are *persecuted* for the sake of justice.

What would mankind say if, following Jesus on Calvary, they saw him turn in sudden anger towards a man who had given him a kick and shout: "Do you know who I am?" No, Jesus did not turn upon those who insulted him to defend himself. He didn't flaunt his true identity at the crowd which was crucifying him. Above all, he did not hate them within himself.

The perpetual newness of the love of Jesus is all here. He had taught it so well and Luke understood it so well:

> But I say this to you who are listening: Love your enemies, do good to those who hate you, bless those who curse you, pray for those who treat you badly. To the man who slaps you on one cheek, present the other cheek too; to the man who takes your cloak from you, do not refuse your tunic (Luke 6:27).

It's unmistakable, the Spirit of Jesus, and unique. Paul, without doubt the best interpreter of this spirit in the depths of the heart of Christ, when he wants to outline the Christian's position before God and the world, says in the epistle to the Philippians:

> And your minds must be
> the same as Christ Jesus:
> His state was divine,
> yet He did not cling
> to His equality with God
> but emptied Himself
> to assume the condition of a slave,

and become as men are;
He was humbler yet,
even to accepting death,
death on a cross (Phil. 2:5).

This is a summary of all the virtues and all the perfections. This feeling of Jesus, this desire to lower himself to obey the Father and save man will for ever remain the climax of the love of Christ.

That is why truth and justice are not enough and we are invited to go further.

The more we "feel we must" abase ourselves in imitation of Jesus, the more humility will reign in our hearts, and peace flow into our lives.

In these lines lies the secret of sanctity.

16.
The God of the impossible

An accident in the middle of the desert paralysed one of my legs. When the doctor arrived—eight days later—it was too late; I shall be lame for the rest of my life.

Stretched out on a mat in the cell of an old Saharan fort, I looked at the marks made by time on the mud wall, whitewashed in lime by the soldiers of the Foreign Legion. The heat made it difficult to think. I preferred to pray. But there are certain moments when prayer is not easy.

I remained silent, trying mentally to take my soul beyond the compounds of my room into the little Arab-style chapel where I knew the Eucharist was. The Brothers were working some distance away, some in the fields, some in the workshop. My leg was hurting terribly, and I had to work up the force to stop my mind wandering. I remembered Pius XII once asking in one of his audiences, "What does Jesus do in the Eucharist?" and he awaited the reply from us students. Even today, after so many years, I do not know how to reply.

What does Jesus do in the Eucharist? I have thought about it often.

In the Eucharist Jesus is immobilised not in one leg only, but both, and in his hands as well. He is reduced to a little piece of white bread. The world needs him so much and yet he doesn't speak. Men need him so much and he doesn't move!

The Eucharist is the silence of God, the weakness of God.

To reduce himself to bread while the world is so noisy, so agitated, so confused.

It is as though the world and the Eucharist were walking in opposite directions. And they seem to get further and further from one another.

One has to be courageous not to let oneself be carried along by the world's march; one needs faith and will-power to go cross-current towards the Eucharist, to stop, to be silent, to worship. And one needs really strong faith to understand the impotence and defeat which the Eucharist represents and which is today what the impotence and defeat of Calvary was yesterday.

And yet this powerless Jesus, nailed down and annihilated, is the God of the Impossible, Alpha and Omega, the beginning and the end. As John describes Him in the Apocalypse:

> A judge with integrity, a warrior for justice. His eyes were flames of fire, and his head was crowned with many coronets; the name written on him was known only to himself, his cloak was soaked in blood. He is known by the name, the Word of God. Behind him, dressed in linen of dazzling white, rode the armies of heaven on white horses. From his mouth came a sharp sword to strike the nations with; he is the one who will rule them with an iron sceptre, and tread out the wine of almighty God's fierce anger. On his cloak and on his thigh there was a name written: The King of kings and the Lord of lords (19:11).

Jesus is God of the Impossible; my powerlessness shows his power; my insignificance as a creature shows his being as the creator.

From Job, in his struggle with his creator, God asked an act of trust, by pointing to the magnificence of creation.

> Where were you when I laid the earth's foundations? Who decided the dimensions of it, do you know? Or who stretched the measuring line across it? What supports its pillars at

> their bases? Who laid its cornerstone when all the stars of the morning were singing with joy? (Job 38:4-7).

Today, a saying of Jesus' in the Gospel impresses me more than this quotation about the power of the creator and the absolute powerlessness of the creature: "It is easier for a camel to pass through the eye of a needle than for a rich man to enter the Kingdom of heaven" (Matthew 19:23).

This expression comes to my mind every time I see a camel on the track, and it makes me smile. If he had said 'A horse or an ox. . . ' but no, a camel, with that hump! Of course a camel can't be made to pass through the eye of a needle!

To create the firmament is certainly a sign of great power, but to make a camel pass through the eye of a needle seems to me greater still; it's quite impossible.

In fact, to the worried and amazed apostles who exclaimed, "Then it is impossible to be saved," Jesus calmly replied, "What is impossible for man is possible for God."

"For you all things are possible," Jesus was to say to the Father in the prayer of Gethsemane. Omnipotence is an attribute of God's.

The real qualities of my humanity are insignificance, weakness, misery, powerlessness. There must be a meaning to this. One must think about it carefully. Is it possible that sin, which invaded the world soon after man's creation and which seems at times so inexplicable, has nothing to tell us about God's omnipotence?

Is it possible that the human weakness we see in old age, sickness and death should be something which simply afflicts us and has no further meaning?

When I think of my evening examinations of conscience, it is always a question of things not done or done badly; I can never list positive things.

And even if I can achieve inner peace for a moment, I still have a deep sense of my inadequacy and wretchedness and I have to admit my incapacity to make my love greater.

The memory of the blanket I denied Kada and the awareness of my being unable to make an act of perfect love keep returning to my mind.

I have experienced the same thing in prayer. Left to myself, with my own strength, I have felt the painful reality that without God's help we cannot say even "Abba, Father."

There are moments when God makes us feel

the extreme limits of our powerlessness; then, and only then, do we understand our nothingness right down to the depths.

For so many years, for too many years, I have fought against my powerlessness, my weakness. Often I have refused to admit it to myself, preferring to appear in public with a nice mask of self-assurance.

It is pride which will not let us admit this powerlessness; pride which won't let us accept being inadequate. God has made me understand this, little by little.

Now I don't fight any more; I try to accept myself. I try to face up to myself without illusions, dreams or fantasies. It's a step forward, I believe. And if I had made the step while I was still learning the catechism I should have gained forty years.

Now I contrast my powerlessness with the powerfulness of God, the heap of my sins with the completeness of his mercy, and I place the abyss of my smallness beneath the abyss of his greatness.

I seem now to have reached a means of encountering him in a way I have never known before: a togetherness I had never experienced before, an awareness of his love I had never previously felt. Yes, it is really my misery which attracts his power, my wounds which shout after him, my nothingness which makes him throw himself open to me.

And this meeting between God's totality and man's nothingness is the greatest wonder of creation. It is the most beautiful betrothal because its bond is a love which gives itself freely and a love which accepts. Really, it is the truth of God and man. The acceptance of this truth comes from humility, and that is why without humility there is no truth, and without truth no humility.

"He has regarded the lowliness of his handmaiden," said Mary when she saw, accepting her nothingness, the essential love of God and felt her flesh become the dwelling place and nourishment of the Word Incarnate.

How wonderful that Mary's nothingness should attract God's all. What sweetness in her prayer when she recognised that she was at the opposite pole from God, where humility not only becomes the acceptance of love, but is one of its demands.

What peace in her total self-giving to him, accompanied by the contemplative gaze at the greatness and perfection of the loved one.

No more perfect relationship exists, and Mary shows in its most perfect form the absorbent thirst of the soul under God's dew.

Thus, after so many years, I feel I have found

the solution to the only real problem we have on earth. I have recognised my powerlessness and this was grace. In faith, hope and love I have contemplated the all-power-fulness of God and this, too, was grace.

God can do everything and I can do nothing. But if I offer this nothing in prayer to God, everything becomes possible in me.

I remember the great rock where I was weighed down by my self-centredness, closed in my purgatory for having denied Kada the blanket.

Within myself I feel the inability to perform an act of perfect love, following Jesus on Calvary, dying with him on the Cross.

Thousands and thousands of years may pass and my position will not change.

But . . . but what is impossible for me, the rich man in the Gospel, is possible for God! It is he who will give me the grace to transform myself; he will make me able to carry out the impossible and remove the obstacle which separated me from the Kingdom1 And so it is a question of waiting, of humble and trustful prayer, of patience and hope.

But the God of the Impossible won't ignore my cry.

17.

The friendly night

When I first came to the Sahara I was afraid of the night.

For some, night means more work, for others dissipation, for still others insomnia, boredom.

For me now it's quite different. Night is first of all rest, real rest. At sunset a great serenity sets in, as though nature were obeying a sudden sign from God.

The wind which has howled all day ceases, the heat dies down, the atmosphere becomes clear and limpid, and great peace spreads everywhere, as though man and the elements wanted to refresh themselves after the great battle with the day and its sun.

Yes, the night here is different. It has not lost its purity, its mystery. It has remained as God made it, his creation, bringer of good and life.

With your work finished and the caravan

halted, you stretch out on the sand with a blanket under your head and breathe in the gentle breeze which has replaced the dry, fiery daytime wind.

Then you leave the camp and go down to the dunes for prayer. Time passes undisturbed. No obligations harass you, no noise disturbs you, no worry awaits you: time is all yours. So you satiate yourself with prayer and silence, while the stars light up in the sky.

Those who have never seen them cannot believe what the stars are like in the desert; the complete absence of artificial light, the vastness of the horizon only seem to increase their number and brightness. It is certainly an unforgettable experience. Only the camp fire with the tea water boiling on top and the bread for supper baking underneath, glows with a mellow light against the sparkling heaven.

The first nights spent here made me send off for books on astronomy and maps of the sky; and for months afterwards I spent my free time learning a little of what was passing over my head up there in the universe.

It was all good material for my prayer of adoration. Kneeling on the sand I sank my eyes for hours and hours in those wonders, writing down my discoveries in an exercise book like a child.

I understood, for example, that finding one's

way in the desert is much easier by night than by day, that the points of reference are numerous and certain. In the years which I spent in the open desert I never once got lost, thanks to the stars.

Many times, when searching for a Tuareg camp or a lost weather station, I lost my way because the sun was too high in the sky. But I waited for night and found the road again, guided by the stars.

The Saharan night is not only a wonderful time for repose; it also provides a restful dwelling place for the soul. After the day—with all that light—the soul closes up like a house without windows to have their shutters unhinged by the wind or burnt by the sun.

I shall never forget the nights under the Saharan stars. I felt as if I were wrapped around by the blanket of the friendly night, a blanket embroidered with stars.

Yes, a friendly night, a benevolent darkness with restful shadows. In them the movement of my soul is not hindered. On the contrary, it can spread out, be fulfilled, grow and be joyful.

I feel at home, safe, fearless, desirous only of staying like this for hours; my only worry that of the shortness of the night so avid am I to read within and outside myself the symbols of divine language.

The friendly night is an image of faith, that gift of God defined, "The guarantee of the blessings we hope for and proof of the existence of the realities that at present remain unseen" (Hebrew 11:1).

I have never found a better metaphor for my relationship with the Eternal: a point lost in infinite space, wrapped round by the night under the subdued light of the stars.

I am this point lost in space: the darkness, like an irreplaceable friend, is faith. The stars, God's witness.

When my faith was weak, all this would have seemed incomprehensible to me. I was afraid as a child is of the night. But now I have conquered it, and it is mine. I experience joy in night, navigating upon it as upon the sea. The night is no longer my enemy, nor does it make me afraid. On the contrary, its darkness and divine transcendence are a source of delight.

Sometimes I even close my eyes to see more darkness. I know the stars are there in their place, as a witness to me of heaven. And I can see why darkness is so necessary.

The darkness is necessary, the darkness of faith is necessary, for God's light is too great. It wounds.

I understand more and more that faith is not a mysterious and cruel trick of a God who hides himself without telling me why, but a necessary veil. My discovery of him takes place gradually, respecting the growth of divine life in me.

"No man may see God and live," says the Scripture, in the sense that to see him face to face is possible only for those who have passed beyond death.

On earth such is the light, the infinity of the mystery and the inadequacy of human nature, that I must penetrate it little by little. First through symbols, then through experience, and finally in the contemplation which I can achieve on this earth if I remain faithful to God's love.

But it will be only a beginning, getting the eyes of my soul accustomed to so much light: the process will go on endlessly and the mystery will remain as long as we are dominated by God's infinity.

What is our life on earth, if not discovering, becoming conscious of, penetrating, contemplating, accepting, loving this mystery of God's, the unique reality which surrounds us, and in which we are immersed like meteorites in space? "In God we live and move and have our being" (Acts 17:28).

There aren't many mysteries, but there is one upon which everything depends, and it is so immense that it fills the whole space.

Human discoveries do not help us to penetrate this mystery. Future millenia will illuminate no further what Isaiah said and what

God himself declared to Moses before the burning bush, "I am who I am" (Exodus 3:4).

Perhaps the sky was less dark for Abraham and the men with the tents than for modern man; perhaps faith was simpler for medieval poets than present-day technicians. But the situation is the same, and the nature of our relationship with God does not change.

The more man grows in maturity, the more he is required to have faith, devoid of sentiment. But the road will remain the same until the last has been born on this earth.

"This is the victory over the world—our faith" (John 5:4).

God asks faith of man and this is the true, authentic submission of the creature to the Creator, an act of humility, of love.

Trust in God; giving praise to the All-Powerful; satisfying our thirst for knowledge in the infinite sea of his Fatherhood; accepting his mysterious plan; entering school to listen to his word; knowing how to wait on him. This is an act of adoration worthy of man on this earth.

But if through pride we do not wish to set out on the path of faith, and we turn our backs on divine reality and close our eyes before the witness of the stars, where does it get us? Will our consciousness of the mystery increase? Shall we find more light somewhere else?

Without speaking of God, of the Incarnation of the Word and of the Eucharist, what do we know of the physical world itself which surrounds us? Or what, indeed, happens after death? What of the suffering of the creatures or the purpose of creation?

What we know is little more than nothing; and what little we know is all relative unless we go to first causes.

We should be overcome when each discovery we make seems to proclaim, 'Have you only just got there?' The advice of Jesus remains true, "If you do not become little children, you will not enter. . ."

What I have tried to say about faith is valid for everyone. No one can escape this reality. It is a gift of God but it needs effort on our part if it is to bear fruit.

God gives us the boat and the oars, but then tells us, "It's up to you to row." Making 'positive acts of faith' is like training this faculty; it is developed by training, as the muscles are developed by gymnastics.

David developed his faith by accepting to fight against Goliath. Gideon exercised himself in faith not only by asking a favorable sign from the Lord through the test of the fleece, but by going into battle with few soldiers against a stronger enemy.

Abraham became a giant in faith by making

the supreme act of obedience which demanded of him the sacrifice of his son.

In Paul's letter to the Hebrews we read:

> It was for faith that our ancestors were commended. . . . Many submitted to torture, refusing release so that they would rise again to a better life. Some had to bear being pilloried and flogged, or even being chained up in prison. They were stoned or sawn in half, or beheaded; they were homeless and dressed in the skins of sheep and goats; they were penniless and were given nothing but ill-treatment. They were too good for the world and they went out to live in deserts and mountains and in caves and ravines (Hebrews 11:2).

But of all the men and women who lived by faith, two reached towering heights.

They lived at the watershed between the Old and New Testaments and were called by God to such a unique and magnificent vocation that heaven was made to wait in suspense for their reply: Mary and Joseph.

Mary became the mother of the Word; she gave flesh and blood to the Son of God; and Joseph must veil the mystery, placing himself at her side so that everyone might believe that Jesus was his son.

For these two creatures the night of faith was not only dark, but also painful.

One day Joseph, engaged to Mary, realises that she is to give birth to a child which he know is not his.

Think of the task of convincing one's betrothed that the mystery of that birth is due to nothing less than the power of God.

No reasoning could give Joseph peace and serenity. Only faith.

And it is precisely this faith which sustained him, placing him next to the mother of God to accompany her in her destiny and take a full part in her mission.

It won't be easy to follow the example of such a man destined to suffer, the spouse of a woman who is to be called the Mother of Sorrows.

The Baby is born.

A few angels came, it is true, to chase away a little of that darkness, but at once the sky closed on a yet greater darkness. The children of an entire village are slain on account of their Baby, and Joseph and Mary, fleeing,hear the cry and lament of the women of Bethlehem.

Why? Why is the All-Powerful silent? Why doesn't he kill Herod? But this is the point: it is necessary to live by faith. Flee into Egypt, become exiles and refugees, let cruelty and injustice triumph. And so it will be until the end of time.

God didn't soften the path of those whom he put beside his Son. He asked of them a faith so pure and uncompromising that only two souls could live up to this demand.

What an adventure, to live for thirty years in a house where God lived in the flesh of an earthly man; to eat with him, listen to him speak, see him sleep, see the sweat on his brow, and on his hands the calluses of weariness and work.

And all this quite simply, as something normal and everyday; so normal that absolutely nobody will unveil the mystery or realise that the carpenter's son is the Son of God, the Word made flesh, the new Adam, heaven and earth.

My God, what great faith!

Mary and Joseph, you it is who are masters of faith, perfect examples to inspire us, correct our course and support our weakness.

Just as you were beside Jesus, you are still beside us to accompany us to eternal life, to teach us to be small and poor in our work, humble and hidden in life, courageous in trial, faithful in prayer, ardent in love.

And when the hour of our death comes and dawn rises over our friendly night, our eyes, as they scan the sky, may pick out the same star that was in your sky when Jesus came upon earth.

Carlo Carretto

In Search of the Beyond

CONTENTS

PROLOGUE

People have asked me whether, in times of protest like our own, I too might find something to protest about.

I have nothing against protest, indeed, I am all in favour of a bit of activity; I like to see a young man jump up on to a table and spontaneously deliver an impassioned tirade against something he feels is wrong and should be put to rights.

What is there to reproach him for?

Surely we are all agreed that things are not as they should be.

A member of the older generation, wedded to the established order and to principles of economy, may be anxious lest window-panes and furniture should begin to fly back and forth with the words – and I have in fact been told that in one far-eastern country the students virtually razed their old university building to the ground, so intense was their anger and the violence of their protest. But now that I am approaching death, and since I am familiar with the language of the Apocalypse, the cost of one building makes little impression on me compared with the cost of the great devastation at the end of time.

Besides, life has taught me one thing : that he who protests loves, and he who protests much loves much. There is only one thing I have never managed to understand : why those who are challenged do not come out into the open as well, into the very centre of the fray, and cry out with all their strength : 'You are right, brothers, things are going badly, and it is our fault. You are right to rebuke us. We have made bad use of our power, we have abused your trust. Forgive us and help us to change.'

Above all, I cannot understand why there are thinking people who get upset, ecclesiastics who are shocked, and so on, when people protest against the Church, and make use of hallowed phrases like 'living the Gospel', 'we must be poor', 'we must return to the sources'.

I would go down to the market place clad in sackcloth and ashes and say quite simply: 'You are right, my sons, we have forgotten Jesus, and deviated from his teaching. We need to change and become converted; we must effectively build up a Church which will be the Church of the poor, the charismatic Church, the Church of the Spirit, the Church . . . '

How splendid such a universal protest would be, a world-wide protest in which fathers and sons would take hold of one another crying, 'We are all blackguards!' A protest in which priests and people would unite in a single cry, a common prayer: 'Our fathers sinned, and we have sinned ourselves, we are all sinners'. In the end we would have sinned ourselves, agreement on one point which is basic to man's life on earth, and which it is good to recall from time to time: we are not perfect; the Church is the Church of sinners; each one of us is moving onwards towards perfection, but . . .

Here we might ask ourselves a question.

What is the underlying reason for the fact that our generation sets out so persistently and energetically to emphasize that things are going badly? The answer is that preceding generations, with equal persistence and energy, took every opportunity to say how well everything was going, especially in the Church.

I remember when I was a schoolboy and reading history books for the first time. It was not difficult to see that certain crimes had been committed by persons of consequence – this cleric, for example, or that pope.

Overcome with doubts, home I would go to express my bewilderment. The invariable response was a cuff from my mother, who, with her conditioned respect for clerical language and dress, would tell me, 'You don't criticize the parish priest.'

If I went to the parish priest and told him that in all conscience I could not understand how Pius IX had failed to grasp certain details in time . . . and so on, the heavens would open. I would find myself listening to a sermon on the Church, holy and spotless, without wrinkle or blemish, and I would return to school with that narrow, prejudiced outlook which has been such a cause of scandal to intelligent, open-minded individuals in our own day.

What we need now is patience, a great deal of patience, and we must endure – though without fear – the choppy seas that will inevitably rock the Church.

If we do so, besides realizing that we are all sinners, that it is important that we should keep ourselves in humility, we shall come to understand something else : that the Church is not in men's hands, but in the hands of God, and that he alone – not we men who in our presumption think we are safe and secure simply because we are in the Church – has power to still the wind and calm the waves.

But it is not with men that I want to take issue.

I am filled with compassion for them.

All of them.

Nor is it with myself. I have already gone in for too much self-scrutiny; so much so, in fact, that I became discouraged about the possibility of ever achieving anything worth while.

I pity myself, too, and I assure you that I am sustained now by the theological virtue of hope, not by confidence in any virtue of my own; it is faith in Jesus that lights up my night, not faith in myself or my own faculties, which are weakening with the onrush of time.

I want to take issue instead with God, with my God.

With the One who has pursued me ever since my childhood and still pursues me.

The One whom I learned to know and love in the Church of my adolescence and youth, so rich in mystery and feeling, in colours, ornaments and lights.

The One who drew me into the desert in order to purify my faith and strip my altars bare, who led me under the Cloud of Dark Knowledge of himself that I might sense his Mystery, his Darkness, his Silence and his Transcendence.

The One in whom I have recognized the God of Abraham, the God of the prophets, the God of the Psalms, and above all the God of Jesus Christ and his Gospel, the God who is living in the Church and in the Eucharist, yesterday, today and for ever.

The God who is the source of my being, who is with me and around me, and who draws me into the unfathomable abyss of his own designs, towards the vision of himself, which will be eternally new.

He is the one with whom I want to take issue.

What is more, I am not the first to do so, and I know there is one particular kind of protest that is pleasing to him.

I mean the protest that springs from love. He is always ready to listen to that.

Did he not listen to the protest of Abraham, his friend? When, outside Sodom, God revealed to the patriarch his intention of destroying the city, Abraham made this protest:

' "Are you really going to destroy the just man with the sinner? Perhaps there are fifty just men in the town. Will you really overwhelm them, will you not spare the place for fifty just men in it? Do not think of doing such a thing: to kill the just man with the sinner, treating just and sinner alike! Do not think of it . . ." Yahweh replied, "If at Sodom I find fifty just men in the town, I will spare the whole place because of them."

'Abraham replied, "I am bold indeed to speak like this to

my Lord, I who am dust and ashes. But perhaps the fifty just men lack five : will you destroy the whole city for five?" "No" he replied, "I will not destroy it if I find forty-five just men there." Again Abraham said to him, "Perhaps there will only be forty there." "I will not do it" he replied "for the sake of the forty."

'Abraham said, "I trust my Lord will not be angry, but give me leave to speak : perhaps there will only be thirty there." "I will not do it," he replied . . .' (Gen 18 :23–30).

And so on as the figure gradually decreases in a dramatic exchange in which one thing is at stake : the salvation of those men. It is precisely about this that I want to protest. No longer capable of finding any alternative approach, I want to take issue with God in defence of contemporary man. I want to act like that other formidable protestor, Moses, who, when confronted with God's plan to destroy his idolatrous people in the confines of the desert, said to him : ' "Yahweh, why should your wrath blaze out against this people of yours whom you brought out of the land of Egypt with arm outstretched and mighty hand? . . . Leave your burning wrath; relent and do not bring this disaster on your people. Remember Abraham, Isaac and Jacob, your servants, to whom by your own self you swore and made this promise : I will make your offspring as many as the stars of heaven . . ." So Yahweh relented and did not bring on his people the disaster he had threatened' (Ex 32 : 11–14).

This the the kind of challenge that pleases God, and I too would have recourse to it, rather than sit back insisting that things are going badly and that the world deserves to be destroyed.

In the end, of course, by saving others I save myself, which is obviously not a matter of indifference to me.

My reasoning is simple :

Mankind today is in the desert, just as the people of God were with Moses on the mountain. Now, as then, men are demanding meat instead of manna. And now, as then, men have fashioned for themselves a golden calf.

So what is one supposed to do?

Start talking about destruction and punishment, like some uninspiring hack preacher?

Or beg God to teach man a lesson?

There is no need for that.

We are quite capable of punishing ourselves, and as far as destruction is concerned, we already have at our disposal all the means necessary for wiping mankind off the face of the earth.

And, in any case, the rainbow still spans the heavens at high noon after the rain, a reminder that the destructive flood was an experience of humanity's childhood, while now . . .

Yes, now humanity no longer looks on itself as a child, it has achieved adulthood. And adults cannot be threatened with disasters. Even when they do occur, people no longer look on them as coming from God. Theirs is a world from which God is absent. They may not have reached a point of total denial but they cannot conceive of God as having any interest in human concerns, as being involved in the details of daily life. The Bible, which is the one book which really marries heaven and earth, still lies on their tables, but they misguidedly persist in searching through it for an alternative reading – an adult reading.

They have begun to react against the dense veil of unsophisticated imagery that surrounds the things of God and women and sin and the world beyond, and they endeavour to tear it aside with a display of self-assurance that is frankly infuriating.

Poor things! They do not realize that by tearing aside that veil of symbolic language, which in its very simplicity conveys all the mystery of God and of things, they will find themselves naked and unprotected in the actual presence of the Mystery. They will no longer understand anything at all.

Nor will they see anything.

The Mystery is a light more blinding than thousands of simultaneously exploded atomic bombs.

If you attempt to gaze on it directly, you are blinded and enter into a darkness that is your own, not God's. He knew this, and devised for our sake certain precautionary measures. Christ knew it, and issued his terse warning: 'Unless you change and become like little children you will never enter the kingdom of heaven' (Mt 18 : 3).

This is the crux of the matter, and knowing the danger to which my generation is exposing itself, I wish to take issue with God.

I am not afraid that God will destroy the world, but I am afraid that he may abandon it to wander blindly in the sophisticated wasteland of contemporary civilization.

I am not afraid that he will allow us to want for food and medicines, but I am afraid that he may abandon us to the temptation against faith. I will not presume to say that I have experienced the terrors of the night of the spirit, and I do not know whether that night is the same as the one described by St John of the Cross. I only know that it is a terrible experience to find oneself with one's faith exposed before the stark Reality of God.

And there is one way, and one only, of coming through the experience: the way of childhood, littleness, humility, persevering prayer, tears. It is not easy, I admit, because before resolving to become little we are only too inclined to try every other way imaginable. In nearly every case the way of humility and tears is chosen only when one feels defeated and at a loss where to turn. The parable of the wedding feast described by Luke tells how, in order to have his table full, the king finally commanded his servants, 'Go to the open roads and the hedgerows and force people to come in . . .' Lk 14 :23). And it is sad to think that we possibly begin to search for God only because we no longer know where else to go, and only when, let down by beauty, by health and by our dreams, we are prepared to open ourselves to the One who still loves us, and makes use of our misfortunes to compel us to enter at last into the kingdom of his love.

This is why I want to challenge my God.

Lord, my God, pity your people, and do not be over-severe with them. I realize that as a result of the riches of the land in which they live, and the pleasure it gives them, your people no longer hunger after the promised land; but, Lord, be patient for a little while more; you will find they will come to understand in the end.

I know that they spend too much time trying to reach the stars that you yourself call by name, and leave so many of their brothers to die of hunger, but, Lord, you will see that some good will come of it. You will see that from the porthole of some space ship one of them will celebrate your greatness. To see a man standing on the moon and hailing the earth that you have loved so intensely, and for which you gave up your life – surely that is something beautiful, Lord?

Lord, have pity on man.

I have confidence in him, even though he has revealed himself to me in all his colours.

One thing I ask you, above all. Do not try his faith beyond the limit, do not put him through that overwhelming test.

If he *will* get himself into all kinds of trouble through his childish, arrogant desire to know everything, by all means chastise him, but do not abandon him to his darkness.

I fear for the man who no longer knows where his God is.

Make him aware of your touch through his experience of created things, make him recognize your presence behind the veil of all present realities.

Lord, bring upon us all the misfortunes that, in your justice, you might have prepared for us, all except that of being the last witnesses to the Invisible.

PART I

'And he did this so that all nations might seek the deity and, by feeling their way towards him, succeed in finding him. Yet in fact he is not far from any of us' (Acts 17:27).

Chapter One

RETURN TO THE DESERT

The goodness and merciful love of God have led me back to the desert. During the day my eyes feed on the light from the stupendous sand-dunes of Beni Abbès; and at night I spend hour after hour absorbing the peace that pours down from the stars, strewn in myriad profusion throughout the galaxy. Its lambent glow seems to have been created expressly for me as a strong sweet reminder of the luminous Cloud of the Dark Knowledge of God while I make my journey through the desert of life. I feel happy, as never before, happy to the point of tears.

And as they fill my eyes the world becomes more compelling in its beauty than ever, and in the depths of my being I am aware of the movement of God.

In such moments everything seems to remain suspended in an eternal present, while the many miles that separate me from my 'yesterday' contrive to deepen the 'mist of forgetfulness' of things, releasing in me the joy of finding myself alone with Him, the Eternal, the Infinite, the Transcendent, and strengthening my resolve to break for a while with everyday things in order to give myself in complete self-surrender to the Absolute.

The desert, in biblical thought, is not a goal but a passing stage, which is how Elijah understood it: 'he walked for forty days and forty nights until he reached Horeb, the mountain of God' (I K 19 : 8). The exodus from slavery to freedom takes place in the desert: 'Remember how Yahweh your God led you for forty years in the wilderness, to humble you, to test you and know your inmost heart – whether you would keep his commandments or not. He humbled you, he made you feel hunger, he fed you with manna which neither you nor your fathers had known, to make you understand that man does not live on bread alone but that man lives on everything that comes from the mouth of Yahweh. The clothes on your back did not wear out and your feet were not swollen, all those forty years.

'Learn from this that Yahweh your God was training you as a man trains his child, and keep the commandments of Yahweh your God, and so follow his ways and reverence him' (Dt 8 : 2–6).

In the Gospel the desert marks a period of preparation for Christ as he stands on the threshold of his active mission : 'Immediately afterwards the Spirit drove him out into the wilderness and he remained there for forty days and was tempted by Satan. He was with the wild beasts, and the angels looked after him' (Mk 1 : 12–13).

It provides some respite from the pressure of the crowd : 'Then he said to them, "You must come away to some lonely place all by yourselves and rest for a while" ' (Mk 6 : 31).

It is a milieu suited to prayer : 'After sending the crowds away he went up into the hills by himself to pray' (Mt 14 : 23); or to prolonged meditation : 'Now it was about this time that he went out into the hills to pray; and he spent the whole night in prayer to God' (Lk 6 : 12); or to quench the thirst for absolute aloneness with the Father : ' "Stay here while I pray." And going on a little further he threw himself on the ground and prayed that, if it were possible, this hour might pass him by. "Abba [Father]" ' (Mk 14 : 32–35).

If the prophets did so, and if Jesus did so, we too must go out into the desert from time to time.

It is not a question of transporting oneself there physically. For many of us that could be a luxury. Rather, it implies creating a desert space in one's own life. And to create a desert means to seek solitude, to withdraw from men and things, one of the undisputed principles of mental health.

To create a desert means learning to be self-sufficient, learning to remain undisturbed with one's own thoughts, one's own prayer, one's own destiny.

It means shutting oneself up in one's room, remaining alone in an empty church, setting up a small oratory for oneself in an attic or at the end of a passage in which to localize one's personal contact with God, to draw breath, to recover one's inner peace. It means occasionally devoting a whole day to prayer, it means going off into the loneliness of the mountains, or getting up alone in the night to pray.

When all is said and done, creating a desert means nothing more than obeying God. Because there is a commandment – arguably the most forgotten of all, especially by the 'committed', by militants, by priests – and even bishops – which requires us to interrupt our work, to put aside our daily tasks and seek the refreshing stillness of contemplation.

'Remember the sabbath day and keep it holy. For six days you shall labour and do all your work, but the seventh day is a sabbath for Yahweh your God. You shall do no work that day, neither you nor your son nor your daughter nor your servants, men or women, nor your animals nor the stranger who lives with you. For in six days Yahweh made the heavens and the earth and the sea and all that these hold, but on the seventh day he rested' (Ex 20 : 8–11).

Do not be afraid that your momentary withdrawal will be detrimental to the community; and do not be afraid that an increase in your personal love for God will in any way diminish your love for your neighbour. On the contrary, it will enrich it.

Let us here recall something which is both important and awesomely true : loving our fellow men, devoting ourselves to the human community with which we must totally identify, achieving a humble, vital understanding of the poor – these are demanding, exhausting undertakings. Only a strong personal love for God can effectively sustain and preserve them in all their freshness and divine newness. It is man's nature to harmonize these two loves, to fuse them into a balanced dialectic. Even the closest and most demanding relationships – mother and son, or husband and wife – require periods of absence, moments of separation, precisely in order that those involved should come to a new and deeper appreciation of the forces that bind them together.

'Place the tents far apart, draw near with your heart', says the Tuareg proverb, and if this applies to the nomad, accustomed to wandering freely through uncharted territory, imagine how much more true it must be for us westerners, living like sardines in our high-rise flats, and hemmed in by the crowd.

It is man's destiny to be alone; that is why he needs to train himself, prepare himself, become mature enough to 'stand alone'. And the desert was designed expressly for this maturing process. To refuse to accept the desert is to deny the vertical dimension of existence – one's relationship with God, the need for prolonged prayer, the face-to-face exchange with the Transcendent.

I would be unhappy if the great emphasis laid on the comunity aspect of Christianity, the shift away from yesterday's individualism, the joy of praying together in a renewed liturgy, were to flourish to the detriment of the solitary aspect of our existence. Among many young people and progressive priests today we find a very realistic awareness of the fact that God reveals himself to us in the very act of love by which we establish, live in and develop our communities, but I would not wish this to signify the abandonment of the arduous path of personal prayer, which alone can bring us to a fully mature union with God and mature contemplation. I would hope, finally, that in heeding Christ's words, 'for where two or three meet in my name, I shall be there with them' (Mt 18:20), we shall not allow ourselves to forget those other words of his, 'When you pray, go to your private room' (Mt 6 : 6).

Those who make Christianity a purely personal affair are certainly mistaken, but those who are willing to consider only the horizontal implications of Christ's teaching would be equally mistaken. This would turn the Gospel into a sociological tract, and it would lose its savour. The truth stands at the precise point where the two dimensions meet. It is not for nothing that the symbol of Christianity is the cross – the realization of the two loves, even on the material level, lived out until martyrdom : love of the Father and love of one's brethren.

Chapter Two

THE PARABLE OF CREATION

This morning I have come out on to the dunes before sunrise. Yesterday's wind has carefully combed and smoothed the sand, and the traces of its passage over the ridges are there in all their splendour and mysterious freshness. The ocean of sand stretches out before me as far as the horizon, where the dawn light heralds the coming of day.

There are few sights in nature so unspoiled as a sea of dunes under the blue sky of the Sahara! It is like seeing the beginning of creation and the spiritual content is so powerful that the visible and the invisible are perceived as a single reality.

Sand and sky separated by a single horizontal line: nothing else.

Yet it is the parable of creation which begins to unfold here, revealing its underlying meaning.

No simple, innocent, childlike eye, opening on to this sight, could possibly be in danger of doubting.

God is here, just as you are here, and the sand and sky are here.

You can start speaking to him immediately.

This is the way in which he is present.

The very elements that go to make up the scene are his words. His speech is contained within things, his thought is expressed in the reality that surrounds me.

Everything is a symbol which introduces me to the dark knowledge of him and prepares me for something that is to come, and yet is already come.

I feel him there, searching me out, coming to meet me, I feel him embracing me already, like someone who has been waiting for a long time, knowing that I would be coming.

Filled with grateful love, I reach out to touch that beauty which in his beauty, I ponder the harmony which is his harmony, I stand spellbound by the newness which is his newness. And it is easy for me to say to him :

'Bless Yahweh, my soul.
Yahweh, my God, how great you are !
Clothed in majesty and glory,
wrapped in a robe of light !

You stretch the heavens out like a tent,
you build your palace on the waters above;
using the clouds as your chariot,
you advance on the wings of the wind;
you use the winds as messengers
and fiery flames as servants'

(Ps 104 : 1–4).

God presents himself to you like this. Welcome him.

A horizontal line with a bit of sky above and a bit of sand below is all that is needed.

And yourself before it, watching, watching, watching.

Do not ask for anything, just contemplate. Do not let yourself be led astray by the evil tendencies of your heart.

Can you not see that your heart is sick from its own cunning and would rather interrogate than contemplate. Already, instead of remaining in ecstasy, it wants to rebel. Totally wrapped up in its own doubts, it does not even give your eye time to scan the full sweep of the horizon before demanding a sign from the Invisible one who is present, saying, 'Give me a different sign from the one you have given me.' Why do you do this, my heart? Are the signs that already surround you not enough?

Can he show any greater power than the power he has shown in creating? Can he increase the perfection of the perfection he has already given, or the beauty of the beauty that is already there? Why does my heart react like this?

No, I will not ask him for another sign. The things I can see are enough. No one asks his own mother for a visiting card as he emerges from the womb; that would be tactless to say the least. My mother is not required to introduce herself to me in order to explain who she was before I appeared on the scene.

And by the same token I ask no sign from my God who is present in his creation, immanent in things and yet transcending them.

Indeed, I will rely on the signs he leaves of himself, signs that will not fail to guide me in my search, but bearing in mind one very important thing, a kind of *sine qua non* for all relations with the Transcendent One : 'Unless you change and become like little children, you will never enter the kingdom of heaven' (Mt 18 : 3).

This saying of Christ is straightforward enough, but it also contains a warning : you will never enter, never enter, never enter.

But then what?

If this doorway into the Invisible is closed to me, where will I find one that is open?

If I cannot enter the kingdom, where will I find refuge?

But now be peaceful, my soul, stop thinking about the warning that made you tremble.

Contemplate what lies before you.

It is God's way of making himself present.

A horizontal line with a bit of sky above and a bit of sand below is all that is needed.

The sand is the symbol of visible realities, the sky of those that are invisible. I say symbol, because in fact the sky is not any more invisible than the earth.

It is the same thing.

The invisible is neither on earth nor in heaven.

The invisible is the transcendent, the *beyond*, the other side of creation's fabric.

The invisible is the possibility to create visible things freely.

The invisible is all that did not need to be created, the Eternal, the Unchangeable.

The invisible is God.

And why is he invisible?

It is not because he enjoys hiding from you, but because you are as yet unable to see him. You will see him later.

Do you want a comparison?

Go backwards, backwards in time, and imagine yourself in your mother's womb.

Enclosed within the womb, you can touch your mother with your feet, with your hands, with your whole body. You are aware of her, you feel and touch her, but you do not see her.

The time for that has not yet come.

But can you really have any doubts about her – her presence, her reality? Even though you cannot see her.

You began life in your mother's womb, and in all beginnings there are things – many things – that must be accepted without understanding.

Only faith and hope can throw any light on the beginning: faith, which is the eye of the reality you cannot see, and hope, which is the conviction that you will be born when it is time.

In the beginning you have a thousand ways of experiencing the presence of the one who will bring you to birth, but you must accept your limitations, your own immaturity, inexorably bound up with the passage of time which does not belong to you and whose child you are.

Your moment will come!

And when it does, after the lightning flash of the Apocalypse, you will emerge from the womb of time, along with the rest of creation.

Then you will see God face to face, you will touch the Transcendent with the finger of your love. No comparison has helped me as much as this one to understand the reason for the darkness of faith, and why we must remain small before the mystery of Being.

We live in the womb of things, in the womb of history and the contingent; we are immersed in the process of becoming.

Only the Apocalypse, at the end of time, will open up to us the vision of the divine Transcendence, of the *beyond*, and then we shall see God face to face.

But then everything will be complete and explained.

In the meantime there is nothing to do but wait.

In fact, living is waiting.

Now I turn back to look at the tenuous line of the horizon, lit up now by the sun which, in the meantime, has risen before me.

The sand becomes pale ochre in colour, and the sky, dominated now by the masterful presence of the sun, loses something of its transparency.

I no longer seem to see creation as it was at the beginning, but creation as it will be at the end.

This sand which runs through my fingers is all that remains of past history, of the civilization which flourished in a Sahara that was once alive, teeming with life.

Some of these civilizations have left a record of themselves, superb, incredibly well-preserved inscriptions, evidence of a high degree of development.

Now cities and villages alike have disintegrated. The sun and wind of the Sahara have reduced them to sand, mountains of sand.

Nothing has been able to resist the relentless rhythm of time, the searing wind which consumes the granite.

Will the steel of our own technological civilization be able to resist any better?

Will the vast complex world we know today be able to resist? The civilized world of science and culture?

And the others that are still to come, the civilizations of the future, will they hold out against the forces of time, against the sun and the wind?

No, they will not resist. New York, Paris, Moscow, Peking, Athens, Rome, all will become like these sand dunes.

It may be that the heat will simply be replaced by cold, the cold of the end of the world.

Everything will be reduced to sand, because sand is the symbol of death, and everything must die.

Some people imagine the possibility of a connection, or better, some kind of real continuity, between the level of technology and maturity reached by human civilizations and the kingdom of God. But they are wrong, there is no such continuity.

The kingdom belongs to a different order.

If there *is* any connection it is a symbolic and not a real one. If there is a link it is in the fire of love, and in the white heat of the charity we drew on for the difficult task of constructing the earthly city.

The new heavens and the new earth which have been promised by the Spirit and form the substance of our faith will be truly new, and not just the old things remade as if new. God is not waiting for anything from us before he re-fashions, re-creates, heaven and earth. His new work in no way depends on the stage we may have reached.

What do you want him to wait for?

Seeing that he himself said, in a moment of sadness: 'But when the Son of Man comes, will he find any faith on earth?' (Lk 18 : 8).

Do you expect him to wait when we are possibly on the verge of blowing the world up with one of our atomic bombs?

God is God, and he is God precisely because he has no need of anything we may have to offer (Ps 117 : 27). Our technology will end up in the sand, just like the first wheel constructed by some gazelle hunter on these same Saharan plains.

Our sociology will end up in the sand, just as the legislation of the ancient civilizations finished in the sand. I am making a new heaven and a new earth, says Christ in the Book of Revelation, and it is as if he were saying : I am making another universe because the old things have passed away. And faith consists in believing that God has this power.

At this point I can well imagine that some people are worried, even scandalized. I hear them say : 'What is the good of all our efforts, our exertions, our work? Will anything remain of the earthly city?'

Yes, love will remain.

The house will disappear, but the affection that held us together will remain. The workshop will disappear, but the toil and sweat which earned us our bread will remain. Human revolutions will be forgotten, but tears shed in the cause of justice will remain. Our old bodies will disappear; the wounds of our sacrifice and the scars of our struggles will remain – but in newly created bodies, transparent and divine; we will be sons of the resurrection and no longer the slaves of death. Indeed, a first pledge of this hope is given us in the resurrection of Christ.

This is why the fact of the resurrection of Jesus assumes such significance in the Good News as preached by his first companions. If Christ is risen, the question of my own joy, fulfilment and happiness no longer presents any problem. It is all a question of waiting.

Waiting, in fact, is what my history, my prayer and my hope are all about. Now I kneel down, and opening the Book of Revelation I read :

'Then I saw a new heaven and a new earth; the first heaven and the first earth had disappeared now, and there was no longer any sea. I saw the holy city, and the new Jerusalem, coming down from God out of heaven, as beautiful as a bride all dressed for her husband. Then I heard a loud voice call from the throne, "You see this city? Here God lives among men. He will make his home among them; they shall be his people, and he will be their God; his name is God-with-them. He will wipe away all tears from their eyes; there will be no more death, and no more mourning or sadness. The world of the past has gone."

'Then One sitting on the throne spoke: "Now I am making the whole of creation new," he said. "Write this: that what I am saying is sure and will come true." And then he said: "It is already done. I am the Alpha and the Omega, the Beginning and the End. I will give water from the well of life free to anybody who is thirsty; it is the rightful inheritance of the one who proves victorious; and I will be his God and he a son to me"' (Rv 21 : 1–7).

'The Spirit and the Bride say, "Come." Let everyone who listens answer, "Come." Then let all who are thirsty come: all who want it may have the water of life, and have it free.

'The one who guarantees these revelations repeats his promise: I shall indeed be with you soon. Amen; come, Lord Jesus' (Rv 22 : 17–20).

Chapter Three

THE POOR OF YAHWEH

What creation tells me is only a beginning.

The revelation conveyed to me by heaven and earth in their splendour, their immensity and their harmony, marks no more than the beginning of a dialogue which will go on for a long time, occupying me throughout my life here, and beyond.

I should add immediately that while this dialogue has a beginning, it has no end, because the two speakers, God and man, are eternal and are to live in the same dwelling.

It would be strange to live in the same house without speaking to one another, and stranger still not to know one another.

Yet man has been created to know God, to speak with God.

The knowledge may be slow or quick to develop, the dialogue with him may prove easy or difficult to sustain, but I would say that ultimately neither can be avoided.

It is almost impossible to dissociate oneself from the plan of God, which is precisely this, 'that all nations might seek the deity and, by feeling their way towards him, succeed in finding him. Yet in fact he is not far from any of us, since it is in him that we live, and move, and exist' (Acts 17 : 27).

No, God is not far from any one of us, he is with us and he always has been.

If we have learned to recognize his presence in creation, then we will find it embodied in his Revelation; if his word has reached us through the symbolic language of what we see, it will penetrate our spirit through the mystery of the Word.

Scripture will bring fulness to the message of the mountains, the seas and the stars; the Bible will draw man into this dialogue with God.

The Book of Genesis and the Wisdom literature will bring out the meaning of the dawns and sunsets. The story of Abraham and the Book of Job will throw light on the mystery of suffering.

The Book of Exodus will draw attention to the slavery of sin, and through the proclamation of the Law the waywardness of man's heart will be corrected.

In the miracle of the Red Sea man will discover the possibility and the hope of salvation, and in the Song of Songs the why and the wherefore of love.

He will find in the Psalter the language of prayer, and in the mysticism of the prophets the vocation to intimacy with the Eternal.

Yes, the mystery of creation finds in the Bible a book that is worthy of it, while the Bible finds in Nature the most conclusive witness to its truth.

In the hands of God, both contribute as one to the dialogue with man; together they serve him as receivers, on which he picks up the wavelength of his God in the eternal spaces of Being.

What, then, is God saying to man through creation?

What is God saying to man through the Scriptures?

One thing and one only: that God is God and man is man.

The consequences follow of their own accord; what matters is that man should realize that God is God and that man is not God.

It may seem almost absurd to keep on insisting on this truth, but it is not so: for our mistakes, our uncertainties and our unhappiness almost always stem from our having ignored one or other term of the equation.

To acknowledge that God is God is to achieve complete peace, to enjoy an optimistic outlook on life; it means believing that everything is regulated by the loving omnipotence of a Being who will lead everything to its goal, and who, being God, is the eternally New, and in whose presence every creature will quench its thirst and achieve its own fulfilment.

Ultimately it implies *adoration* which is simply the jubilant response to creation, the smile of the son towards the father, the joyous and trusting approach of one who has not towards the One who has, of one who cannot towards the One who can, of thirst towards the source, of nothing towards the All. I would suggest that the deepest and the most comprehensive truth which emerges from the contemplation of nature as *the belief that God has created and is creating* and of the Scriptures as *faith that God has revealed and is revealing himself* is this : that man is the poor one of God, that man is rightly defined as *the poor one of Yahweh.*

This expression 'poor', which nature teaches you to understand in terms of hunger, need, sweat, drought, sickness and death, which the Bible will enrich with its thought, its prayer and its experience, and which Jesus will make his own with exile, hard work and the harsh realities of daily life, is without any doubt the most complete, comprehensive and authentic one of all, placing man in the presence of his God, the creature in the presence of his Creator.

> 'Listen to me, Yahweh, and answer me,
> poor and needy as I am;
> keep my soul : I am your devoted one,
> save your servant who relies on you'
>
> (Ps 86 : 1–3).

The poor of Yahweh !

How rich in meaning these words are for the man who lives in God, who seeks God and loves him.

It is a peace-bearing phrase, a ray of light, a piercing shaft of love. This unassuming, humble attitude of supplication and dependence wraps the soul round like a cloak, shines like a lamp to light up the way, and serves as a staff for the journey through the desert.

It causes his prayer to well up within him :

'I waited and waited for Yahweh,
now at last he has stooped to me
and heard my cry for help.
He has pulled me out of the horrible pit,
out of the slough of the marsh'

(Ps 40 : 1–2).

'I love you, Yahweh, my strength . . .
Yawweh is my rock and my bastion,
my deliverer is my God.
I take shelter in him, my rock,
my shield, my horn of salvation'

(Ps 18 : 1–2).

It becomes the driving force behind all his rejoicing and praise of God :

'God, you are my God, I am seeking you,
my soul is thirsting for you,
my flesh is longing for you,
a land parched, weary and waterless,

(Ps 63 : 1).

The unshakable basis of his peace :

'In God alone there is rest for my soul,
from him comes my safety;
with him alone for my rock, my safety,
my fortress, I can never fall'

(Ps 62 : 1–2).

'Yahweh, our Lord,
how great your name throughout the earth !

Above the heavens is your majesty chanted . . .
I look up at your heavens, made by your fingers,
at the moon and stars you set in place –
ah, what is man that you should spare a thought for him?'
(Ps 8 : 1, 3–4).

The inexhaustible source of his prayer of petition :

'Look after me, God, I take shelter in you.

To Yahweh you say, "My Lord,
you are my fortune, nothing else but you" '
(Ps 16 : 1–2).

His constant yearning :

'As a doe longs
for running streams,
so longs my soul
for you, my God'
(Ps 42 : 1).

The most reliable place of refuge in times of danger :

'Save me, God ! The water
is already up to my neck !

I am sinking in the deepest swamp,
there is no foothold'
(Ps 69 : 1–2).

The realization that God is his goal :

'God, you are my God, I am seeking you.'

Man is the poor one of Yahweh, and Jesus, who is the perfect man, will stand before God, in the name of all men, as *the poor one of Yahweh. Blessed are the poor*, and he will transform what was originally an attitude of painful submission into one of joyful, loving acceptance. It is rightly said that humility is truth, in which case, the truth that God is God creates humility in man's heart, and this humility serves as the foundation of the entire spiritual edifice.

Man before God is the poor one *par excellence.*

But he is a poor man who can rely on Another to satisfy his needs.

This is the source of that attitude, characteristic of the poor man who has the courage to go on asking even for what seems impossible.

David asks that he might conquer Goliath with the power of five stones and a sling.

Joshua, that he might bring down the walls of Jericho with the crooks of shepherds who have come from the desert.

There is no limit set on the request. Everything depends quite simply on the maturity that has been achieved through faith, and on absolute confidence in the power of God.

The poor man is really poor, but the poor of Yahweh has God at his disposal.

The realization of this is enough to make one's head spin.

God at the disposal of my faith! What an awesome thought!

Jesus has left us an echo of that sense of vertigo. We are told in the Gospel of his being tempted by the possibility of changing stones into bread, or of casting himself from the pinnacle of the temple without doing himself any harm.

He says himself that he recovered his equilibrium by crying out in the midst of temptation: 'You must not put the Lord your God to the test' (Mt 4 : 7).

Yes, it is a terrible thing to feel that God is at the disposal of our poverty.

All things are possible for him who believes. That is the secret of the poor of Yahweh.

I am nothing, but God is my all.

I have nothing, but God is the fulness of being and I will lose myself in him. I believe this is the most radical experience man can have here on earth, the most dramatic struggle man can have with God, the face-to-face encounter of Israel with Yahweh in the night of the Passover under the moon of bare faith. And I also believe that nothing gives greater glory to God than this struggle on the bastions of the invisible; and that nothing gives him greater consolation than this cry which springs from the mouth of man who is caught up in the struggle with no weapon other than his own weakness, but with unshakable confidence in God's will to involve himself in what concerns him as a poor man.

I feel such a strong sense of brotherhood with all those people who have been and are aware of their radical neediness, but who yet believe in *the God of the impossible.*

Brother of Abraham, poor in his old age, impotent and alone, but trusting in the promise that is to make him the father of many nations.

Brother of Moses, who, inwardly aware of his vocation to liberate his people, had nothing but the poverty of a motley crowd of shepherds with which to confront the army of Pharaoh.

Brother of Job, who, having become, on his miserable dunghill, the very incarnation of poverty, would give evidence before the whole world of his proven faith. 'This I know : that my Avenger lives' (Job 19 : 25).

I am bound, in fact, as a brother, to all the poor, the destitute, the starving, the weak, the sinful, the despised, who have no one to rely on but God. But, above all, I am the brother of Mary, who had the courage to offer to God the poverty of her humble nature as an insignificant and unknown woman when confronted with the dark mystery of becoming the mother of Christ, and the constancy to accompany him unquestioningly to the Cross, to the ill-treatment, spittle and blood.

Chapter Four

THE POOR MAN PUT TO THE TEST

There is not only the vertigo that comes from feeling the power of God within our grasp; unfortunately we experience the same sense of vertigo when, as everything becomes dark ahead of us and his light is obscured behind the storm clouds of trial, we cry out that we no longer believe in him. Nothing is more self-evident than the existence of God and nothing is more obscure; nothing causes us greater elation than the feel of our hand in his, and no darkness is more painful than our moments of bare faith. Through faith we believe that God created the world, and theorizing about it can help us, but it is not enough. We can truly say that all the proof needed to demonstrate his presence to us is there already, and at the same time be terrified at the thought that nothing further can be added to shake our incredulity.

Faith is neither a feeling nor a mental process; it is an act of self-surrender in the dark to a God who is indeed darkness as far as our human nature is concerned. And he is darkness not because of an absence of light, but rather because we are overwhelmed by the reverberations of a light to which we are as yet unaccustomed, here in the restricted world of our own unfolding history.

The area in which reason and faith operate, and in which there is an interplay of light and shadow belonging to the two clearly distinct worlds, the visible and the invisible, is a terribly complex one. When the light which emanates from the Cloud of Unknowing reaches the earth on which we are journeying, it forms, as it were, a *mist* (St Paul) which surrounds everything and forces us to *feel our way* (Acts), putting us on our guard and inducing within us a continual state of anxious expectation.

An expectation which obliges us to fix our gaze on what lies ahead, and gives us a glimpse of the unexpected patch of sunlight which is to come. And it is on this uneven terrain that, sooner or later, God will be waiting for us, as he waited for Abraham, as he waited for Moses, as he waited for Job. Normally God leaves us to live in our tents, like the young Isaac under the eye of his father. As cherished sons in our Father's house, he leaves us to enjoy our laughter and to run, glad and carefree, on the hills of a life that is rich in peace and every other blessing. In moments like this we have no doubts about him and faith comes as easily as the heartbeat of the young, as the deep healthy breathing of those who are in good health. But one day . . .

' "Take your son," God said [to Abraham], "your only child Isaac, whom you love, and go to the land of Moriah. There you shall offer him as a burnt offering, on a mountain I shall point out to you" ' (Gen 22 : 1–2).

This is the moment of testing.

The skies darken, and faith is as starkly naked as the uncovered blade which cuts the flesh.

And then one says to oneself : 'Is it possible that a God of love could demand such a sacrifice? Perhaps faith is just a trap? A psychological illusion? Is it possible when children are dying of hunger, when the innocent are being killed and the wicked man triumphs? When earthquakes destroy the houses of the poor and drought reduces further still what little rice they have? This is the moment of testing, the moment of scandal ! And in the face of our anguish heaven remains closed and hostile and our question unanswered.

Why, Lord?

Why, Father?

But this God whom we are invoking has taken up a challenge – a challenge in which we ourselves, without wishing it or perhaps even realizing it, are the stakes.

'Satan said [to God]: "But Job is not God-fearing for nothing, is he? Have you not put a wall round him and his house and all his domain? You have blessed all he undertakes, and his flocks throng the countryside. But stretch out your hand and lay a finger on his possessions: I warrant you, he will curse you to your face"' (Job 1 : 9–11).

It was Satan who initiated the challenge, and God is caught, as it were, in a trap.

'Perhaps it is true that Job only believes in me and loves me because I have showered him with blessings and filled his life with joy?'

And so it is that God abandons Job to adversity and he is harshly afflicted with every kind of material adversity. The challenge is accepted; Job loses his flocks, his sons are killed, his lands laid waste.

But what is Job's own response to all these misfortunes?

'"Naked I came from my mother's womb, naked I shall return. Yahweh gave, Yahweh has taken back. Blessed be the name of Yahweh"' (Job 1 : 21).

But the challenge is taken still further, and Satan says to God: '"Skin for skin! A man will give away all he has to save his life. But stretch out your hand and lay a finger on his bone and flesh. I warrant you, he will curse you to your face"' (Job 2 :4–5).

The trial of strength intensifies, and God still accepts the challenge in man's name: '"Very well, he is in your power. But spare his life." So Satan left the presence of Yahweh.

'He struck Job down with malignant ulcers from the sole of his foot to the top of his head. Job took a piece of pot to scrape himself, and went and sat in the ashpit. Then his wife said to him, "Do you now still mean to persist in your blamelessness? Curse God, and die." "That is how foolish women talk," Job replied. "If we take happiness from God's hand, must we not take sorrow too?" And in all this misfortune Job uttered no sinful word' (Job 2 : 7–10).

Job did not sin, he affirmed his faith, and by repeating his conviction : *I know that my Avenger lives*, in the midst of such dreadful trials, was to bear witness before all men – a witness as enduring and resplendent as any precious stone.

Naked and covered with sores, like the man who survives the night of the senses and passes through the night of the spirit, Job succeeded in reaching the frontiers of the invisible, there to gaze through his tears at the horizon were the sun is on the verge of rising.

But how hard it is !

St John of the Cross speaks of the great compassion we should feel for *those who remain in the night*, those who succumb to the powerful attraction of the senses, or are led astray by spiritual pride and cast themselves to the ground howling and cursing; for those, sick with rationalism, who bring the canons of reason into matters of faith and claim they can break into the stronghold of the mystery with the pocket knife of reason; that they can look into the light of *the dark knowledge of God* with their short-sighted human eyes.

For this precisely is our tragedy : we think we know, when in fact we know nothing; we think we can see, when in fact we are blind. What do *we* know of death, of eternity, of the purpose of things, of suffering, of what was before us, of what will be after us?

We imagine we have a plan, when in fact we have not; we believe we know what is good for us, when all the time we may be working to destroy it.

All too often, our one concern is to remain at home undisturbed, however dull and joyless it may have become.

We are afraid of adventure, of the new and the mysterious.

If it were left in our hands, we would ask God to stay here on our level, when all the while our happiness depends on our moving upwards towards him.

We would willingly ask him to spare us all suffering, though it is genuinely for our good that we should suffer a little.

We know nothing, or practically nothing, about our eternal destiny, and we cling so tenaciously to what we believe is for our good. Affluent and overfed ourselves, we think that the only evil in the world is hunger; because *we* get upset by pain and privation, we think that the only problem to be resolved is that of providing bread and better hygienic conditions for the Third World. Of course these are serious problems for which solutions must be found, but what we fail to recognize is the far greater wretchedness of some rich people who die of boredom and drugs in comfortable bourgeois houses, and who stifle their personalities beneath their accumulated wealth and their self-centredness.

What we lack is true perspective, and this distorts the whole picture of our lives.

When all is said and done, we still believe that our home is here on earth, and that death, which takes us away from it, is somehow a mistake.

But the reality is diametrically opposed to this, and it is useless for us to try and alter things. The earth, whether we like it or not, is *not* the ultimate reality, and one day we shall discover that death was an invaluable and wise friend.

Is it not so?

This is the truth, this is the mystery, the one immense mystery in which we are all involved, and it is useless to worry about it, to complain, to wish things were otherwise: this is how things are.

We live surrounded by the contingent, the provisional; we are caught up in the process of evolution, of becoming, and the restlessness that clings to us like a second self is the sign of this. As I said earlier, we are still in the womb which is preparing us for birth, and anyone who is still in the womb is not in a convenient position to look into the face of the one who bears him.

It is necessary to trust, to believe, to hope, to accept.

Ultimately it is a question of patience because, as Scripture says, 'Your endurance will win you your lives' (Lk 21:19).

Besides – and it is time this was said – if this earth were the goal of creation, we really would have something to complain to God about, and could legitimately hand him the prize for incompetence as creator.

My knowledge may be limited, but I know enough not to be satisfied with what I see around me or, worse yet, with what is within me.

To be so would be absurd, a great mistake, a cause for scandal even. How could one understand death if earth was one's home and one was taken far from it? Who would not blaspheme in the face of innocent suffering, the ruthlessness of tyrants, the disasters produced by hostile nature? As if to relieve God of his responsibility, or else driven by an unshakable and incurable optimism, there are those who say: 'It is true that things are going badly, but we only have to get together in a spirit of goodwill, and the situation will improve; with the help of our doctors we might even succeed in overcoming death; we will certainly not have any more starving people, and with our technology we will build a habitable world – or one that is reasonably so'.

And then, just at the crucial moment, an earthquake swallows up entire cities at a time, or seasonal disasters reduce to nothing both the hard work of millions of poor people and the economic calculations of governments. There is obviously something here which does not quite add up and causes me to doubt the efficiency or goodness of God himself.

No, Job was right: 'Yahweh gave, Yahweh has taken back. Blessed be the name of Yahweh.' And Anna was right when she said, 'Yahweh gives death and life, brings down to Sheol and draws up; Yahweh makes poor and rich, he humbles and also exalts' (1 S 2:6–7). God is not the reliable protector we imagine him to be according to the negative, domestic dimensions of our faith; he is a demanding God who, in order to heal me, is quite capable of crushing me, and who, to save an entire people from paganism, can abandon them to exile, hunger and nakedness. *God gives, and God takes back* – a hard truth for someone to swallow who has accustomed himself to a sort of lightning-conductor God, a wonder-worker who cures personal ills; or to a theology of limited range, largely developed in *ex voto* shrines and merely concerned with rational explanations of the mystery, ready to justify a God who might send you to hospital or leave you unemployed.

God has absolutely no need to be justified by our theological pretensions. There is no point in attempting to justify him before the mystery of things that do not turn out as we would like them to.

And it is a waste of time to place all the blame on Adam. In any case, he is not here to listen to us. Whether we like it or not, it is all part of the mystery of God, it is God who gives and who takes away, and until we can get back into the way of attributing to him – as does Job and the Bible – both what is good and what is evil, without getting bogged down in a morass of casuistry whose sole purpose is to evade the mystery, we will never succeed in making a radical act of faith. As long as we are accustomed to see the evils from which we suffer as no more than the work of evil men, we shall only learn to hate them and try, like Marxism, to overthrow them.

Marxism is evil only in so far as it involves a direct denial of the Transcendent, and, in building up society, completely excludes all agents apart from man. And what a lot of Marxism has seeped into the lifeblood of contemporary Christianity!

Not in the sense that there are Christians who are tempted to engage in guerrilla warfare and to approve the use of violence, but in the sense that they have been penetrated by a more subtle poison.

'Do not look to God for bread, look rather to governments, technicians and silos.'

'What has God to do with the cultivation of fields, with the productivity of the earth, with chemical fertilizers?'

They have become 'enlightened', 'up-to-date', 'liberated' from the sacred, which attributes certain powers to the blessed water used on rogation days or to the prayers of some unlettered woman.

They have stepped out of the world of mystery and can no longer recite the Our Father meaningfully because they no longer believe that God intervenes or even wants to intervene in such banal human concerns as the harvesting of rice.

In fact, they have replaced the Our Father with words that make more sense, and have credited technicians with a greater power than they actually have. *You* give us this day our daily bread.

But the technicians do not always succeed in doing so, and things end up in a mess.

If there is one prophecy that should be proclaimed loud and clear in the leaden sky of contemporary rationalism it is this: 'Listen, Israel: Yahweh our God is the one Yahweh.' He is the God of the impossible, the mysterious God who has rescued you from the powers of darkness and hatred and led you to the land he promised to your fathers (Deuteronomy).

Believe in him, place your trust in him. He rescued you from the land of despair and doubt and led you into the desert in order to purify your heart. Do not be afraid, Israel, saying: what are we to eat, what are we to drink now that we have become so numerous that the land seems incapable of containing us all.

Is my arm shortened or my power diminished? Yahweh asks. Come, put me to the test – go to the temple and pray – give up your evil ways, sever your links with impiety and usury, and then come to me, and you will find out whether or not I am able to pour out on your heads a torrent of blessings, the overflowing river of my bounty (Zechariah).

Do not be afraid, Israel, I am with you. When you pass through fire and water, call on me and I will save you. When you see the dry bones strewn on the vast plains of death, trust in me. Those bones will rise. The Lord has spoken (Ezekiel).

I am your God, and there is no other.

From the rising of the sun to its setting, so wide is my mercy towards those who fear me and call on my name.

I am God, yesterday, today and forever.

We have therefore reason for weeping when the voice of prophecy is silent in the Christian community, or when prophecy itself is reduced to merely human dimensions.

It means that the poor one of Yahweh is betraying his God, placing his trust in man instead.

But what will we say when the Gospel is reduced to sociology, and pastors become mere political agitators or organizers of 'good works'?

Who will prophesy then?

Who is going to say that bread is a gift from God when even the priests regard it as a gift from the Americans, and Christians think they can have it in greater quantities simply as a result of careful planning?

Never more, perhaps, than today have we run the risk of reducing the Bible, and the Gospel in particular, to a guide for good behaviour, a belated support for democracy and the equality of all men.

If he follows this road, the poor one of Yahweh will be overwhelmed by the duplicity of men, and having strayed from the path that led him to the desert where his heart could be purified, he will die of hunger and thirst far from God.

May God forbid!

Chapter Five

THE BEYOND

Here we come to the heart of the matter, to the precise point where faith – and not only faith – plays its determining role and provides the answer for anyone who tries to penetrate the beyond. The Book of Job, and everything that we have said so far, only makes sense if, having enabled man to penetrate the heart of things – and nothing can do so more effectively than suffering and love – it brings him out of the experience quickened with renewed life. Things have been given to us that we may penetrate them, but through the dynamic process of becoming, we come out on the other side of them towards the Infinite, the Eternal, the Unchangeable. We know that nothing can stop short man's course in the world of the contingent, the temporary, and that there is a goal which surpasses everything, drawing us towards a point in which everything will be accomplished and explained.

It is like the descent of turbid, impetuous torrents towards the great ocean of peace. The restlessness of Ulysses, the Greeks' awareness that everything is in a state of flux, and most of all, the eschatological perspective of biblical thought, are all indications of this fact. There is one book in the Bible which is perhaps the most important as a witness to the unsatisfied longing of the human heart in its never-ending search for that which is : the Book of Ecclesiastes.

It is a strange book, almost too easy to read, but not so easy to understand.

When I was young, and was introduced to the Bible for the

first time, I was quite surprised that the Church had included this among the canon of inspired books. I felt it was a pagan book, slightly dangerous.

Now that I am older and somewhat more experienced in the search for unity and the synthesis of all things, I must admit that it is one of the books that I find most persuasive. For if Job bears witness to the existence of God beyond, and in spite of his suffering, Ecclesiastes bears witness even more powerfully to God's existence beyond pleasure. He had the courage to say: this life is tedious . . . can you not see? You insist that you like it? I tell you that it no longer has any interest for me. You still feel the pull of the pleasures of this world? For myself, I am fed up with them.

It is precisely in human pleasure, in the delights that the world offers me, that I have discovered the emptiness of things and the thirst for something totally different!

How it rings true, this book of wisdom! Listen.

'I thought to myself, "Very well, I will try pleasure and see what enjoyment has to offer." And there it was: vanity again! This laughter, I reflected, is a madness, this pleasure no use at all . . .

'I did great things: built myself palaces, planted vineyards; made myself gardens and orchards, planting every kind of fruit tree in them. I had pools made for watering the plantations, bought men slaves, women slaves; had home-born slaves as well; herds and flocks I had too, more than anyone in Jerusalem before me. I amassed silver and gold, the treasures of kings and provinces; acquired singing men and singing women and every human luxury . . .

'I then reflected on all that my hands had achieved and on all the effort I had put into its achieving. What vanity it all is, and chasing of the wind! There is nothing to be gained under the sun' (Ecclesiastes 2 : 1–11).

It takes courage to say things like that, especially in a piece of sacred writing, and they can only be said – if they are not to become blasphemy – if the speaker is fully aware that the new reality he is looking for, the good he seeks as the one thing necessary, belongs to another dimension, is further on, existing beyond the realities of this world. The expression *there is nothing to be gained under the sun* can only be used by the man who has already made the earth his own, just as the opinion that culture is of little significance can only be held honestly by the man of culture, and only the rich man and the artist can say that riches or art are trifles.

Otherwise it is impertinence or superficiality. Life is understood by the man who is dying, and things are appreciated by someone who is giving them up or giving them away.

This is how Ecclesiastes sings of the approaching disappearance of created things :

'Light is sweet; at sight of the sun the eyes are glad. However great the number of the years a man may live, let him enjoy them all, and yet remember that dark days will be many. All that is to come is vanity.

'Rejoice in your youth, you who are young; let your heart give you joy in your young days. Follow the promptings of your heart and the desires of your eyes.

'But this you must know; for all these things God will bring you to judgment.

'Cast worry from your heart, shield your flesh from pain.

'Yet youth, the age of dark hair, is vanity. And remember your creator in the days of your youth, before evil days come and the years approach when you say, "These give me no pleasure", before sun and light and moon and stars grow dark, and the clouds return after the rain; the day when those who keep the house tremble and strong men are bowed; when the women grind no longer at the mill, because day is darkening at the windows and the street doors are shut; when the sound of the mill is faint, when the voice of the bird is silenced, and song notes are stilled, when to go uphill is an ordeal and a walk is something to dread.

'Yet the almond tree is in flower, the grasshopper is heavy with food, and the caper bush bears its fruit, while man goes to his everlasting home. And the mourners are already walking to and fro in the street before the silver cord has snapped, or the golden lamp been broken, or the pitcher shattered at the spring, or the pulley cracked at the well, or before the dust returns to the earth as it once came from it, and the breath to God who gave it.

'Vanity of vanities, Qoheleth says. All is vanity' (Ecclesiastes 11 : 7–12, 8).

No, the earth no longer interests me. I am weary of it. It gives me increasingly less pleasure. I remain just as long as I need to remain in order to learn to love, to pay something towards the cost of the redemption, but it no longer attracts me as once it did. I have come to realize that it is in my interest to move on. And this is an important sign.

I am familiar with the changing seasons of life, I have lived through its loves, I have rejoiced in each as it dawned. Now I am looking round for yet other seasons, for another love, for another dawn.

I have lived down here long enough to convince myself that we were not made for the earth, that the earth is not our paradise, and that it has been of service to us only as a great preparation for something else. Above all, it carries within it the all-too-familiar seeds of decay, and as the years pass I find it increasingly wearisome, while my soul fixes its sights with assurance on the One who always has the power to captivate, the uniquely, truly and eternally new : God.

Yes, conceived in Genesis by the love of God, we attain self-awareness in Exodus, consciously and painfully collaborating with God, and we are brought forth at last into eternal life beyond the Apocalypse, beyond history, when all things will have delivered their message and each one of us made his choice freely.

So man's basic condition here on earth is one of waiting, he is at home with insecurity, suffering characterizes his everyday experience and his hope lies in the final transformation of all things. The efforts made by each succeeding generation to create a state of earthly happiness and stability inexorably come to grief after the first few attempts, leaving in their wake a more pronounced lack of self-confidence in man and a pessimism more bitter than even death itself. What does retain its validity is the goodwill of 'men of goodwill', together with the love that went into the effort to create, and the increasingly manifest approximation to the divine model of the Kingdom in which every man is a man and all men are equal, but . . . how can this man be satisfied with things on an earthly scale, when God has planted in the depths of his being the awe-inspiring seed of the divine and opened up before him the infinitely vaster, more perfect perspectives of the Kingdom of God? If, as Christ has said, the Kingdom is already within us, how can man possibly still his longings in the realm of his own humanity, however beautiful, however fascinating it may be?

Sooner or later he will break through the barrier and gallop through the fields like a thoroughbred that has been enclosed for too long within the narrow confines of its stable.

Once he becomes aware of his true nature as a son of God, how can he be content to be no more than a son of man?

This is the real source of man's restlessness, of his unconscious urge to search for novelty, of his desire to discover the beyond and breach the walls of the invisible.

We have germs of eternal life within us, seeds of divine life. Such germs or seeds, though planted within our human nature, must now begin to germinate, put down roots and bear flowers and fruit in an unfamiliar soil that does not belong to this earth at all, and which is defined in the Gospel as 'the Kingdom'.

Already there is blood flowing within me that I have inherited neither from my mother nor from my father, but directly from God.

In short, the supreme truth, the most exhilarating piece of news, the most disconcerting fact is this: *I am not simply the poor one of Yahweh, I am the son of Yahweh.*

This sonship is not juridical, it is real. Born a child of man, I am reborn in grace, a child of God.

This is not just playing with words; it is a fact, the basis of our greatness and our motive for hope.

Do you believe in evolution?

I do myself, and I became an evolutionist, not by studying the skeletal structure of prehistoric animals in order to observe the successive stages in the great chain of being, but because I experienced it within myself. I became aware, in the depth of my being as a man, of the tension, the *evolution* of becoming a son of God. Through my own religious experience I came to realize that the phrase 'son of God' is neither rhetorical, nor symbolic; it describes a reality.

At this point perhaps I may be permitted a short digression by way of illustration. I recall that Mgr Olgiati told me a similar story when he wanted to explain to me what it means to be an adopted son of God. It was his stock story, and I shall now tell you mine. At Tazrouk in the Hoggar the Little Brothers had a fraternity among the ex-slaves of the Tuareg, poor families who lived by cultivating a bit of grain and a few vegetables along the *oued*.

The *oued* of Tazrouk was a haven of peace and the brothers too had their garden, where they worked the soil.

But what a labour it was to draw something forth from that sand! If there was not a drought, the locusts descended, and if one escaped the locusts there were caterpillars instead. And what is more, rabbits used to come in from round about and make short work of the little bit of green that had been acquired as the result of so much effort.

By way of self-defence, therefore, one was compelled to set traps, and these became the source of a bit of meat which was generally not too bad – as long as it was not fox or jackal.

One evening a flight of storks appeared in the sky above Tazrouk, bound for the north : it was spring at the time.

Descending in wide circles, the birds came to pass the night on the *oued*. In her efforts to find somewhere to alight, a beautiful female stork put her foot right into one of the traps. All that night she lost blood, and when the dawn came, and her companions realized what was happening, it was too late. All attempts to save the poor bird were useless : she died that same day and we buried her at the edge of the *oued*.

But then began the drama which involved each one of us intimately. The flight of storks set out once more for the north, but the partner of the dead stork stayed behind at the *oued*. That evening we saw the wretched bird come down near the garden, in the same place that his partner had been trapped, and fly round and round, crying and showing by obvious signs that he was looking for something. This went on until sunset. The same scene was repeated next day. The flight of storks had possibly reached the Mediterranean by now, and yet this lone bird was still there, searching for his companion. He stayed for the entire year. Each day he would go off in search of food, and at sunset we would see his outline against the sky over the garden, as he came down in the usual place, crying, searching and finally going to sleep in the sand where, perhaps, he could still detect the smell of his partner's blood.

The brothers became accustomed to the stork, as he did to them. He would fly into the garden and come over to take whatever morsel of meat or moistened bread the brothers offered him.

It was moving to see how sensitive this creature was to the love and attention of the brothers, who, feeling themselves to be somehow responsible for his bereavement, redoubled their attentions.

I remember the look in his eyes, his habit of cocking his head on one side, the regular movement of his beak, and the way he had of staring at me, as if he were trying to catch hold of me and escape from his solitude.

I for my part tried to understand him, but I remained myself, and he remained a stork. I remained imprisoned within my limitations as he did within his – limitations fixed for us by nature.

There was no possibility of communication.

And yet this migrant had done, and knew how to do, extraordinary things, things that I myself would have been incapable of doing.

He had left the hot countries – Mali, perhaps, or Niger – and he had travelled hundreds of miles with neither compass nor radar; he was capable of continuing his journey without a map, until finally he came back to the same roof-top, the same chimney-pot as last year and there built his nest. And yet . . . for all his skill as a long-distance navigator, he would not have known how to read my language or interpret the intonation of my voice.

The following spring another flight of storks reached the *oued* of Tazrouk. This time our friend joined it, and set out once more for the north.

I have often thought about that bird as I searched for a comparison or tried to explain the gulf that exists between the nature of animals and the nature of man. Comparisons are of limited value, but they can help us in our weakness.

There is also an unbridgeable gulf between the nature of God and the nature of man – there is the fact of transcendence.

And herein lies the mystery kept hidden, as St Paul says, through many centuries, and revealed to us in the fulness of time.

God, in his love, decided to bridge the gulf, making it possible for man to become in every respect his son.

It is as if, with a power I do not in fact possess, I had somehow enabled the stork to achieve the impossible and become my child, and therefore capable of 'understanding me', of 'communicating with me', of living my life, sharing my intelligence, my love, my will.

For to confer a nature, to establish a parent–child relationship, does not simply require a legal act recorded in a ledger in a registry office; in reality it means ensuring that the one who is adopted as 'son' can share the same preferences and customs as his father; that he can share his parent's nature – which means sharing the power of perceiving, loving and willing. This is the mystery: what theologians call our participation in the divine nature, and which St Paul celebrates in the Epistle to the Ephesians when he recapitulates the plan of God.

'Blessed be God the Father or our Lord Jesus Christ, who who has blessed us with all the spiritual blessings of heaven in Christ. Before the world was made, he chose us, chose us in Christ, to be holy and spotless, and to live through love in his presence, determining that we should become his adopted sons, through Jesus Christ for his own kind purposes, to make us praise the glory of his grace, his free gift to us in the Beloved' (Ep 1 : 3–6).

John also describes it in the magnificent prologue to his Gospel:

'But to all who did accept him, he gave power to become children of God, to all who believe in the name of him who was born not out of human stock or urge of the flesh or will of man but of God himself' (Jn 1 : 12–13).

Born of God, I who was born of a man and a woman whom I learned, from my earliest years, to call mother and father! What a profound mystery! Nicodemus was right to be perplexed by Jesus's statements.

How can one bridge the unbridgeable?

Given the fact that God offers us such a priceless gift, how are we to make it a reality for ourselves? How can we turn it into something authentic, living, true?

If God was prompted by love to make so radical an offering, how could man respond adequately? How could he freely make it his own?

Who would show us the Father's house, familiarize us with his language, his customs, his will?

Who, in short, would 'reveal' God to us?

Enable us to approach the heart of his inexpressible knowledge?

Make it possible for us to make the transition to another nature which spelled complete darkness in terms of our understanding, our language?

Who would overcome the problem of God's otherness, bridge the gulf that separates creature from Creator, man from God?

Who would make it clear to me what I ought to do?

Who would pass on to me his own life, his personal knowledge?

Listen . . .

Chapter Six

JESUS

'O unsearchable mystery! God has taken our human nature, he has deigned to be born of the Virgin in order to make us sharers in his own divinity' (Liturgy of Christmas).

In order to achieve the impossible, the God of the impossible took the first step himself. What man was unable to do for himself on his journey towards God, God has done by stooping down towards man. To enable man to take his place in the family of God, God entered the family of man. With the Incarnation for the first time the unbridgeable was bridged from above to below. Something that had never happened before – that One from above should come down to us – happened in Jesus.

The invisible became visible, the intangible became tangible in Christ. History has been shocked into new life since Jesus came to play a part in it: the cosmos has become a sacred offering since the Word took flesh from a woman living within the cosmos.

God has become man, the Word has become a child, Immensity has accepted limitations.

The infinite has become finite.

The unknowable has made himself known.

Omnipotence became a child.

The immutable accepted suffering.

The Perfect one took on the burden of sin.

Life was attained through death.

Love was expressed as resurrection.

Jesus became our brother.

What happened is so amazing that it leaves us speechless with wonder; the fact is unique enough to justify our incredulity. And we should not be surprised if many people remain puzzled. We should be surprised by the contrary.

In order to proclaim that God became man, we need the invincible courage of faith.

In order to believe that Jesus is the Christ, the Son of the Living God, we need a revelation from the Father.

We need absolute humility of mind and heart if we are to enter into such a mystery as this. There is no point in discussing it.

Leave men to seek and to love, and they will find.

Each of us has his own history; each must follow his own path with patience and perseverance. Sooner or later our history, our path will meet up with, and intersect the history of Jesus, the path along which he is travelling.

Then – but only then – comes the moment of choice, of acceptance, of the yes or the no. One thing, however, is certain : until we have accepted him and borne our witness that he is the Son of God, something will be missing from our life, for us the sunlight will be mixed with shadows, at dawn we will be filled with nostalgia, and our nights will be restless.

It is inevitable !

If you have ever met anyone who has found the answer to the mystery of life or peace of heart, without Jesus, come and tell me about him, for I have never come across such a one.

As for me, I began to know Jesus as soon as I accepted Jesus as the truth; I found true peace when I actively sought his friendship; and above all I experienced joy, true joy, that stands above the vicissitudes of life, as soon as I tasted and experienced for myself the gift he came to bestow on us : eternal life.

But Jesus is not only the Image of the Father, the Revealer of the dark knowledge of God. That would be of little avail to me in my weakness and my sinfulness: he is also my *Saviour*.

On my journey towards him, I was completely worn out, unable to take another step forward. By my errors, my sinful rebellions, my desperate efforts to find joy far from his joy, I had reduced myself to a mass of virulent sores which repelled both heaven and earth.

What sin was there that I had not committed? Or what sin had I as yet not committed simply because the opportunity had not come my way?

Yet it was he, and he alone, who got down off his horse, like the good Samaritan on the way to Jericho; he alone had the courage to approach me in order to staunch with bandages the few drops of blood that still remained in my veins, blood that would certainly have flowed away, had he not intervened.

Jesus became a *sacrament* for me, the cause of my salvation, he brought my time in hell to an end, and put a stop to my inner disintegration. He washed me patiently in the waters of baptism, he filled me with the exhilarating joy of the Holy Spirit in confirmation, he nourished me with the bread of his word. Above all, he forgave me, he forgot everything, he did not even wish me to remember my past myself.

When, through my tears, I began to tell him something of the years during which I betrayed him, he lovingly placed his hand over my mouth in order to silence me. His one concern was that I should muster courage enough to pick myself up again, to try and carry on walking in spite of my weakness, and to believe in his love in spite of my fears. But there was one thing he did, the value of which cannot be measured, something truly unbelievable, something only God could do.

While I continued to have doubts about my own salvation, to tell him that my sins could not be forgiven, and that justice, too, had its rights, he appeared on the Cross before me one Friday towards midday.

I was at its foot, and found myself bathed with the blood

which flowed from the gaping holes made in his flesh by the nails. He remained there for three hours until he expired.

I realized that he had died in order that I might stop turning to him with questions about justice, and believe instead, deep within myself, that the scales had come down overflowing on the side of love, and that even though all men, through unbelief or madness, had offended him, he had conquered for ever, and drawn all things everlastingly to himself.

Then later, so that I should never forget that Friday and abandon the Cross, as one forgets a postcard on the table or a picture in the worn-out book that had been feeding one's devotion, he led me on to discover that in order to be with me continually, not simply as an affectionate remembrance but as a living presence, he had devised the Eucharist.

What a discovery that was!

Under the sacramental sign of bread, Jesus was there each morning to renew the sacrifice of the Cross and make of it the living sacrifice of his bride, the Church, a pure offering to the Divine Majesty.

And still that was not all.

He led me on to understand that the sign of bread testified to his hidden presence, not only during the Great Sacrifice, but at all times, since the Eucharist was not an isolated moment in my day, but a line which stretched over twenty-four hours: he is God-with-us, the realization of what had been foretold by the *cloud* that went before the people of God during their journey trough the desert, and the *darkness* which filled the tabernacle in the temple at Jerusalem.

I must emphasize that this vital realization that the sign of bread concealed and pointed out for me the uninterrupted presence of Jesus beside me was a unique grace in my life. From that moment he led me along the path to intimacy, and friendship with himself.

I understood that he longed to be present like this beside each one of us.

Jesus was not only bread, he was also a friend.

A home without bread is not a home, but a home without friendship is nothing.

That is why Jesus became a friend, concealed under the sign of bread. I learned to stay with him for hours on end, listening to the mysterious voices that welled up from the abysses of Being and to receive the rays of that light whose source was in the uncreated light of God.

I have experienced such sweetness in the eucharistic presence of Christ.

I have learned to appreciate why the saints remained in contemplation before this bread to beseech, to adore and to love.

How I wish that everyone might take the Eucharist home, and having made a little oratory in some quiet corner, might find joy in sitting quietly before it, in order to make his dialogue with God easier and more immediate, in intimate union with Christ.

But still that was not enough.

Jesus did not overcome the insuperable obstacle presented by the divinity and enter the human sphere simply to be man's saviour. Had that been all, his work would have remained unfinished, his mission of love unfulfilled.

He broke through the wall surrounding the invisible, and came down into the visible world to bear witness to 'the things that are above', to reveal to us 'the secrets of his Father's house', to give us in concrete form what he called eternal life.

What exactly is it, this famous 'eternal life'?

He himself defined it in the Gospel: 'And eternal life is this: to know you, the only true God, and Jesus Christ whom you have sent' (Jn 17:3). So eternal life is, first and foremost, knowledge. It is a matter of knowing the Father, knowing Jesus. But it is not a question of any external, historical, analogical knowledge which we could more or less imagine, possess perhaps, even now; it is rather a question of real, supernatural knowledge which, although it is still surrounded here by the darkness of faith, is already the same as the knowledge we will have when the veil is torn aside and we see God face to face. It is a question of knowing God *as he is*, not as he may appear to us or as we may imagine him. This is the heart of the mystery I have tried to describe as *the beyond*, and which is the key to the secret of intimacy with God and the substance of contemplative prayer.

In giving us 'eternal life' Jesus gives us that knowledge of the Father which is already our first experience of living, here on earth, the divine life; which is a vital participation, here and now, in the family life of God; and which means that while we remain sons of man, we are at the same time sons of God.

Then there is the knowledge of Jesus. We will never find words adequate to describe what the simple phrase 'to know Jesus' contains and means for us.

For God established Christ as a bridge between heaven and earth, between the seen and the unseen; he constituted Christ as author of salvation and teacher of his brethren; as the restorer of the original plan of the Father and the one before whom every knee should bend, on earth, in heaven and under the earth.

Jesus is the Image of the Father, the centre of the universe and of history.

Jesus is our salvation, the radiance of the God we cannot see, the unquenchable fire of love, the one for whom the angels sigh, the Holy one of God, the true adorer, the eternal High Priest, the Lord of the Ages, the glory of God.

Jesus is also our brother, and as such he takes his place beside us, to teach us the path we must follow to reach the invisible. And to make sure that we understand, he translates into visible terms the invisible things he has seen – as man he acts as

God would act; he introduces the ways of the family of God on to the earth and into the family of man.

All this is called the 'Good News'.

Whatever Christ does as man in the Gospels, it is as if God were doing it in heaven.

What Jesus says in the Gospels is what he has heard the Father say in heaven.

The Gospel is the way in which we can live here on earth as the saints would live in heaven.

The Gospel is everything.

It is the unique model; it is invisible perfection made visible in Christ's manner of life.

For a Christian there should be no other book from which to draw inspiration, no other model to imitate.

The Gospel is a living person: Jesus Christ.

If the Gospel prefers poverty to riches it means that the Father sees things this way, and will judge us according to his standards, not ours:

If the Gospel looks for mercy and forgiveness it means that such behaviour is habitual with God and we should bring our own actions into line with it.

If the Gospel believes in the Resurrection there can be no reason for doubting it.

If the Gospel shows preference for the simple life of the poor, of shepherds and artisans, so much so that it wanted the Son of God to be poor, a humble workman, those of us who are not poor, simple workmen must look to ourselves. We could be in for some nasty surprises.

If the Gospel tells us that it is better to find oneself minus an eye or an arm in the kingdom of heaven, than physically intact in hell, we should get used to paying less attention to our appearance and concentrating more on our salvation.

If the Gospel tells us we are sons of the Father in heaven what reason have we for doubting it?

Why not be at peace and rejoice?

PART II

'Be happy at all times; pray constantly; and for all things give thanks to God' (I Th 5 : 17).

Chapter Seven

THE RUSSIAN PILGRIM

I have discovered a really extraordinary story, and I want to tell it here.

It is about a young Russian, born in a village in the Ural province. Having been orphaned at the age of three, and lost an arm when he was seven, he had one unique blessing – his grandfather who taught him to read the Bible.

A series of misfortunes punctuated his youth : his house was destroyed by fire, and tuberculosis deprived him of his young wife.

He kept to his hovel, weeping.

Then he felt he could no longer go on living where he had suffered so much and where his memories were so painful.

He gave what possessions he had left to the poor, took a knapsack in which he put a bit of dry bread and a Bible, and became a pilgrim. For thirteen years he walked the roads of Russia, living on alms and visiting monasteries and churches; he accustomed himself to living in the solitude of the steppes and fields, and he had one great desire : to be able, one day, to reach Jerusalem.

We meet him, when he is thirty-three, the Lord's own age. Let us allow him to speak for himself – it is more interesting :

By the grace of God, I am a man and a Christian. In my life a great sinner; my status, homeless pilgrim; general circumstances, poor and perpetually on the move from place to place.

As for possessions, I have a knapsack on my back with dry bread in it, and a Bible in my pocket. That is all.

On the twenty-fourth Sunday after Pentecost I went into a church to pray during the Office. Someone was reading from St Paul's First Epistle to the Thessalonians, where he says 'pray constantly'.

These words made a great impression on me, and I wondered how it was possible to pray constantly, given the fact that everyone was bound to be involved in a certain number of activities in order to support his life. I looked it up in the Bible, and there I read with my own eyes exactly what I had heard during the Office. It is necessary to pray constantly (I Th 5:17), to pray in the Spirit on every possible occasion (Ep 6:18), in every place to raise one's hands up reverently in prayer (I Tm 2: 8).

However much I reflected, I did not know what decision to make. How, I said to myself, can I set about finding someone to explain these words to me? I will make the rounds of the churches where there are well-known preachers, and perhaps I will find what I am looking for.

And I set out on my journey.

From then on I heard many excellent sermons on prayer, but they were instructions about prayer in general – what prayer is, why it is necessary to pray, what are the fruits of prayer. But how to pray constantly – nothing was said about that. I even heard a sermon on the prayer of the heart and on continual prayer, but no one suggested to me how such prayer could be achieved. So attendance at sermons failed to give me what I was looking for.

This being so, I stopped going to them and decided to seek out a wise and experienced man who would explain this mystery to me, seeing that my spirit was inescapably drawn to it.

I searched for a long time: I would read the Bible, and wonder whether somewhere there might not exist some master of the spiritual life who could serve me as a wise and experienced guide.

I took to the road once more, without really knowing where to go.

I was depressed by my failure to find what I was looking for, and to console myself, I would read the Bible. I had been walking like this along a main road for five days, when one evening I met a little old man who looked like a religious. In response to my question, he said he was a monk who lived as a hermit, along with some other brothers, some ten kilometres away, and he invited me to stay with him.

'At our house,' he said, 'we receive pilgrims, we attend to their needs and offer them shelter.'

I was not too keen to go with him, and replied : 'My peace of mind does not depend on my being housed, but on spiritual instruction; I am not looking for food, since I have plenty of dry bread in my sack.'

'But what kind of instruction are you looking for, and what is it you want to understand? Do come with me, brother. We have some experienced *staretz* who could give you spiritual direction, and set you on the right path in the light of the word of God and the teachings of the Fathers.'

'But look, Father, it is about a year now since I heard the apostle's injunction, "pray constantly", during the Divine Office. Not knowing how the phrase was to be understood, I set about reading the Bible. And there too I found many passages containing God's command that we should pray constantly, in all circumstances, in all places, not only in the course of our daily work, but while we are asleep as well : "I sleep, but my heart is awake."

'This struck me very forcibly; I could not see how such a thing was possible, nor the means to achieve it. Such violent longing and feelings of curiosity were roused within me that the words did not leave my mind, day or night.

'From then on I became restless and unsure of myself.'

The *staretz* made the sign of the cross and began to speak. 'Thank God, my brother, who has filled you with this irresistible attraction towards constant interior prayer. Recognize it as the call of God, and find your peace once again in the thought that the response of your will to the word of God has been severely tested.

'God himself had enabled you to grasp this, and it will certainly not be thanks to any worldly wisdom or desire based on empty curiosity that you will reach the heavenly light of interior prayer. On the contrary, it will be through poverty of spirit, simplicity of heart, and actual experience.

'You should not be surprised that you have heard nothing profound about the act of prayer itself; that no one has taught you how to achieve this constant activity of the soul.

'In fact people preach a great deal about prayer, and there are many recent books on the subject, but the authors' arguments are almost always based on intellectual speculation, on rational principles, and almost never on the actual experience of prayer nourished by deeds. More is said about the attributes of prayer than about its essence. One man will tell you precisely why it is necessary to pray; another will illustrate for you the power and the advantages of prayer; a third will describe the conditions that are necessary in order to pray well, the attentiveness, devotion and purity of soul that are required, and so on and so on.

'But what prayer is and how one learns to pray – questions which are fundamental – preachers rarely tell you these days, because they involve something far more demanding than all their arguments, and require not so much academic knowledge as mystical understanding.

'And the sad thing is that only too often their superficial human wisdom leads them to judge God by human standards. Many make the mistake of thinking that it is the methods and the good actions which produce the prayer, whereas in reality prayer is the source of all virtues and all good works.

'They wrongly take the fruits and outward effects of prayer to be the means of achieving it, and in so doing diminish its power. This is a point of view entirely contrary to the passage in Scripture, where St Paul says: "First of all, I urge you to pray" (1 Tm 2 : 1). Many good works are demanded of the Christian, but the work of prayer ranks above all because without it no other good can be achieved.

'Without frequent prayer, one cannot find the way that leads to the Lord, nor can one know the Truth, crucify the flesh with its unruly passions, or be inwardly enlightened by the light of Christ and unite oneself to him in the work of salvation.'

Continuing our conversation in this way, we had without realising it made our way to the little monastery. In order, therefore, not to leave the wise old man before I had satisfied my desire to learn, I said quickly: 'Please, reverend father, *you* explain to me what constant interior prayer is about and what one must do to achieve it. I can see that your experience is deep and genuine.'

The *staretz* granted my request and invited me in.

'Come with me, and I will give you a book of the writings of the Fathers which will help you to understand clearly what prayer is, to learn to practise it with the help of God.'

We entered his cell, and the *staretz* addressed me with these words: 'The interior and constant practice of the Jesus prayer involves a continuous, uninterrupted invocation of the name of Jesus with the lips, with the heart and with the understanding, together with awareness of his presence at all times and in all places, even during one's sleep. It is expressed in the words: Lord Jesus, Christ, have mercy on me!

'Anyone who makes habitual use of this invocation experiences great consolation as a result, and feels the need to repeat it over and over again. After a while, he cannot do without it, to such an extent that he hears it repeated within him without his having spoken it with his lips.

'Now do you understand what constant prayer is?'

'I understand perfectly, father,' I cried, full of joy, 'but now, in the name of God, teach me how I can reach this state myself.'

'We will discover together in this book how one learns to pray. It is called the *Philocalia*, and it contains fully detailed teaching, elaborated by the Fathers, on interior prayer. It is such a useful and perfect book that it is considered to be an essential guide to the contemplative life.'

So the *staretz* opened the *Philocalia*, chose a passage from St Simeon, and began to read: 'Remain seated, in silence and alone; bow your head, close your eyes, and breathe gently; try to direct your imagination and thought processes to within your heart; and as you breathe in and out say: Lord Jesus Christ, have mercy on me, in a low voice, or even simply interiorly. Try to drive all other thoughts away, and repeat this exercise frequently.'

I listened, attentive and wondering, trying to memorize all that the *staretz* was saying to me. We passed the entire night away in this way, and went at dawn to recite matins without having slept at all.

As he said goodbye, the *staretz* blessed me and told me to come back to him in the course of my study of prayer.

In church, I felt within me a burning zeal which impelled me to study this constant interior prayer with great care, and I begged God to help me.

Then I went in search of somewhere to live, since I could not stay in the convent guest rooms for more than three days.

Fortunately I knew of some lodgings only four miles away. I went to find a place there and God helped me. I offered my services as watchman to a farmer, in return for being allowed to spend the summer alone in a hut at the bottom of the garden.

Thanks be to God, I had found a really peaceful spot. It was there that, using the method I had been shown, I set about practising and learning more about interior prayer, going from time to time to visit my *staretz*. For a full week, in my garden solitude, I worked hard at my study of interior prayer, following exactly my *staretz*'s advice. At first everything seemed to go well. Then I began to experience a great sense of weariness. Boredom, laziness and an unbearable desire to sleep descended on me like heavy clouds.

Full of misgivings, therefore, I went back to the *staretz* and described my condition to him.

He received me kindly, and said :

'My brother, what you are experiencing is the war the powers of evil have declared on you – for the world fears nothing more than the prayer of the heart. Satan tries to make things difficult for you, and to give you a distaste for prayer. Your humility must still be put to the test, for it is too early as yet to attain something so sublime.

'Here are some beads with which you can begin to recite three thousand invocations a day. Standing or sitting, lying down or walking, keep repeating to yourself : Lord Jesus Christ, have mercy on me. Say it softly, without hurrying. This is how you will arrive at that uninterrupted activity of the heart.'

Joyfully I took in what the *staretz* said, and made my way back to my hut. Exactly and faithfully, I begun to put what I had heard into practice. I had some further difficulty for a couple of days, then it all became so simple that when I was not repeating the prayer, I felt the need to start saying it again, and it ebbed and flowed within me easily and gently, with none of the tension of the first few days.

I told the *staretz* about this, and he commanded me to repeat it six thousand times each day, adding, 'Don't be anxious about it, and try to be faithful to what I have recommended. God will have mercy on you.'

All that week, I kept to the seclusion of my hut, reciting the six thousand invocations each day and not worrying about anything else or wrestling with my own thoughts : I simply tried to carry out exactly the precepts of my *staretz*.

What happened?

I became so accustomed to praying that if I stopped, even

for a moment, I experienced a sense of emptiness, as if I had lost something. But as soon as I started again I became light-hearted and happy once more.

I wanted to remain there alone – I had no desire to see anyone, and I was completely happy.

When I went back to the *staretz* I described this joy to him, and after he had listened to me he said : 'Now that you have made a habit of prayer, try to maintain that habit, and strengthen it. Never waste time, love solitude, rise early, and resolve to remain united to God.'

One morning early, I was, as it were, woken up by prayer. I began to say my morning prayers, but it was as if my tongue was tied, and I was overcome with the desire simply to repeat the Jesus Prayer. I began to repeat it and was immediately happy. My lips moved effortlessly, of their own accord.

I passed the whole of that day in a state of joy. It was as though I was detached from everything, and I felt as if I was in another world. I went to see the *staretz* and gave him a detailed account of all this. When I had finished, he said : 'God has given you the desire to pray, and the capacity to do so without effort.

'What heights of perfection, what ecstatic joy, man can experience, when the Lord wishes to reveal the secrets of prayer to him and purify his passions ! It is an indescribable state, and the revelation of this mystery is like a foretaste of the delights of heaven. This is the gift which they receive who seek the Lord with love and with singleness of heart.

'Now you can recite as many prayers as you wish. Invoke the name of Jesus without bothering to count, and comply humbly with the will of God, trusting in his help. He will not abandon you, and will guide you on your way.'

From then on, how happy I was ! What joy to feel within me the fervour of my prayer. Whenever I went into a church, I burned with love for Jesus.

My solitary hut seemed like a magnificent palace, and I did

not know how to thank God for having such an excellent *staretz* to a poor sinner like myself.

But unfortunately I had not much longer to take advantage of his direction : my beloved master died at the end of the summer. Weeping, I took leave of him, and thanking him for his teaching I asked him to leave me, by way of a blessing, the beads he always used to pray with.

And so I found myself alone once more.

The summer came to an end and the garden produce was gathered in. The farmer gave me two silver roubles in payment. I filled my knapsack with bread for the journey and went back to my wandering life.

But I was no longer poor, as I had been previously. Invoking the name of Jesus made my travelling a joyous affair, and everywhere I met with kindness. It seemed that everyone was predisposed to love me.

So here I am on the road once more, constantly reciting the Jesus Prayer which is dearer and more precious to me than anything else. Often I cover more than seventy kilometres a day, and I have no idea where I am going. When the cold bites into me I recite the prayer more attentively, and immediately I feel warmer.

If my hunger becomes too acute, I call on the name of Jesus more frequently and forget that I am hungry.

If I feel ill, or if my legs or my back ache, I concentrate on the prayer and the pain passes.

If anyone offends me, I think of nothing but the sweet Jesus Prayer, and immediately the anger or hurt disappears, and I forget all about it. I have become a bit strange.

I no longer get anxious about anything. External realities have no hold on me. My only wish is to remain alone and pray continually; then I am completely happy.

God knows what has taken place within me; I do not. I only know that I am happy, and that I now understand what the Apostle meant when he said : 'Pray constantly.'

Chapter Eight

UNLESS YOU CHANGE AND BECOME LIKE LITTLE CHILDREN . . .

I have re-read that *Story of a Russian Pilgrim* many times, not merely because it is an authentic mystical text of great purity, but also because from it, as well as from other texts of the same kind, I have gleaned solid supporting material for my own attraction to spiritual childhood. The more involved I have found myself in the world of culture, or large scale concerns, or specialization, the more have I needed to simplify my spiritual life; the more contact I have with Christians with intellectual problems, the more I have tried to safeguard my prayer behind the curtain of lowliness and wisdom of heart. I must admit that, at the end – or nearly – of my journey, I am more attracted by the gentleness of a Pope John, the simplicity of a Père de Foucauld, than by any of the learned observations that have been spoken or written for or against *aggiornamento* in the Church.

I have too often been wounded by 'intelligent' people, disconcerted by unloving champions of orthodoxy or by self-advertising revolutionaries who are incapable of an act of humility.

Wishing to protect my poor soul from the babble of useless talk, I took up once more the simple rosary that my mother had wanted me to recite daily when I was boy.

Either I have seen too much of life, or else I have witnessed too many failures. One thing, however, is certain: that I put more and more faith in the simplicity of the Gospel, and I can appreciate the concern of Christ when he said to his friends : 'Unless you change and become like little children, you will never enter the kingdom of heaven.'

To become like children is not easy for men as riddled with pride as we are; that is why Jesus warned us so uncompromisingly : 'You will never enter !'

I realize that no one will believe me, but I have no hesitation about affirming that a serious beginning is made in the spiritual life the moment a man makes a genuine act of humility. So often for most men the early stages of faith, or, in the case of others its development, is blocked, poisoned, distorted, or relegated to an everlasting tomorrow by our inability to become like a child and to cast ourselves, in the spirit of a child, into the enfolding arms of God's mystery. We try to show God how clever we are, when no class of men is so abhorrent to the Gospel; we want to lay down conditions to the Eternal and Infinite One, but the Infinite does not respond, and the Eternal allows time to destroy us.

This is why I loved and still love that young pilgrim : he has the heart of a child and does not lay down conditions to his God.

So God taught him to pray, and God took him up into his own peace and joy, in spite of his dreadful poverty and his unrelieved sufferings. Although he does not realize it himself, he has undoubtedly reached the end of the journey of prayer : he has become a living prayer. He lives in a state of pure prayer, in a union with God so complete that it recalls the extraordinary experience of St Benedict Joseph Labré who travelled as a pilgrim along the roads that lead from France to the holy places in Rome.

Purified by trials, immersed in the purifying waters of evangelical poverty, detached from material things, the young man became an empty vessel filled by the Spirit of God, a musical instrument, ready and waiting to be played by the supraterrestrial hand that is capable of drawing from it celestial harmonies.

Yet he reached these heights by making use of the simplest means imaginable.

A single phrase, repeated like a single, uninterrupted note, acceptance of the events of daily life as part of the mystery of Providence, a Bible in his knapsack, and a bit of dry bread.

We westerners, who consider ourselves to be so experienced in theological matters, smile condescendingly at such a childish method of prayer – so mechanical, so naive!

Have we never smiled at the rosaries of our grandmothers?

But the fact of the matter is that this young man has passed through the wall that separates us from the invisible, and our elders were contemplatives without realizing it, while we, rich in our thoughts and man-made securities, run the risk of dying of subastral cold, far from Jesus, the Sun of our universe.

For it was Jesus himself who said, in a moment of spiritual exhilaration: 'I bless you, Father, Lord of heaven and of earth, for hiding these things from the learned and the clever and revealing them to mere children' (Mt 11 : 25).

And this is the first thing we must keep in mind as we enter the school of prayer.

The Father reveals himself to little ones; the Father hides himself from the learned.

This is not a joke!

If we want to know God, to become close friends of the Most High, we must acquire the habit of contemplative prayer, made with the eyes of humility and with simplicity of heart.

Yes, to become lowly, lowlier still – as lowly as possible. This is the great secret of the mystical life. And then, having reduced oneself to a single point and become nothing more than a soul which watches attentively and a heart which loves, to get used to a complete reversal of the usual position – the eternal position of pride, and the uneasy position of the ego which always sees itself as the centre of the universe.

At this point let us call to mind one very important thing:

prayer is not so much a matter of talking as listening; contemplation is not watching but being watched.

On the day when we realize this, we will have entered finally into possession of the truth, and prayer will have become a living reality. To be watched by God : that is how I would define contemplation, which is passive rather than active, more a matter of silence than of words, of waiting rather than of action.

What am I before God?

What can I do to be worthy of his revelation?

If he shuts, no one opens, and if he opens, no one shuts. He is the active principle of love, he is before all, he is the one who makes within me his own prayer, which then becomes my prayer.

I do not know what has happened or is happening within you, but I do know what has happened and is happening within myself, and I can tell you this : that it was he who sought me in the first place, and it is he who continues to seek me.

At first it was more difficult to recognize his presence, to feel the movement of his hand, but now that I have *experienced him* it has become easier, even though the locus of encounter between him and myself is darker and the memory of that experience harder to capture. With God I have never had great difficulties in the area of faith and I can only say that in spite of my infidelities, my sins, my egoism, and my superficiality, there is no longer any creature – star or flower, meadow or hill, storm wind or fine weather, ocean or bird – which does not speak to me of him, which is not a message and a symbol, a word and a warning from him. I feel I am in him like a bee in its hive, like a bride in her own home, or, better still, like a child in its mother's womb. This last comparison is the most faithful I have found because it says, in a very real way, that union with God is not something that has to be found because it already 'is', just as the union between the mother and her infant already 'is'. At the most it is a question of becoming aware of it; of fostering it through our adherence to him; of responding to his incessant calls, because in God 'we live and move and have our being' (St Paul).

But it is not only that. To say that we are in God like a child in the womb of its mother is to draw attention (given that comparisons are never quite perfect) to the inequalities that exist in the relationship of the two – between the possibilities, the attentiveness, the awareness and the love of the mother, and the helplessness, smallness, blindness and passivity of the child. Our relationship with God is even more unequal than this. Our blindness is greater than that of the foetus. Our possibilities are even more circumscribed. I am not exaggerating. Look around and see how some great men have ended up, how some dictators have oppressed their people. If their places had been taken by children, fewer disasters would have befallen us. And each one of us could produce endless examples from his own experience to bear out what Christ affirmed in the Gospel : *without me you can do nothing.* And nothing means nothing. Let that much at least be understood.

But if Jesus needed to tell us that without him we could do nothing, his implication was : *but with me you can do all things.*

This is one of the paradoxical results of our union with God : the omnipotence of impotence, the knowledge of ignorance, the courage of weakness – all expressed in the cry of St Paul : *If Christ is with me, who can be against me?*

The child in the womb of God means peace in the midst of the storm, security amid the trial of life, light in the darkness, hope in the face of death.

What matters is that one should let oneself go, live by faith, trust in the Eternal – and above all understand one thing : that our growth depends on laws that are not of our own making, on a will that is more powerful than ours.

What can a child do in its mother's womb but wait, be patient, be still? One of the parables describes well this truth about the unfolding of the kingdom of God in an almost imperceptible manner. It is Mark who recounts it.

'He also said, "This is what the kingdom of God is like. A man throws seed on the land. Night and day, while he sleeps, when he is awake, the seed is sprouting and growing; how, he does not know" ' (Mk 4:25). Nor do we know how, but to accept that he brings it about *without our knowing how* is a hard lesson to learn, and it takes us a long time to learn it by heart.

But when we have learned it, what joy we experience. To be able to live in the knowledge that God works while I am sleeping, thinks of me while I work or pray, and will intervene at the appropriate moment, that God awaits me in prayer, and knows my future.

This is true peace, the foretaste of heaven, and the answer to all my problems about faith.

Chapter Nine

PRAYER AND REVELATION

I said just now that contemplation is not so much a matter of watching God as of *being watched by God*. This is something I have learned by praying.

What do you want me to look at while I am praying? I can assure you that never do I feel so short-sighted as I do when I try to focus my eyes of God.

I would say that it is precisely in prayer that you learn to recognize more clearly than ever your own limitations, your measure as a created, not a creating being, the radical powerlessness of your poverty. And you will experience this above all if you have the courage to make your way in faith to *the frontiers of the invisible*.

When you have passed beyond the stages where sentiments, hymns, preoccupation with your own salvation, immediate results and easy achievements matter, and have reached the realm of mystery, then you understand what this world is.

When you have grown tired of setting up little altars on which to erect images of God, the product of your own fantasy, or worse, your theorizing, or, worst of all, your fears, and you reach the arid sands that separate the finite from the infinite, time from eternity, you have little left to think or say.

And then you realize that if contemplation were to depend on you, it would be a pretty sad, impoverished affair.

Emptied of its creative and imaginative powers, bowed and broken by suffering and dissatisfaction, your being would be able to utter no more than an anguished cry, and contemplation would simply mean staring at a grey horizon under northern skies, in an endless winter.

But through the grace of God, contemplation – true contemplation – does not depend on you. You are not the dawn, you are the land that awaits the dawn.

Your God is the dawn, and later he is full daylight, and later still high noon.

You are the land that waits for the light, the blackboard that waits for the white chalk of the draftsman who walks towards you with that chalk in his hand. Sit down and try to be still; sit still and try to hope. Leave behind you time, space, number, thought, reason, culture, and look ahead.

Look beyond yourself, beyond your helplessness and your limitations, and wait.

Your heart has been tried by suffering and darkness; now allow it to stop relying on the earth it is leaving.

Let your tears flow, to water the arid land of your faith.

Persevere.

Do not think of anything else. God is before you.

God is coming to you.

Contemplation is not a matter of watching, but of being watched, and he is there watching you.

And if he is watching you, he loves you, and in loving you, he gives you what you are looking for : himself.

What other gift could there be for one who had searched so hard.

Our heart is so hard to satisfy.

God alone can fill it.

Things never can.

Yes, God is there before you, watching you.

His look is creative, capable of achieving the impossible.

And just as he looked on the chaos at the beginning, hovered over the waters with the smile of his favour, and drew forth the cosmos, so, looking at you with the same favouring smile, he realizes the final purpose of creation : love.

Take courage, then : God loves you.

I know you do not deserve it, so it is useless to go on saying so : the fact is he loves you.

I know you are tormented by doubts, but do not be afraid. He loves you, and his love is freely given. He does not love you for what you are worth; he loves you because, as God, he cannot help loving you : he is love.

Let yourself go; let him take hold of you.

He accepts you as a son.

I realize that you have fled so many times, that you have preferred strange countries to your own home, but all *that* belongs to the past, so stop thinking about it. The time has come for you to love.

But how can I love someone I do not know, respond to the love of someone I cannot see? I have been told that God is unknowable, and that is what makes the relationship so difficult.

You are right : God is unknowable, but being love, he has decided to make himself known.

Just as God, invisible and intangible, has made himself visible and tangible in Christ – has brought about the incarnation – so, in the same way, incommunicable and unknowable, he has become knowable and communicable through love.

By receiving his love in prayer, you enable him to make you the gift of knowledge of himself; by offering him the clean slate of your soul, you make it possible for him to trace on it the features of his own face. The unknowable becomes known; love crosses over the frontier of the invisible; the *beyond* crosses over onto this side, and becomes life. Jesus has described it as eternal life, defining exactly what he meant in the wonderful words, 'Eternal life is this : to know you, the only true God, and Jesus Christ whom you have sent' (Jn 17 : 3).

Union with God depends on knowledge and love : it is a vital reality.

And so, at last, we arrrive at the crux of the matter – the revelation of the mystery kept hidden for centuries, and revealed to us by Jesus in the fulness of time; the completion of the work of creation itself; the profound inner significance of the passion of Christ; the reason for the presence of the Holy Spirit within each one of us.

It is a question, no less, of bringing about the union of creature and creator, of the Father, who is God, with the son, ourselves. And since, as we have already said, this union is not juridical, but a real and vital union, it involves man's entry into the divine life, the divine life which Jesus defined above all as knowledge.

I cannot love what I do not know, and God, who understands this better than I do, cannot ask us to love him – or better, oblige us to love him with the first commandment: *You must love God above all things* – without first making sure that it is possible for us to know him.

This is not what I would call natural knowledge of God, analogical knowledge, which I can achieve by using my own reason or common sense. It is true supernatural knowledge, the same knowledge, that is, that I shall have when the veil of faith is torn aside and I see God face to face. Only God can give me this sort of knowledge, because only God can tell me 'what he is'.

Simply by assembling every conceivable human argument on the subject of God, I will not succeed in adding one centimetre to my height; but by accepting his revelation I enter immediately into the mystery, I become a member of his family, I live his same life.

These are the things that people ought to be saying in church, instead of wasting time criticizing the capitalists who are not present, or turning the Gospel into a sociological text (one hundred years late) on the message of Marx.

The true measure of the Christian is the divine life within him. His primary concern is that he should know God because such knowledge will bring with it the love of charity, which, as St Paul says, is a good surpassing all others, since it is God himself within you.

If I presume too much in saying these things and in believing them from the depths of my heart, the fault lies with Christ. It was he who said to me in the Gospel: 'I will will reveal myself to him' (Jn 14: 21), and I promise you, that I have prayed for this revelation, I have waited for it, and longed for it with an almost unbearable longing.

And here on this arid meeting ground of the visible and invisible, ignorance of God and the possibility of knowing and loving him, I have played all the cards in my hand.

I have not been disappointed, and should you ask me why I believe in God, I would reply, 'because he has revealed himself to me' and should you ask what is the surest proof I have that I know him, I would reply, 'the fact that I have been with him'. St Thomas's five proofs for the existence of God have been a help to me, but the experience I have had of him in prayer helps me far more, and that is the only evidence I would produce for those of my brothers who are searching.

I am aware that in so saying, I am challenging them to set out on a journey through the desert, to renounce themselves totally, to give themselves to the Absolute; but I also know that the prize makes the hardness of the choice worth while, and what is more I know, as St Paul says, 'in whom I have believed'.

Do not be afraid. Listen to what someone who has already travelled this road has to say, my beloved Angela of Foligno:

'The soul, in the presence of God, is surrounded by darkness, and in that darkness comes to a knowledge of him which is greater than any I could have ever imagined was possible, and so splendid, so certain, so profound, that no heart could possibly invent or understand such a thing in any way at all.

'The soul can say absolutely nothing at all, because there are no words in which she can speak about it and express herself. Indeed, there is no thought or intelligence that can encompass such a thing, so far is it above all other things – just as God cannot be explained in terms of anything else that exists. When I turned the matter over in my mind, I knew with absolute certainty that those who are the most aware of God are the least able to talk about him.

'Precisely because they experience something of that infinite and ineffable good, they are less able to speak about it. May God grant that you remember this when you go to preach. For then you will be at a loss for anything to say about God; at which point anyone else might keep silent, but I would come up to you and say: Go on, brother, speak to me for a while about God.

'And you would be so overcome by the goodness of God, that you would be unable to say anything about him.

'And yet the soul does not lose consciousness, nor does the body lose contact with any of the senses; indeed, consciousness is entire within us.

'But you will say emphatically to the people: Go with the blessing of God, because I can say nothing at all!

'And I realize that everything that has been said in Scripture, and by all men from the beginning of the world up till the present moment seems capable of expressing virtually nothing about the heart of the matter, not even so much as a grain of sand in comparison with the universe.'

As for Angela of Foligno, so for us all. We are aware that the knowledge of God increases within us in the measure that our love for him increases.

But we can say nothing about this knowledge. We realize that it is, as theology tells us, an exquisite, mysterious, personal and dark knowledge of God, but we cannot say a word more about it.

This revelation of himself which God makes to man is the body and soul of so-called contemplative prayer, its breath of life, and it constitutes a genuine participation in eternal life.

'And eternal life is this: to know you, the only true God, and Jesus Christ whom you have sent' (Jn 17 : 3).

But what really matters in all this is the fact that the barrier created by our innate inability to advance in the knowledge of God can be overcome. There is one thing we can do; and it is, so to speak, within our reach: the possibility of loving.

The anonymous author of *The Cloud of Unknowing* says: 'Every intelligent creature, angel or man, has within him two principal faculties: one is called a faculty for knowing, the other a faculty for loving. God is the creator of both, but if, through the former, he remains incomprehensible, he can be perceived through the latter, according to each one's different ability. In this fashion, only the being who loves can, by virtue of his love, perceive him who is sufficient to the full to satiate all the souls and angels of creation.'

And the inexhaustible wonder, the miracle of love, is this: that our practice of it will never be interrupted because God ceaselessly rekindles it. And why? Because, since he can be loved but not thought, love can grasp and hold him; thought never can.

Which means that in the last analysis there exists within us a certain capacity to influence God, to approach God, to clasp him to ourselves: the power, that is, of loving. By loving one can achieve what is impossible through other means; by loving one can find God. This, fundamentally, is the sum and substance of all history, of our own history.

Let us keep this truth before us.

You say you have no faith? Love – and faith will come.

You say you are sad? Love – and joy will come.

You say you are alone? Love – and you will break out of your solitude.

You say you are in hell? Love – and you will find yourself in heaven. Heaven is love.

Chapter Ten

PRAYER AND LIFE

Life and prayer are inseparable.

A life without prayer is a life which fails to acknowledge the essential dimension of existence; it is a life which remains satisfied with what it sees, without discovering the grandeur, the eternal aspect of human destiny.

To plumb the depths of prayer is to discover, affirm and live the fact that everything has this vast, eternal dimension.

The world in which we live is not a profane world, even though we ourselves frequently succeed in profaning it. In itself it came from the hands of God, and is loved by God.

In order to appreciate the value God attributes to this world, it is sufficient to think of the life and death of his only Son. But that is something we come to understand as we pray, just as it is only by praying that we come to appreciate that everything around us has a sacred value in the eyes of God.

Not to pray is to exclude God from one's life, and not only God, but everything that he can signify in the world he created and in which we live.

If we want to learn to pray, we must first of all identify ourselves with every aspect of human reality, with man's destiny and that of the world. We must accept it in its entirety. This, basically, is the essential act which God accomplished in the Incarnation, and which became intercession on our behalf.

Normally speaking, when we think of intercession, we believe it to consist in respectfully reminding God of the things he has forgotten to do. In reality, intercession involves the taking of a step which brings us straight to the heart of a tragic situation; and, as Anthony Bloom points out, it is a step of the same quality as that taken by Christ, who became man once and for all.

We ourselves, as far as the world is concerned, must take the step that will lead us to the heart of a situation from which we must never seek to withdraw.

It is not easy, but the trouble is that we have a mistaken idea of life, just as we have of prayer.

Only too often we imagine that life consists in being immensely active, while prayer consists in withdrawing to some place apart, completely forgetting about our neighbour and our human situation. This is quite wrong : it is a misrepresentation of life and a misrepresentation of prayer as well.

If there are moments or longer periods of time when, in order to establish a personal relationship with God, we create a solitude within ourselves, a temporary state of withdrawal, we do so knowing that he will himself remind us of our fellow men and send us back to them, in order that, together with them, we should give concrete expression to our love.

It is God himself, incarnate in Christ – the most sublime and most vital manifestation of love – who has given to each one of us and to his Church, as his own commandment, the commandment of fraternal love : 'Love one another as I have loved you.' To the extent, that is, of total self-sacrifice.

But let us begin at the beginning. Learning to pray means, above all, identifying oneself with every aspect of earthly existence. Anyone who prays to God must be, or endeavour to become, one who looks on the whole of creation with a sympathetic eye – on all reality, physical and spiritual; on nature and on grace; on the rocks on which he places his feet, and on the angels in whom he believes on the testimony of Christ and who inhabit the invisible world. As long as man is unable to accept creation, he will be unable to enter into a relationship of love with the God who fashioned and sustains it, and who continues to fashion and sustain what he has created.

The whole is a unity, and God is at the heart of this unity.

God is like the face of reality, the heart of the universe, and until I can look on created things with sympathy and understanding, I will not be able to enter into vital communication with the One who willed both my existence and that of the entire universe.

To believe that God is present in my prayer means making room within it for the fulness of his thought, his will, which has been realized and is being realized in creation.

Obviously I may come into contact with things I do not understand, and have to accept through faith, but I cannot begin to pray if I put a question mark over everything and remain for ever on the threshold of faith.

I can say, 'I do not understand this yet, but God will explain it to me in his own good time', but in order to pray, I must begin to say 'Our Father, who art in heaven', which means making a first genuinely serious gesture of optimism.

By saying 'Father', I say a thousand and one important things; and I say above all, 'I am beginning to trust you because you are a father and a father could not betray my hopes.'

You are a father who is hidden from us, but you are still a father, and from now on I can greet you with confidence, even though many things still remain a mystery to me.

A woman who belonged to a society for the protection of animals once said to me: 'I will never be able to believe in God as long as I see animals suffering, and as long as butchers continue to exist.'

I appreciate this woman's confusion – it is certainly a strange thing to watch a cat mauling a bird and to realize that in the created order everything lives at the expense of someone or something else; but if I stop there I will not penetrate very far into the mystery, and my own death will overtake me while I am standing there thinking, without understanding, about the deaths of calves in the slaughterhouses of Paris or Bologna. If the idea of the slaughterhouse was holding this good lady back from God, she should realize that the whole universe is one vast slaughterhouse, and it is not only cattle who pay the price for this.

Yet what do we know about what happens in the heaven of slaughtered creatures? What happens when a gazelle dies, or a rabbit parts with its flesh in the hands of the housewife?

We know nothing, or virtually nothing, and yet we presume to pass judgment on everything. We are like children who say to the doctor who prescribes our medicine, 'bad doctor'!

What I am saying may seem trivial, but it is just such trivial matters as these which keep many people back from a serious life of prayer. They deny themselves the possibility of communication with God simply because they have not yet been able to face the fact that the fire which burns and the knife which cuts the flesh are part of life.

Each one of us is entitled to outline the plan or plans according to which he, in his wisdom, would have created the universe. I believe, however, that on the day when we see God face to face – the day, that is, when things are revealed to us as they are – if those plans still lie hidden in our pockets, we will hurriedly destroy them in disgust as we are faced at last with the truth: 'What a fool you have been! Is there no limit to your self-importance?'

And this will be a good beginning for our entry into eternal life.

Having accepted God's plan for ourselves and the world, we should at least desire to put it into practice.

I say 'desire' because putting it into effect is not always

easy. Many people accept in theory that it is more logical, more sincere, more in keeping with the nature of love to have one wife, but at the same time they are few who conform to this plan.

And yet the plan is clear enough.

There is a design in creation which is visible enough, even to the naked eye. And it is visible, furthermore, because within our conscious minds the Creator of all things has left a model, as it were, a chart which can help us to discover the truth, and a compass to enable us to find our bearings on the chart without getting lost.

And yet . . .

An elderly doctor, who had an exaggerated fear of death, used to say to me, 'If only I had your faith, Brother Carlo! What comfort it would bring me! It is obvious that you are at peace, at one with yourself. But what should I do? I have no faith, and I cannot give it to myself.'

The old doctor used to repeat this little speech for my benefit rather too frequently, and as in the end I had the impression that he was using it to justify himself, thus taking refuge in unreality, I once said to him, 'Doctor, do you really want to have faith? Do you want to die at peace with God and men?

'Well then, let the servant whom you keep as a mistress leave the house. You know quite well that she is poor and only agrees to sleep with you because of her poverty. Make her a small settlement, and then let her go off and start a family.

'Rediscover the friendship and compassionate understanding of your wife, sell your estate and distribute the proceeds to the poor, extricate yourself from your appalling egoism, look at people optimistically and stop saying they are evil . . . then you will see.

'Trust me in what I say. Put your house in order, and within a year you will see your faith grow great like an oak tree, and all your doubts disappear.'

In all this I was wrong about only one thing – the date.

Not a year, but a few days after his decision, he had come to the Eucharist. I realize I am carrying coals to Newcastle in saying all this, but let me insist.

So often our prayer lights upon the right path, uncovers the gushing stream, at the moment when we take a step forward in accepting the will of God, whatever it might be, and at whatever stage it happens to find us.

There is a close link between prayer and life : we frequently look on them as unconnected realities, then we see them as drawing closer together, but by the end of our lives we must see them as a single reality. To pray is to live, and living becomes prayer.

There is something else that needs to be said about the connection between life and prayer, a deeply significant, indeed a divine truth, since it was Jesus himself who said it : 'A man can have no greater love than to lay down his life for his friends' (Jn 15 : 13).

One must transform one's own life into an act of self-giving. From then on it becomes 'prayer' and I suddenly achieve the synthesis, the unity of my being, and I break through into the real.

He who becomes a gift, is in a state of perfection; he becomes invulnerable, he is light.

To be a gift to God, a gift to one's fellow men.

The union of these two elements is what makes the Christian, the authentic human being, the saint.

People today are fond of the expression : make yourself available, and it makes a good beginning.

But one needs to go further than that, even if it is terribly difficult and demanding; one needs to become a gift. A gift is something permanent, something previously offered and therefore not open to question, whereas we are so fond of questioning everything.

A gift is an expression of love, but we are more attracted

by the truth because it is more manageable, easier to grasp.

And moreover . . . each one of us sees his own truth.

And since it often happens that the man standing next to me sees a different one, the clashes begin.

The origin of all wars lies in this separation of truth and love.

That is why it is better to become a 'gift' because the gift is more likely to bring peace – which cannot always be said of that which we call 'truth'.

Had Jesus been satisfied with being Truth, and not become a gift, we would still need to be saved. If, having proclaimed the truth to man, he had claimed their immediate consent to it, we would be in hell. It was precisely when no one believed him that he kept silent and allowed himself to be killed. But in dying he became a gift, and so he saved us.

We must learn from him how and to what extent one can interpret the truth, but above all we must let him teach us when the only thing to do is to keep silence, and to go to the depths in love.

And not to make judgments at such moments.

Above all, not to strike out.

Anyone who strikes out when love and truth are not at one within him, misdirects his blows, and the results are invariably disastrous.

The same applies to the slap a man gives 'in hate' to his own son, and to a papal bull which drives a section of the flock outside the Church. Anyone who does not love is in death, and death can only produce corpses, even when it is surrounded by all the truth in heaven an earth.

Chapter Eleven

AND THE NIGHT SHALL BE CLEAR AS THE DAY

I got up at three o'clock to pray.

Very quietly, so as not to wake the brethren, who were sleeping in the adjoining cells, I went out into the night.

I crossed the courtyard, and found myself in complete darkness.

There was a cold nip in the air, but I was sufficiently protected by my *burnous*.

I left the hermitage buildings behind me, and made for the nearby slope in order to watch the stars.

This, for me, is the best preparation for prayer.

Above my head, in all its magnificence, stretched the winter sky of Beni-Abbès.

The profound darkness resulting from the absence of the moon, which was in its last quarter, made it particularly easy to see the stars.

The constellation Leo was passing through the south-west, with its brilliant star Regulus. Virgo's ear of corn, with its unmistakable glow, dominated the Tropic; next came the Lynx, and then the Great Bear, which rose up in the eastern sky, drawing behind it the tail of the Dragon.

I always count it as something precious when, before embarking on my prayer, I am able to fill my gaze with the pure, mysterious light that comes from the stars.

Everyone has his own method, his own way of going about things. The important thing is to realize that it is difficult to reach the point when one can get down on one's knees immediately. We need some moments of preparation, a little time in which to calm the soul, or to wake it up – a vestige of human prudence, so as not to turn up like brutes for such an exacting task as prayer.

For me, the process of star-gazing was a great help.

Others help themselves by contemplating an arrangement of flowers, a meadow, a sunset, a lamb, the view of a sleeping city from an open window. Some focus their attention on the crucifix; others finger their rosary, thinking of one of the mysteries in the life of Our Lady. The important thing is that we should realize that we are little, and must help ourselves in little ways.

How hard we find it to keep our blessed psyche at peace – our complicated, tormented psyche!

And this wretched body which complains incessantly, which always has something wrong with it somewhere, which troubles one, clamours for attention and weighs one down – oh! what a tiresome burden it can be!

And there is nothing to be done about it: one must bear with the first and look after the second; one must be patient and not press too much; give a shake where necessary, but otherwise leave things as they are. No, it is not easy to establish oneself in a state of prayer, to find a bit of peace, relaxation and calm. There is always something in the way!

People really make me laugh when they say, 'You have to bring everything into your prayer, every aspect of yourself.' It is obvious that they are talking about prayer in the abstract, as one might talk about the polar ice-cap without ever having seen it, or about journeying across the desert when one has never so much as set eyes on a sand-dune. Bring everything? I can tell you I would like to bring nothing with me, to contrive, for an hour at least, to forget myself, my poor head, and my heart. To succeed in keeping my imagination in check, bundling it into some corner or other in order to be left in peace, just for that one hour.

And then there are those who come and tell you, with impressive arguments, that you must bring your fellow men with you, have them present continually.

'My God!' a telephonist once said to me, 'from morning till night I'm harassed by my neighbours, first at home, then in the office, and then in the course of my various social engagements. When can I find five minutes to be alone with God?' The telephonist was right, and not those who ramble on about prayer without ever having had any real experience of it. In order to pray, one needs a modicum of solitude, of detachment and withdrawal. This is what the desert, retreat, getting down on one's knees, is all about. One cannot spend all one's time with the community, otherwise one ends up denying that God is the Absolute. Do not be alarmed. I shall return to my brethren, of course, I shall. Jesus himself compels me to do so, though I assure you that, were it not for him, I would flee to the desert and never come back.

To all community enthusiasts I say: all right, I will give you twenty-three hours, but allow me to have the twenty-fourth alone with God.

To take prayer seriously means giving at least the twenty-fourth hour to God – and to God alone.

Simply because he is God, the Absolute.

He is entitled to expect that I should drop everything for him, just as the visitor who comes to see me has the right to expect it.

How reassuring it is to go into the house of friends, and watch everything stop because you have arrived.

We westerners, with all our rushing, have lost sight of this 'sacred' approach to the welcoming of guests. Here in the desert it still exists, as it did in the time of Abraham, and it is manifested in the most wonderful way. Listen to what the Bible has to say about the way visitors should be received:

'Yahweh appeared to him at the Oak of Mamre while he

was sitting by the entrance of the tent during the hottest part of the day. He looked up, and there he saw three men standing near him. As soon as he saw them he ran from the entrance of the tent to meet them, and bowed to the ground. "My lord," he said, "I beg you, if I find favour with you, kindly to not pass your servant by. A little water shall be brought; you shall wash your feet and lie down under the tree. Let me fetch a little bread and you shall refresh yourselves before going further. That is why you have come in your servant's direction." They replied, "Do as you say."

'Abraham hastened to the tent to find Sarah. "Hurry," he said, "knead three bushels of flour and make loaves." Then running to the cattle Abraham took a fine and tender calf and gave it to the servant, who hurried to prepare it. Then taking cream, milk and the calf he had prepared, he laid all before them, and they ate while he remained standing near them under the trees' (Gen 18 : 1–8).

What has always struck me about the way in which these simple men receive visitors is their ability to put all activity to one side. You, the guest, become the focal point, and they range themselves round you in a circle. If the owner of the tent has planned to go on a journey, he puts it off : now he must concern himself with you. If his wife was thinking of doing the laundry, she piles it all up on one side : now she must see about serving you.

The guest is sacred : everything else is less important.

For the time being you are the one who matters : time is less important. And if the visitor, who has left one corner of the world in order to search you out and spend a bit of time with you, has these rights, surely God has the same right, he who came from heaven itself to find you; who took flesh in order to become visible for you; who became the Eucharist in order to gain entrance to your tent and stay there as long as possible.

Here and only here, in fact, is to be found the meaning of prayer, the power that sustains it, and the hope that gives it life: there is one who seeks you, one who stands before you saying: 'Look, I am standing at the door, knocking. If one of you hears me calling and opens the door, I will come and share his meal, side by side with him' (Rv 3:20). If prayer meant addressing oneself to a mute, unheeding wall, I guarantee the Bible would never have been written. I guarantee that the saints would have grown wise to the fact, and years ago the abbey of Monte Cassino, the monasteries of Mount Athos or in the Tibetan mountains would have fallen into ruin.

Prayer is meaningful because in your presence Another is present, another mouth corresponds to your mouth, another ear to your ear.

In this way it becomes something real, vital, authentic.

Under the impulse of this conviction I managed to get up in the night – and I can tell you it is not pleasant.

And it is filled with this hope that I now prepare myself for prayer. I go back down the slope and re-enter the hermitage. It is the same one that Père de Foucauld, thirsting for prayer, built for himself in this desert of Beni-Abbès.

The room, poor as any other, with walls of beaten clay and earthen floor covered by a layer of beautiful clean sand from the dunes, is of an extreme simplicity.

The bright flame of the sanctuary lamp, fed by the purest olive oil, flickers and casts its light into the semi-darkness.

I wrap my soul round with that light, and my body with the *burnous* which keeps me warm, and kneel down on the sand to pray.

You will ask me: why did you go back inside?

Could you not pray under the stars? Would it not have been easier?

Is not nature the principal reminder we have of Almighty God?

And you might even be right, but you must listen to my

explanation. There is no absolute law about praying in church. One can find God perfectly well out under the stars, or in the midst of the city crowds. We have all tried these things out ourselves. But . . .

There are three really important things in my life: the Cosmos, the Bible and the Eucharist.

I could pray outside under the stars, which represent the Cosmos for me; I could pray with the Bible, which is the Word of God; but if I can I prefer to pray before the Eucharist, which is the very presence of him for whom everything was created and who was revealed by the Bible as saviour of the world.

The Eucharist recapitulates the Cosmos for me; the Eucharist recapitulates the Bible for me. All three bear the divine within them, and all three are worthy to be there while I am praying, but the third is the greatest.

The Eucharist is the fulness of the gift, it is the pearl hidden in the mystery of Scripture, the treasure in the field of the Word of God, the secret of the King. In the Eucharist God becomes a presence beside me on my path, bread in my knapsack, friendship close to my heart as a man. To those who have not the courage to say there is nothing there and leave the tabernacle unattended; to those who behave as though there were no living presence there, I would say: assume that it *is* true; assume that under the sacramental sign there is the living presence of Jesus. Assume that the faith of the Church, which has always accepted this mystery of faith, is the authentic response to such a sublime reality; surely I am justified in coming to spend a bit more time here in his presence.

You will say: but the Eucharist was made to be eaten, Jesus said so himself. That is true, and I shall eat it tomorrow, and the day after tomorrow, and so on to the last day of my life; but between one meal and another, one *agape* and another, is Jesus absent from me? Has he given me his body and withheld himself? Has he given me his blood and denied me his friendship?

I need bread, but I assure you I feel the need of friendship quite as much, and nothing gives me the friendship of Jesus more than the Gospel and the Eucharist.

You will tell me I am old-fashioned to go on believing in visits to the Blessed Sacrament. Still, I *do* believe that Jesus is present in the Eucharist not only during the mass, but also between one mass and the next: always. And how helpful this belief has been to me; what great things this presence has given me!

It was here, before it, that I learned to pray.

When, in the desert, my novice master left me alone for eight days; when, later on, I remained alone in a hermitage for forty days, I would have gone mad had it not been for this presence answering to the needs of my presence, this love responding to the demands of my love.

It is here that I have felt the presence of God most strongly; it is here that I have experienced for myself Christ's dramatic recapitulation of the history of salvation.

And I always come back here when I want to make my way to the threshold of the invisible, because the Eucharist is the surest doorway opening on to it.

Here I am, then, alone before that door – or, rather, that window – which opens on to the invisible at the extreme limits of human reality. Faith alone is my guide, and I assure you that I know, both in my heart and in my flesh, what 'mystery of faith' means.

To find oneself confronted by a piece of bread, and to believe that it is the presence of Jesus, involves an act of faith: reason is inadequate.

But faith is bare, dark and frequently painful.

Once I get past the barrier of my feelings, however, and cast myself with confidence into the abyss of God, my faith is joined by hope, and love sustains me. Just as each of the three Divine Persons seeks the other two within the framework of the unity, so each of the theological virtues gathers to itself the other two theological virtues. And as soon as you succeed in holding them strongly within your grasp, keeping them united before you, you can fashion a sword sharp enough to cut through to the invisible.

The sign of bread both conceals and points to the presence of Jesus; faith, hope and charity cut through the barrier that separates me from him and reveal his presence. It is Jesus himself, Son of God and son of Mary, Jesus of Bethlehem, of Nazareth, of the Last Supper, of Calvary, Jesus of the Resurrection, yesterday, today and the same for ever.

Now leave me with him for a while – with him, who chose to come to me as bread so as not to overwhelm me. Let me contemplate his life and his Gospel, as told by the Eucharist.

This bread speaks to me of humility, of lowliness, of self-giving. It tells me the parable he invented to explain me and to explain himself, it epitomizes for me his preferences, which find in the bread the model and symbol dearest to him. Bread, not a stone; bread, not luxuries; bread, not arms; bread, not punishment; bread, not gold.

Above all, it tells me that it is with this bread – with which he became bread – that he will nourish me for eternal life. '... anyone who eats this bread will live for ever' (Jn 6:58).

But was it not for that reason that we started on our way: he towards us, and we towards him? Was it not to find some point of contact between heaven and earth that we persevered to the frontiers of the Eternal? to discover the *beyond* that we have left created realities behind us? And do I not place myself in the Father's presence to receive the gift of divine sonship? Yes, in the Father's presence, before Jesus, the window that opens on to the invisible.

For Jesus is the one who will enable me to see the Father and will speak to me of him.

Jesus is the One Who Reveals, in the fullest sense of that word. And in revealing himself he will reveal the Father to me: '. . . I shall . . . show myself to him' (Jn 14 : 21) in a supernatural revelation which is 'eternal life'. 'And eternal life is this: to know you, the only true God, and Jesus Christ whom you have sent' (Jn 17 : 3).

There is no need to say much, to think much. The sooner you manage to arrive at a state of quiet, of attention, of loving passivity, the better it is.

The advice of the Russian pilgrim is valuable in this connection. Gather up the whole of your being into a single expression of love: 'Lord Jesus Christ, have mercy on me'; and repeat it, repeat it in peace, without worrying about anything else. As a fourteenth-century English mystic put it, fashion that invocation into a sword for yourself, and with all the strength of your love, pierce the cloud of unknowing that stands in your way.

The Eucharist is like the cloud which accompanied the people of God on their desert journey; like the pillar of fire which pointed out the way through the depths of the night.

And the night shall be clear as the day.

Chapter Twelve

THE PRAYER OF THOSE WHO HAVE NO TIME TO PRAY

Every time I happen to write something on the subject of prayer, my desk is inundated with letters such as this:

'Brother Carlo, you know what you are talking about, but what you have written applies to you and to other religious like you. What am I expected to do? I am completely caught up in my work, and I have not a moment to draw breath . . .

'If only you knew what my days are like! I have family obligations, the office makes its demands, and what with parish work, parish meetings, reading in order to keep myself up to date . . . I can tell you, prayer becomes something which . . . and so on.' Or again: 'I have read everything you have written on prayer, and since it is a subject that interests me, I have given it a great deal of thought. I would like to pray, but how do I set about it? My life is one long struggle to beat the clock.

'It's an achievement if I manage to get to mass on Sundays and make the sign of the cross night and morning – but even that is done in a hurry. All the same I am unhappy about it, and I would like to remedy the situation, since I feel things cannot go on like this: I am on edge, no longer at peace with myself, and my faith is growing weaker. Sometimes I am afraid . . .'

And elsewhere: 'You have said some fine things about prayer . . . but come over to Montecitorio and you will see what happens to your good intentions about praying!'

Yet another example: 'Dear Carlo, since I became a priest, I have lost the habit of prayer – or at least of praying spontaneously as I once used to. I excuse myself by saying that it is the structure that stifles us, and it is true, it does, but I still do not feel fully justified. I am not happy or at peace with myself; I seem to have forgotten that I am a child of God, and have become a servant of the Church: catechism classes, baptisms at all hours, sung masses, and those confounded requiems that even manage to put me off the mass that I used to love so much, visits, meetings and gatherings of all sorts.

'When can I pray? The Divine Office has become unbearable for me; administering the sacraments is like working a slot machine. If I go on like this, goodness knows where I will end up. I must admit that I was much happier when I was a minor official in a small-town industrial concern, and that I used to feel more at home with my prayer when I put my advertising to one side and said the rosary with friends, or went to serve mass in the parish church without pocketing two thousand lire as I do today. That money makes me feel ashamed!'

And another: 'Dear sir, I am a young mother, and I never get out of the house. How can I manage to pray always, as you say in your book? Please teach me.'

And so I could go on to the end of the book . . .

Indeed, I think the problem is enormous if concern about it among Christians today is as widespread as this would suggest, and I must confess that the temptation to write this book came more as a result of those letters than from any idea of producing a treatise on prayer.

It may not come off, and perhaps by the end I will not even have succeeded in touching the surface of the problem, but one thing I must say: *In Search of the Beyond* is a good title for the writers of the letters quoted above, and for all who are immersed 'in things'. In order to get beyond created realities it is necessary to start from the inside. And he who is surrounded by them is right to be 'inside' – to be involved.

The mother must be in her home; the politician must be in political life; the priest in his ministry. Prayer is not an escape but an illumination from within; it is not flight but a *fiat* of acceptance; it is not a spiritual or psychological antithesis but a human–divine totality; not a distraction but a purification.

Yes, each one of us must be involved in his particular task, his love, his work, up to his neck, to the extreme limit of his powers. But God has not condemned us to work, to the family, to our social life, to destroy us but to realize our potential. God does not call us to relationships and contact with our fellow men in order to break off our relationships and contact with himself.

It is clearly a question of understanding. More often than not our uneasiness is due to confusion and want of courage. Sometimes we misunderstand what it means 'to pray'. If, for example, an industrialist, who already has more than he needs and more work than he can manage, continues to spread the net of his involvements without really knowing why, one might very well suggest to him : cut down on your work and take more interest in your soul and your family.

To the priest who is threatened with the prospect of losing his taste for prayer because of his routine and all those masses for the dead one can say : renew the parish liturgy, achieve a greater measure of participation, separate it from the humiliating rota of mass stipends, organize your pastoral duties more efficiently, and seek help from the laity – perhaps you will end up finding a bit of time to spend in adoration and to pray a bit longer.

But it is not always a question of badly organized time. One often meets people, especially nowadays, whose vocation it is to be crucified by a timetable.

In our evolving society, enormous pressures are exerted on

certain nerve centres of society, and underneath there is an individual bearing the brunt of it all: a poor woman who, besides being a wife and mother, is forced to go out to work in order to pay the rent; a nursing sister who has to do the work of three people because there is always someone on leave; or else a badly paid clerk who has to take on extra work in order to pay for his son's education; or a politician who has become the symbol of sanity in all situations and chairman of all the committees; the unfortunate teacher who leaves school exhausted, and is then eagerly awaited by all the christian organizations of the area; and finally, a poor priest who is devoured by all and sundry in a city that has lost its sense of humanity and reason.

One often wonders how people manage to put up with pressures like these. Some doors and some telephones are real instruments of torture; calculating machines and assembly lines can be real crosses for contemporary man. How is one to pray in situations like these?

I would like to write something especially for the benefit of these brothers of mine, because they have, I must confess, been something of a reproach to me in my religious life. When I found myself in the desert, having left behind me my life as a layman with its professional and apostolic commitments, one of my own crosses was the thought that, without intending to, I had, as it were, abandoned the trenches.

When all is said and done, Carlo, you have chosen the easier path. The desert is a luxury compared with some of the demands made today in the dough of the world. Yes, it is true – even granted that I have not exactly escaped to an island paradise. I used to pacify myself with the thought that it was the Lord not I who had made the choice, since vocation is his affair and he is the one who distributes the burdens.

But no more of that. Instead let us try to say something to those who come in from work exhausted, and struggle continuously in order to establish some kind of equilibrium between their life and their prayer. I would say : begin here. Write this prayer on the back of some picture that you value and repeat it frequently until you know it by heart. It was written by Père de Foucauld, and reads like a simple paraphrase of the Our Father. It goes like this :

'My Father
I abandon myself to you.
Do with me as you will.
Whatever you may do with me
I thank you.
I am prepared for anything,
I accept everything
Provided your will is fulfilled in me
And in all creatures.
I ask for nothing more
my God.
I place my soul in your hands.
I give it to you, my God,
with all the love of my heart
because I love you.
And for me it is a necessity of love,
this gift of myself,
this placing of myself in your hands
without reserve
in boundless confidence,
because you are
my Father.'

And remember that Père de Foucauld wrote these wonderful words at a time when he was wearing out the camels and the nomads of the caravan in order to get to the other side of the great Erg – and undertaking such arduous exploits that they will remain in the memories of courageous and proven men.

And remember too that he repeated the prayer on the evening after he had recorded in his journal : 'Today I had to receive more than 400 people in my hermitage. What will become of your religious enclosure, Brother Charles of Jesus?'

To receive 400 people as demanding as the Arabs, or even worse, the Tuareg – where, one asks oneself did this hermit find the time? And where did he find the time to write his famous Tamasek dictionary, and at the same time to translate the Bible into Tuareg, and maintain relations with everyone as he did? He was alone, remember, and had to build his own *šriba*, do his own cooking, and wash his tunic from time to time. And yet it is the same Père de Foucauld who writes in another place in the Journal: 'Today is a holiday and the people of Beni-Abbès are enjoying themselves. They certainly won't come to seek me out in the hermitage. What joy to be able to remain alone and to pray for eight hours at a stretch! What happiness, Jesus, to contemplate you in the host; to put my requests before you; to love you.'

I think that, in the difficult struggle to create a balance between work and prayer, the first secret we need to discover in ourselves is this: the desire to pray. I am convinced that the desire takes the place of prayer, provided it becomes prayer as soon as possible.

It is not enough to complain, saying: 'Where am I to find the time to pray,' In fact one needs to ask oneself in all honesty whether this question has not become an excuse to cover up one's bad conscience. If I have no time, I am not obliged to go to church or to make an hour's adoration, but if I find that I can in fact salvage a few moments, then I must not hesitate. If I do, I prove that my desire was not genuine, and that my complaints were unjustified.

To pray is to love, and loving God is like loving men – that much is obvious. Words count for nothing here. If a man loves his wife, there is no need for him to explain his absences, his commitments, the fact that he has to be away. She understands perfectly well, and even though she might long to be with him more, she knows inside herself that distance cannot separate her from the man she loves.

Read the *Song of Songs* again. You cannot find any difference between the passionate love of the bride for her husband and that of the soul for God. One might almost say they were the same thing : certainly the way in which they are expressed is the same.

And exactly the same thing happens to those of us who love God. So when you are very busy, do not ask yourself whether you have time to pray; ask yourself if you have time to love.

Can love not go on living when two who love are far apart? Cannot love arouse feelings of tenderness in you every time you think about him, or fill you with an indescribable longing at the mere recollection of his existence?

Maybe I could turn my prayer into short expressions of affection, telling him, 'Jesus, I love you', while I am putting the baby to sleep; or, 'Good morning, Jesus,' when the telephone rings, 'no one will usurp your place in my heart.' Or else, in the evening, as I walk home through the anonymous crowd after work, 'Jesus, have mercy on us, we are sinners'.

No, nothing can separate me from my God. Certainly not my activities; certainly not mankind. Not even death!

And if I love him, I will find my own way of telling him so in a foreign country, and I will find a way, even if men have destroyed all the churches and profaned all the tabernacles in my own country.

Because prayer is like love : it transcends space and can be lived anywhere, since wherever you love, Love is there, for God is Love.

Think back over the story of Joseph, sold into slavery by his brothers. It is the story of a young man cut off from his tribe, from his familiar way of life and, I would add, from his way of praying with Jacob, his father. He is a slave in Egypt, sold to Potiphar, a rich man of the country. Thanks to his endurance and intelligence, he became his master's steward.

But he has not forgotten the God of Abraham, the God of Isaac, who remains in the centre of his heart, as it were, in the tent in which he himself had lived since his childhood. And when the moment of testing comes and Potiphar's wife tempts him with her beauty, Joseph consults his God in the depths of his heart, as he used to once in the tent of Jacob. You may not do this, says his God; I may not do this, he says himself, echoing that voice and that will.

If you do not give yourself to me, says the woman, I will tell my husband you have seduced me. And in order to have some valid piece of evidence, she snatches his cloak from him.

You may not do this, says the voice of his God, have confidence in me. Be faithful to the law of your God. I am the God of Abraham and Isaac . . . And Joseph goes to prison as a result of his resistence thanks to the woman's vindictiveness.

Perhaps there was something missing from Joseph's prayer?

And who knows how long it was since he had taken part in the sacrificial rites of his now far-distant tribe. And yet . . . at the appropriate moment his own prayer, his true prayer, the prayer that was like a chain of love binding him to his God, vibrated in his heart. And what a prayer it was! It welled up like a melody, like a freshwater spring, like a symphony which all the angels would come down to hear.

No, churches, formulae and methods are not essential to prayer: what is essential is that I should love, because love is the highest form of prayer – it is the fulness of prayer.

And what is more, love quickens the confidence which becomes a constant element in the soul, a mode of being, a habit, a continuing reality. I believe in him – I trust him – I love him.

Is there any prayer more vital than that? Make it your own, and you will pray all day long, even in the midst of the crowd.

Does the lover forget his beloved because of his occupations?

Are the unexpected longings that come upon him suddenly like a flash of lightning, less charged with love than the long hours they have spent together?

It seems to me that this is the secret of prayer, if one has no time to pray – and let us remind ourselves that Christ came, not to restrict but to set us free.

The more we free ourselves from the structures, from the formulae, from our idols, the better we succeed in simplifying our spiritual life and the more our union with God becomes a reality. And union is always the response to the call of love.

So churches and formulae are not an essential part of prayer, but they can help, and in the normal course of events should help. Each of us knows this by experience, and we will not be mistaken if we say that so many of the episodes in our spiritual history are connected with this church or that shrine.

This explains why it is so important that places of prayer should be carefully chosen, as welcoming as possible, clean and peaceful; above all there must be silence, and a complete ban on those strident, discordant noises that invade our psyche when it is already exhausted and severely tried by the tribulations of daily life.

And here I would like to pass on a piece of advice to my many friends who are united by their common desire to safeguard their prayer in these troubled times.

Why not make an oratory for yourself at home?

Yes, at home, where you live and love and suffer.

My life as a Little Brother has taught me to do this, and I cannot tell you how useful I have found it.

When a Little Brother moves into a new district, a different shipyard, an unfamiliar shanty town, one of those places where poor people live, and where he wants to live as a poor man, he creates his own base by renting a cottage, a hut or an attic.

After that, the first thing he thinks of in his new home is the oratory. In a corner, if there is only one room; in some other place if there are several rooms: what concerns him is that he should provide himself with a place to pray. No Little Brother should rest until he has succeeded in carving out from his abode – however poor – the surroundings that will enable him to pray more easily. These are more important than the kitchen or the bedroom, because it is there that he will find his moments of consolation, however bitter, and of prayer; there he will be able to localize, as far as is possible, his overwhelming encounter with God.

Often a mat is sufficient – placed before a wall on which he hangs a picture of Our Lady and a crucifix, and screened off on one side with a sackcloth hanging. Frequently, however, the furnishings may be more ambitious, and the result will be a delightful little chapel, receiving its light from above – as it would in a poor but peaceful attic. I feel this advice is both important and useful, especially now that cities have become so sprawling and churches are frequently far away; now that we have to exert ourselves to the utmost to remain faithful to Christ.

In this way a very busy person can more easily answer the call to prayer, find somewhere to spend a silent moment or two during the evening and a quiet corner where he can read the Gospel with his wife or pray with his children before they go to bed.

And what about considering one of those little chapels where people gather in groups to recite Vespers or Compline, or else those 'house churches' where the priest can come from time to time to celebrate mass and, God willing, leave behind him the living presence of Christ in the Eucharist?

As the laity becomes increasingly self-aware and spiritually vigorous, as the fruits of the Council ripen on the tree of the Church, these things will be realized; of that I am certain.

How beautiful it will be, the city of tomorrow, studded with those lights in the darkness – lights that proclaim the presence of Jesus in the houses of men.

PART III

'I want to proclaim the Good News by my life.'
Père de Foucauld

Chapter Thirteen

MAN TOO IS AN ABSOLUTE

The first time I stayed for any length of time in the desert, and acquired a taste for it, I experienced the profound longing to stay there forever, which is not surprising!

A superficial acquaintance with the world one is leaving behind is enough to convince one that not much will be lost by abandoning the city and (somewhat more difficult) its inhabitants.

The deep peace I enjoyed during the long, healing silences, the delight of the clean, luminous horizons of the Sahara, the pleasure of the solitude and, better still, the face-to-face encounter with God, were gifts that outmatched anything my youthful dreams had given me, or the heavy demands made on me by my involvement as a human being in the earthly city.

And yet, underlying this human longing to hide among the dunes, and live in a small desert *tsar* among poor and simple people, was a certain uneasiness of conscience. Do you want to remain in the desert because you like it, or in order to seek God?

Do you love the desert because you no longer love men? Are you trying to stay here because the idea of going back there is distasteful to you? 'If so, go back,' said my conscience; 'If so, go back,' said my superior. I remember one conversation I had with the man who at that time, in the name of God and of the Church, was acting as my spiritual director. 'Carlo, during these years of solitiude you have discovered God as the Absolute and you have fallen in love with him. But now you must discover another absolute : man. Before, perhaps, when you spoke of working for the apostolate, you were doing so under the impulse of nature. Now you must do it under the impulse of grace. Originally, perhaps, you enjoyed it, now you must do it because it costs you something. And remember one important truth, which made of Père de Foucauld one of the prophets of our time : one must live out the life of contemplation among one's fellow men. And if you want one phrase that sums up his thought on the subject, remember this : 'Present to God and present to men.' And so I found myself back in the world, in the midst of all the confusion, surrounded by my fellow men.

Things had changed, however, and above all my vision of man had changed. Man too is an absolute, I would repeat to myself each time someone came to visit me in the fraternity, distracting me from my prayer.

But does prayer simply mean remaining on one's knees?

That could be so convenient in times of stress.

And then I realized in a new way that even prayer can become an escape. Yes, an escape from reality when that reality is charity, love. I was forcibly reminded of this by the words of the prophet Isaiah :

'Hanging your head like a reed, lying down on sackcloth and ashes? Is that what you call fasting, a day acceptable to Yahweh? Is not this the sort of fast that pleases me – it is the Lord Yahweh who speaks – to break unjust fetters and undo the thongs of the yoke, to share your bread with the hungry, and shelter the homeless poor, to clothe the man you see to be naked and not to turn from your own kin? Then will your light shine like the dawn and your wound will be quickly healed over . . . Cry, and Yahweh will answer; call, and he will say, "I am here" ' (Is 58 : 5–9).

Man too is an absolute, and you must seek, love and serve him just as you seek love and serve God. Jesus left us in no doubt about this inexorable and simultaneous movement into the two dimensions, the horizontal and the vertical.

The closer you come to him as you ascend the slopes of contemplation, the greater grows your craving to love men on the level of action. The perfection of man on earth consists in the integration, vital and authentic, of his love for God and his love for men.

It is quite useless to look for convenient escape routes : there are none, because Jesus himself welded together into one single commandment the two elements that men, in their apathy, only too frequently separate : 'You must love the Lord your God with all your heart, and your neighbour as yourself.'

And since, with our skill in casuistry, we found it easy to separate what he had joined, he established another with the authority of his blood, shed to the last drop : 'I give you a new commandment : love one another just as I have loved you.'

After that, anyone who wants to go on arguing can do so, but he should not then delude himself that he is a close friend of Christ. To separate our love of God from our love of our fellow men is a fundamental betrayal of the Gospel ideal.

To take to one's prayers when the village is burning and the inhabitants crying for help is to create an untenable excuse for one's own laziness and one's own fear.

That is why a Church that concentrates on its own ritual and is not aware of the sufferings and anxieties of men, of the chains that bind them, is a dead Church, with nothing more to say about the heart and mind of its founder.

That is why the scandal of piety based on processions, masses for the dead, and private devotional practices unrelated to the evangelization of the poor, gets swept to one side by the protest of those who still believe in the inexorable power of the word of God.

But that is not enough. Having said that man is an absolute, we can go much further. And above all far from the bourgeois outlook which has been inherited by our generation, sick with its egoism and its racism, its liberalism, its communism and its culturalism. Each one of these 'isms' involves a fundamental denial of the absolute in man, which explains why the Christian, while he can learn something from all of them, can find in the Gospel alone a radical answer to the question of why man is an absolute.

Man is not an absolute for the racist or the colonialist, since they believe that some men are superior to others, that the whites are nearer to God than the blacks; and with the arrogance of their strength, they end up by crushing the weak.

Man is not an absolute for the liberal, because every time a conflict of interests emerges between production and freedom, production and unemployment, production and the human life of the worker, liberalism always opts for production, and condemns the human being to the slavery of irrational objects, or abandons him to the living death of unemployment.

Man is not an absolute for the communist – events in Hungary and Czechoslovakia have revealed this clearly enough – because communism, although it began with the clearly defined and sincere intention of freeing man from his slavery to capitalism and from need, is compelled to crush this wretched man every time he sets himself up against the party line, or the national interest, which is the same thing.

And, finally, man is not an absolute for culturalism, because only too often culture is self-absorbed, forgetful of the illiteracy of the masses. Someone who is bent on reaching the moon is not going to be very interested in the fact that millions of human beings are dying of hunger. Jesus alone has given convincing proof of his fundamental belief in man as an absolute; it was because of that belief that he did not hesitate to die on the cross to save him.

One final point.

The discovery that man is an absolute inevitably leaves you

with the consuming desire to graft him on to the original trunk of every absolute : God himself.

As long as man remains separated from God, he is in danger of becoming corrupt, confused, distressed, morally disintegrated.

Cut off from the source of its being, which is God, the life of man is unable to find fulfilment, beauty, peace.

Man without God is, *ipso facto*, a lung without air, an eye without light, a heart without love.

The man who does possess God fully appreciates this, and wonders how anyone could possibly live without him.

This is the driving force behind every apostolate.

It is not a question of handing on a formula, but of 'being', 'peace', 'light'.

We evangelize with our lives before we do so with our words.

Anyone who reduces the Gospel to a formula will be an efficient administrator, but a prophet, never.

Jesus came to bring fire not the catechism to the earth.

Anyone who is content to catechize, without announcing the Good News in his own life, will find he is writing in the sand, which the wind of passion will carry away. The mounds upon mounds of catechisms that have been turned inside out in our parishes and chewed over in seminaries have helped to produce the present crisis in which everything is known about Christ and about the Church, but no one any longer believes either in the Church or in Christ. The catechism, without life and without witness, is like medicine given to a dead man.

Only God, who is life and gives this life of his to those who, in Christ, believe in him, can say : 'I tell you myself, you shall live.' (Hosea). We live, by faith, not by religious knowledge, be that knowledge as deep as the ocean.

If, in recent years, our parishes and seminaries had appreciated this, we would not be confronted now with the crisis of faith of so many priests and lay people, who were also veritable mines of religious knowledge.

And it is not as if we had not been told by our fathers. The *contemplata aliis tradere* made this absolutely clear. You must pass on the fruits of your contemplation, not your wisdom, or worse still, your culture.

Only the man who contemplates the face of God, and is carried beyond himself in so doing, can effectively say to his brother : come and see, and understand for yourself how sublime he is !

To lead others to contemplation : this is the soul of every apostolate. Come and see, come and try for yourself, come and experience, come with me on to the holy mountain.

What persuades your brother to follow you is the grace of God, which is never lacking, and your own conviction, your experience, your example – of which there can never be too much.

As I prepare to speak about community, about our task in the contemporary world and our apostolate to our fellow men, I would like to sum it all up in a famous phrase of Raissa Maritain : 'contemplation in the market place'.

And I also want to emphasize that there exists no human preparation for the task of evangelization, or if there does, it is within the framework of God's plan, which nearly always eludes us.

But what does exist, as something we are all capable of grasping, is the fact that for each one of us evangelization is but the reflection of the light of the beatitudes, which shines in our faces with increasing intensity as we draw near to Jesus, the divine model. To every man who is living in darkness, evangelization comes like the moon, rising above the darkness of his way. But moonlight is always the reflection of the original source of light – the sun.

Christ is the sun of the earth, and in every man's night someone or something is needed to reflect its light, someone who had first absorbed it himself. Ensuring that the light of Jesus is a living reality within you is the one indispensable condition on which your ability to shed light on someone else who is close to you depends.

If you want to be an apostle, do not look around for something else. Your wisdom does not matter; only your capacity to absorb the light of God that comes to you in Christ matters.

And it comes, first and foremost, in so far as you live the beatitudes which are the most authentic and radiant summary of the Good News and of the thought of Jesus. So begin here, first by reading them over and then by striving to live them within yourself :

> 'How happy are the poor in spirit;
> theirs is the kingdom of heaven.
> Happy the gentle :
> they shall have the earth for their heritage.
> Happy those who mourn :
> they shall be comforted.
> Happy those who hunger and thirst for what is right :
> they shall be satisfied.
> Happy the merciful :
> they shall have mercy shown them.
> happy the pure in heart :
> they shall see God.
> Happy the peacemakers :
> they shall be called sons of God.
> Happy those who are persecuted in the cause of right :
> theirs is the kingdom of heaven'
>
> (Mt 5 :3–10).

Chapter Fourteen

BLESSED ARE THE POOR IN SPIRIT

When Pope Innocent III, who was a pessimist by nature and obsessed by the vision of sin, wrote in his little book *De contemptu mundi* that man is like an uprooted tree, saw before him Francis, the poor man from Assisi, with joy and humility and freedom in his eyes, and he felt as though that tree had been replaced in its upright position, that man had recovered all the lost splendour of his primeval integrity. If one is to rediscover the original beauty of nature as God created it, all one has to do is to make oneself poor, to become poor, to be poor. Which means that the wealth which clings to our bodies, our minds and our hearts, makes us truly ugly and absurd.

But meanwhile let us see what significance the words 'the poor' have for Jesus, as well as their opposite, 'the rich'.

In this connection we need to begin by drawing attention to something very important. Few words have undergone greater changes of meaning in the course of centuries than 'the poor'. The Council came like an invitation to conversion from God to each one of us, and we stood on its threshold with momentous but no longer meaningful words. And yet, which makes it all the more serious, these are very words of Jesus himself.

For most Christians who talk about renewal in the Church, the word 'poor' means the beggar, the shabbily dressed, the underpaid, the man who is starving in Latin America, the children who are dying of hunger in Africa or India. That is to say, the poor are synonymous with the destitute.

This explains the watchword of those short-sighted revolutionaries, which turns the Church of the poor into an ill-defined but tough form of social action for the emancipation of the least privileged classes. But if they were right, we would be a good century behind the Marxists, who have far more vigorously and effectively dealt with the problem and not with the heirs to the one genuine revolution of love which is that of Bethlehem.

Those words with which Jesus challenged his followers and which embody his entire programme 'blessed are the poor' – I wonder what impression they must make on the man of common sense who has the other concept of 'poor'. It is like saying: Blessed are the Biafrans who are dying of hunger, blessed are the peasants who have not enough to feed their children, blessed are the children of north-east Brazil who die, as often as not, before they have learned to use their reason, or even their limbs. If they are blessed, why work to take away their blessedness? Especially we Christians. If the word 'blessed', as used by Jesus, means anything, and if it applies equally to what we understand as blessedness, then it must be contrary to his desire to work and take measures to alter their condition of blessedness, diminishing it by bringing them bread, clothes and improved social conditions.

The fact is that ignorance of the things of God has reached such alarming proportions that people are no longer familiar with even the most rudimentary terminology, and the inner meaning of the Gospel gets distorted. And this is true not simply of lay people standing on the sidelines of the Church, but of ecclesiastics who have studied theology, and who are at times, however unintentionally, incapable of explaining anything to the people.

The poor man in the biblical sense is not the beggar, the starving or the unemployed; he is the average man, who has a house, children and work, who dresses like everyone else, does the shopping and goes to the office, who buys an overcoat when he is cold and goes to the doctor when he is ill. He is the average human being – the minister, the bishop, the peasant, the craftsman, the old man, the boy, the mother, the poet, the worker.

He is everyman!

But who can claim to be poor in the biblical sense? The man who comes to understand, under the pressure of suffering or in the light of God, what it means to be human.

The man who discovers his own limitations, who enters into the mystery of what it means to be a creature rather than a creator.

Anyone, that is, who knows he is sick, small, weak, vulnerable, ignorant, sinful, needful of everything; who stands at the mercy of history and of wickedness in high places, prisoner of hostile circumstances, who has learnt humility and discretion from the pain and anguish of his experience, who is thirsting for help and for love. The poor man, in short, is the man who has discovered his own limitations. He is blessed and he becomes blessed, if he accepts such limitations as coming to him from the hand of God in order that the Kingdom might become a reality within him. Naturally the beggars, the starvelings, and the ragamuffins are included in this category – indeed they are! – but they are not the only ones, and nowhere is it said that they are blessed *because* they are without food. Only someone who accepts his misfortune out of love becomes 'blessed', otherwise, whatever his material poverty, he might well be spiritually rich. Thus we can say that each one of us forms part of the Church of the poor, and when the community joins in reciting the prayer of the psalmist:

> 'Listen to me, Yahweh, and answer me,
> poor and needy as I am;
> keep my soul: I am your devoted one,
> save your servant who relies on you'
> (Ps 86:1–2),

everyone, whatever the social category to which he belongs, can lend his voice to the chorus without feeling ashamed of his origins, of his work in the earthly city, of his responsibilities as master or servant.

I say this, and it is painful to have to do so, because people continue to twist the meaning of certain words. Sooner or later, beset by those who believe that Christ came to found a religion for down-and-outs and that in order to become converted one must abandon the earthly city, or at least become a worker or a trade unionist, the well-dressed woman or business man will not be able to set foot inside a church.

When Jesus spoke of or to the poor he had in mind the whole of mankind, and not a particular category of men. He had no intention, that is, of establishing some kind of inverted racism or of preaching a religion suitable only for a handful of initiates or a group of fanatics. By establishing the beatitude of poverty as the basis of his programme, he brought it fairly and squarely into the wider context of reality as a whole.

Nothing, in fact, is more real for each one of us than the fact of being poor. For simply by being born we are poor, children who have need of everything; by living we are poor, creatures thirsty for everything; in our dying we are poor, leaving everything behind us. Has man not been defined as the poor of Yahweh?

And did Jesus not make this title his own by becoming man? From the crib to the cross, from Bethlehem to Calvary, from exile to work, from the misunderstandings to the physical blows.

In saying that we are poor, Jesus is not telling us anything new. This is the reality and life has been given us that we might deepen our understanding of the fact.

But there is a new element in what Jesus said : his declaration that this is 'blessed', his explanation, that is of the fact that, had we accepted our poverty in a spirit of love, peace, trust and conviction, we would have been blessed, we would have experienced some measure of happiness, even here on earth.

I have no hesitation in saying that most of the suffering in our individual lives is due to the effort required of us to face reality, rather that to any of the genuine misfortunes that may befall us.

There are some people who go through life refusing to accept themselves. I have known women who would have been wonderful people, had it not been for the complex some minor physical defect produced in them. Some people cannot even cross the road without reflecting gloomily that they are too short, or a little overweight, or that their beauty is marred by a facial blemish or a nose that is out of proportion.

It is sad to have to say so, but that is how it is.

The beatitude of poverty could liberate us from those forms of slavery too, and then, having been freed by Christ, we would be able to see the supreme beauty of the spirit shining in all its transparency, even in the face of a man who is physically deformed. That was how Pope Innocent III regained something of his optimism when he saw Francis – saw a man untrammelled by complexes, authentic through his total acceptance of himself, a man without a mask. The mask is wealth, and we can never say so too emphatically.

When the Gospel speaks of riches it is not referring to the roof over our heads or the food from which we derive our strength. When it speaks of riches it refers to the banquets of the rich man Dives, banquets from which Lazarus is excluded. When it speaks of poverty it is referring to the man who demolishes the old barns in which he can amass no further riches, in order to build new ones as vast as his own unbridled concupiscence (Lk 12:16–21). When it speaks of riches, it says: 'But alas for you who are rich: you are having your consolation now' (Lk 6:24). The 'riches' of the Gospel does not apply to 'that which is needful', but to all that is left over, all that is pure luxury, all that is hoarded, refused to others, concealed.

It applies to the way we look after ourselves and exclude our brothers from the feast. And they are equally excluded when it is a matter not of food or clothing, but of culture, of the word of God, of dignity, peace or love.

This first beatitude Jesus preached in his sermon on the mount is so all-embracing and the heedless Christians of our age have reduced it to such mean, unattractive 'charity'.

The poor man is not simply the man who is aware of limits to his own material wealth; over and above this, he is one who sets bounds to his own spiritual pride and surrounds his heart with barbed wire, as it were, to safeguard it from the vanity of useless and dangerous affections.

Because – and let us be quite clear about this – if the possession of capital riches is ugly in men who exclude their brothers from the feast, much more ugly is that spiritual wealth which encourages the idea that whites are superior to blacks and keeps them away from the table of the God-given equality of men. Those who are proud and spiritually rich cause more hurt than those who are rich in money and material goods. There is no limit to the presumption, to the complacency and sense of superiority that exudes from the expression of someone who is convinced that all truth and culture belong to him. The Gospel is less sympathetically disposed to these riches of the mind and heart, and Jesus's words 'Woe to you who are rich' sound a far more serious and warning note for the 'wise' of this world than for someone who, by defrauding his brothers, buys a larger vineyard than he actually needs.

Go to the universities, go to the centres of culture, to the clubs where men assume the title of 'master'. Go into the political circles, move among those who feel they are invested with the divine mission to command, to promulgate laws, to interpret the truth.

Go with your New Testament in your pocket. You will be sickened by all this spiritual and intellectual pride, this struggle to get ahead regardless of anyone else, this lust for possessions.

There is one category of men whose arrogance exceeds that of all others: self-confident religious people who act as proprietors of religion; who, instead of serving, make use of divine things for their own ends, and instead of taking the last places, force their way up to the first, raining down the deadly blows of their abused power as they go (Mt 23).

It is not insignificant that Jesus was killed by a clique of this kind; that he felt, almost to the point of despair, that as far as the Pharisees of the Temple were concerned his message was a dead letter from the moment he uttered it.

And let us bear in mind that each one of us has it in him to become a Pharisee, capable of crucifying Jesus anew in his own heart, as long as he forgets to be poor, poor, poor.

But what exactly does it mean, to be poor?

What was Jesus trying to say when he set before us the beatitude of poverty? What a continual crisis of conscience the answer to a question like this manages to provoke in contemporary Christians!

Caught up as they are in our so-called welfare state, they feel the need to see things clearly, to understand at least what attitude they should adopt in the face of such grave responsibility. You will not find a gathering of dedicated lay people that fails to register some echo of it. Must we really sell everything that is superfluous? Can I buy myself a new coat? Can I allow myself the luxury of a holiday abroad? Must we pool everything and live like the Christians described in the Acts of the Apostles?

But the answer is not so simple, and the more one gets bogged down in casuistry, the more one senses the empty rhetoric of words; the more one listens to fanatics who would like to turn everything upside-down, the more likely one is to go home discontented and restless. The fact is that we mistake the way; and we would like to obtain the fruit without paying attention to the tree on which it has to ripen. Poverty, divine poverty, the beautiful bride of St Francis, is a sweet, ripened fruit, not the answer to a problem. And it is a sweet fruit that grows on a tree that contains within itself all sweetness: the tree of love.

The tree of love is not the tree of social justice (often it is that as well, but not always), or the tree of philanthropy; even less is it the tree of the arrogant display of one who wants to prove to me that he is better or more generous than others.

The tree of love is the tree of love, and only someone who loves can appreciate this and live the life of evangelical poverty. Poverty without love is a form of mutilation not a blessing.

Which explains why I must begin to love before I set out to solve the problem of poverty.

Yes, that is where I must start. I must love my fellow men, love them until I really grasp that they are my fellow men, my equals. Once I have learned to love them with a love that is true, authentic and uncalculating, such love will lead me on to ever greater heights. But first it will lead me downwards. Step by step it will force me to come down from the heights of my presumption until I reach the humble level of equality. Slowly but surely it will rid me of the arrogant conviction that I am better, more intelligent, more gifted than my neighbour. It will strip the mask of social convention from my face, destroy my false family or racial values – my belief that my skin is fairer, my blood more distinguished, my culture older, my religion better founded.

That is how I will become poor, poor in spirit first of all, poor of heart.

To stand poor beside the brother I love means being his equal in terms of cultural values, intelligence and human dignity far more than in terms of money. At all events, I can offend far more cruelly through my spiritual superiority than I can through my economic superiority. Do the developing nations who are just now emerging on the scene of history feel nothing of this with regard to the richer nations? And surely the

Alabama negro is far more easily stung by the presumptuous condescension of the white man than by his financial superiority? Riches in the evangelical sense, Jesus's threat, 'Alas for you who are rich', is purely and simply that terrible word applied to the man who thinks he is better than his brother, richer than he is, and who, in his wealth, closes his heart to love – that genuine love which looks for equals, creates equality, makes us equal.

If you really want to understand in what sense love is a condition for poverty of spirit, just look at two lovers. Imagine that one is economically privileged, the other culturally so, and then watch what happens when they fall head over heels in love with one another. The first will disclaim his riches and try to give them to his beloved; she will play down her education in a spirit of humility, seeking to share it bit by bit, in patience, understanding and hope, with the man she loves until their respective offerings balance one another.

Love creates equals, makes equals. That is its nature. Love lives, breathes and fulfils itself in equality; and evangelical poverty lives, breathes and comes to fruition in equality: evangelical poverty, which, in imitation of Jesus, who although he was God made himself poor out of love, and equal to us, in order to enrich us with his own riches, is the most radical expression of that love.

Obviously evangelical poverty also involves austerity where money, food, clothing and lodging are concerned, and in this sense the man who is poor in the way the word is usually understood today is to all intents and purposes 'poor' in the gospel sense, and can become 'blessed' if he accepts his neediness with love. But the subject is not a simple one, and we must earnestly beg God for light in order to come to an understanding of Jesus's preferences, which unfortunately are not our own. One needs to be quite bold nowadays to tell someone he is blessed when he finds it hard to pay his rent, balance the family accounts, and has to put off buying an overcoat or a pair of shoes until next year.

And yet it is true, and in order to prove it to us, Jesus put himself in the category of those who have to cope with just such difficulties and many others besides. He was a poor artisan in an insignificant village in the provinces; he had to work for his living; he certainly had to put up with social conditions which were, to say the least, worse than ours; he had to admit that he had nowhere to lay his head; and scarcely had he given up his work as an artisan in Nazareth to devote himself to his mission, when he was obliged to submit to the humiliation of accepting help from a number of wealthy women.

But still he said 'blessed are the poor'.

Perhaps when he said it he saw further than we do.

Above all, he saw the opposite – he saw what happened to someone who was not poor.

He saw where wealth leads – and avarice, and the accumulation of money, and attachment to things.

He saw, and he could say with conviction :

> 'Woe to you who are rich,
> woe to you who are satisfied,
> woe to you . . .'

This is a serious matter, and I can assure you that, from the little I know of Jesus, I prefer not to hear myself addressed in these terms. We have good reason to be on our guard.

Suppose Jesus really is the Son of God, and suppose that everything St Matthew records him as saying about the last judgment is true : 'Go away from me, with your curse upon you, to the eternal fire . . .' (Mt 25 : 41).

I would be anxious to say the very least.

I would not feel entirely at ease.

I who love a good night's sleep, would toss and turn in my bed . . . and finally I would get up . . .

And rather than run the risk of such a terrible end, I would sell vineyards and houses – all, in short, that was superfluous – and distribute the proceeds to the poor.

When all is said and done, I want to be at peace with myself; I prefer to be happy with few possessions than ill-at-ease with too many.

And then . . . to feel one's head throbbing with phrases of the kind Jesus spoke in cold blood: 'What gain, then, is it for a man to win the whole world and ruin his life?' (Mk 8:36).

Briefly, if Jesus said 'blessed are the poor' and if he confirmed this with the corresponding 'Woe to you who are rich', he had his own good reasons. He cannot deceive us, as anyone who has had any really deep experience of him knows.

One only needs to see where riches can lead to understand the 'blessed are the poor'.

One only needs to know what goes on in the soul of a rich man to convince oneself that it is better to live as a poor man.

One only needs to list the effects produced by this cursed wealth in a society, a family or an individual, to recognize how right Jesus was.

Ultimately, the love of God has one purpose in view as far as we are concerned: to save us.

The thoughts of God are thoughts of peace, not of affliction.

And so, since he wills to save us, he wishes us to discover for ourselves and live in the conditions best suited to the achievement of this end. The condition of the poor man is the condition most conducive to salvation. Someone who is obliged to work hard for his living runs less risk of damnation than someone else who, surrounded from birth by pleasures and plenty, weighs his soul down with a far greater burden of concupiscence, vanity and pride.

Perhaps at this point it would be a good idea to take an overall look at the mystery of salvation, and of the way God sees man on earth, how he thinks of him. We have not far to look, because in the Gospel we have the prototype of man, the unique model; the most outstanding example: Jesus Christ.

Jesus is the man *par excellence*, the perfect man, man without limitations, the man who enjoys the Father's approval.

Since Jesus could choose – he was unique in this respect, being God – when he became man, he chose to lead the life which is described for us in the Gospels, a life which is familiar to us from beginning to end.

And what was the result of that choice? What type of man did he become? He made his own the most ordinary life-style there ever has been or is ever likely to be here under the sun: that of the worker, of the man who lives by his own labour, who finds himself moving between two extremes, the two ugly exaggerations of ostentatious affluence and destitution, the man who experiences sufferings and limitations, and out of those sufferings and limitations learns the value of bread and water and a home.

The man whose dignity depends on his own toil, and not on the mask he inherits from his parents.

The man who helps to weave the fabric of society, and shuns all deceit and malpractice.

The man who bends his back to his task, and earns his happiness with the sweat of his brow.

The man who does not go in for double-dealing, who does not try to get the better of others, who is discreet, humble and straightforward.

The man who exists, as it were, within each one of us as the model of what God wills us to be. Our unhappiness and our lack of freedom are determined by the extent to which we fail to approximate to this model.

And when we look carefully we discover that both the model, made manifest in the person of Jesus, and the pattern we discern within ourselves is none other than the famous 'poor man of Yahweh' whose epic story is recorded in the Bible, which also expresses his hope and his prayer.

For is not Elijah the poor man of Yahweh? and Moses? and Abraham?

Do not the prophets express in their own lives this same poverty of mind and heart and body?

Jeremiah, Amos, Ezechiel and Micah – are they not simple men, unassuming, patient and prayerful?

It seems to me that from Genesis to the Book of Maccabees, over the centuries, that is, leading up to the appearance of Jesus, there is no room within the context of authentic biblical religion for any type of religious person other than the so-called 'poor man', exemplified by Christ in all his splendour.

There is no room for the powerful, the braggart, the self-confident, the 'self-made man', the rich, the triumphalist, the man who rides roughshod over others and lives off the blood of the poor. Or if there is room, it is on the 'other side'; and, just as in the Gospel the rich man, Dives, provides material for some sad and distressing parables, giving substance to a condemned world into which the powers of evil erupt with their full force throughout the course of history under the providential control of God's saving will, so such a man serves as a source of purification for the just man, and to try his patience.

It is as simple as that, even if, in the vast struggle that goes on here on earth as a result of our freedom to love God or not, each one is free to decide which side he will be on.

For my own part, I prefer to look for a place among the poor who have the capacity to love.

Chapter Fifteen

BLESSED ARE THE MEEK

I would like to write this chapter on the beatitude of meekness over the recently dug grave of Martin Luther King, or that of our noble brother Gandhi.

Both came close to Jesus by seeking to understand to the full, that is, to the point of shedding their own blood, the value and efficacy of the great revolution which the Son of God came to unleash on this poor earth, sick with hatred and violence: the revolution of meekness.

I would like to dip my pen in the tears and blood of all martyrs for peace, of all victims of violence and hatred, of all those who have confronted the sword of abused power with the weakness of their own flesh, after the shining example of the man who willed to offer himself as an unresisting lamb to the teeth of the wolves: Jesus.

First, then, a very brief preamble.

When God wanted to find images through which to convey something of himself to our minds and hearts, he chose two and only two: the dove and the lamb.

The dove indicates the vitality, the gentleness and the agility of the Spirit, while the lamb represents the meekness, the unpretentiousness and humility of Christ, the divine victim.

The man who prides himself on his shrewdness chooses instead the lion or some such animal, imagining, in his folly, that he will conquer the earth more quickly by the use of force and the abuse of power.

People have been trying to conquer the earth for many thousands of years, and still no one has succeeded. The fact is that the lions, tigers or serpents emblazoned on the standards of the aggressor are confronted with other lions, other tigers, other serpents, all of whom have the same significance and inevitably clash with the first. The story of what happens next is terribly simple and terribly monotonous: in the evening, when the battle is over, the two opposing armies lie in a lake of blood surrounded by heaps of ruins and incalculable evils.

There they rest a while, the worst of the wounds get bound up, the great fear is to some extent forgotten, the lion is sewn back in place on the standard with an even more ferocious grimace; then they begin all over again, thinking that this time things will go well and in the wake of victory will come true and lasting peace, our own peace. Tell me, is not the whole affair a tragic farce, to be explained by one single word: you are mad, all mad?

But then was this not the very conclusion Jesus himself came to as he was dying on the cross?

Was it not he who, at a time when people were not accustomed either to joke or to lie, said that 'madman' was the appropriate title for man? In fact, while he was dying a victim of man, he turned in his agony to his Father, and pronounced his own judgment on man: 'Father, forgive them; they do not know what they are doing.' And that is the true definition of the madman.

But do you imagine that man, who is thus defined by Jesus as 'mad', accepts the description, believes that he is mad? On the contrary; if anything, he applies the term to those who went before him, to those who failed to assess accurately the forces involved in earlier wars, who committed this or that error; but himself, mad? Oh no! and he will actually prove to you that he is not.

Indeed, speaking of madmen, who is the arch-madman of them all? There he is: the arch-madman, Jesus Christ, who during his trial was dressed in a white garment and silenced with derisive and mocking words.

You too are mad, you who want to conquer through non-violence, to win the earth with meekness.

You are mad, you who dreamed of beating down swords into ploughshares and spears into sickles (Is 2 :4).

You are mad, you who wish to turn the defenceless other cheek to the hatred of the enemy. (Mt 5 :39).

We are not mad like you, and there are some follies that we do not commit : we do not even think of them.

So runs the argument, and echoes of this tremendous dialectic ring in our ears every time people discuss the problem of how to achieve some social advance or liberate a people; how to realize a man's personal dignity or bring the human race a step nearer to the attainment of justice. And it is when one picks up this echo, deep as the heart of man, that one comes to realize just how irreconcilable are the two spirits that produce it : the spirit of the world and the spirit of Jesus.

Each calls the other mad and is answered in the same terms.

History has shown, and will go on showing to the end, which of the two is right; which of the two, the meek or the violent, will more truly possess the earth; which of the two is happier, the man who destroys his enemy or the man who lives with him under the same roof.

The incompatibility between the world and Christ is total, and I will certainly not be the one to persuade the lion that the lamb is right. I only want, and in all humility, to offer a helping hand to those who have not yet chosen between the two camps and the two systems; those who, as Christians, have savoured the beauty of the Gospel message, and suffer when they feel compelled to side with the others, simply because they have the impression that violence is more decisive, or worse still, as is frequently argued nowadays, that it features as an inevitable element in the process of history.

'If we do not fight, if we do not make use of guerrilla warfare we will achieve precisely nothing, and in any case we are not fighting for ourselves, but for the poor we wish to liberate.'

This is the dilemma, and on the walls of so many Christian homes hang the virile photographs of prophets of a liberating hope more persuasive then the liberating hope of the Gospel.

It is not that I do not appreciate the way in which they have paid and continue to pay personally for their beliefs. They are worthy indeed to take their place beside us at the workbench to inspire us, to help us with their courage and their strength of purpose.

This I accept; but knowing Jesus as I do, I wonder whether such men might not have achieved far more in the revolution for justice had they taken up the cause of meekness and non-violence.

You say that one cannot do without arms, and I answer in the name of Jesus that this is not true, that one can do without them, and obtain greater results. This is why we can be helped by the witness of those two great prophets of non-violence : Gandhi and Martin Luther King.

They believed in the beatitude of meekness, not only for themselves, but for all; not only as a subject of meditation and chosen by individuals, but as a subject for meditation and chosen by entire peoples; not only as an instrument of individual peace, but as an instrument of universal liberation.

And yet how hard it is to believe in meekness!

In no other situation more than in this one do Jesus's words apply : 'If your faith were the size of a mustard seed you could say to this mountain, "Move from here to there", and it would move' (Mt 17 :2).

Faith the size of a grain of mustard seed is not much, but we do not have even that. In other words, we do not believe Jesus. We are, without willing it, on the other side. His words outrage and scandalize us; or at the very least they surprise us : how can the wolf be driven off unless his body is riddled with bullets?

How far removed from the streets of modern Gubbio is the spirit of St Francis!

The wolf returns only to be hunted down with bill-hooks, and people want to see the pavement stained with his blood . . . and yet for a moment hope seemed to revive.

I have seen so many young people, so many women believers in non-violence, allowing the police to carry them off bodily, without offering any resistance, like the negroes in the southern states who boycotted the public transport services in American cities and travelled on foot.

It seemed that one generation had at last understood, and no longer wished to repeat the mistakes of its fathers who had cut each other's throats and achieved nothing whatsoever in the process. There was a spate of songs in which people sang of their desire to put flowers in the cannons. And then . . . it only needed someone to come along and say that non-violence was non-productive, that it was necessary to engage not in war, but in guerrilla warfare, and there was a marked resurgence of confidence in the power of arms.

How easily a bit of sentiment can change the direction of the wind for someone whose faith is weak!

As long as non-violence gave the impression that it was strong, strong enough to sway public opinion and governments as well, people professed non-violence; as soon as they could be convinced that their tactics had been understood and the powerful had grown wise to it all and were laughing in the faces of the non-violent, back came the grim, forbidding looks. The fact is that for too many non-violence was an attitude, not a faith. Fundamentally, instead of being a blessing, meekness was a pose. A mere nothing was needed to make it disappear.

I once saw a man on hunger strike. When he realized that no one was watching him, and that the papers no longer mentioned him, he went off to a restaurant and had a good meal.

So many are non-violent for show!

So many are meek in order to be seen to be meek!

Jesus would call them 'hypocrites', and he would be right.

No, the beatitude does not concentrate on results, it concentrates on the face of the Eternal, the Unchanging, the One who said: 'I have overcome the world.'

The beatitude does not involve the winning of a victory now, it depends on having faith in him who has already overcome.

Beatitude consists in being meek.

The result does not always depend on us, and we will not always be carried along in triumph. The beatitude can also lead to death, as it did in the case of Martin Luther King and of Gandhi, but it leads to a happy death and happiness such as this does not come to an end when the weapons of the violent have succeeded in tearing our wretched bodies apart. Happiness, like God, is eternal, and when I leave this earthly life, I entrust to him the task of making my blood fruitful.

The fruits may come a hundred years later, perhaps: he knows, and I know in whom I have believed.

Anyone who is unable to separate his own virtue and commitment from this hypothetical human result will be a revolutionary for this divided world but not a revolutionary for the Kingdom of God. Had Jesus been concerned about results on that Good Friday evening, he would have stopped acting meek and perhaps called down legions of angels to destroy the earth. But then what? What would have been the point of destroying the earth? What advantage could there be in ruling over a world of the dead, a desolate land where he, as the strongest, had overcome?

How would we react to him? Are you satisfied now? Did you come to win corpses?

Would a victory like that be worthy of God?

No, Jesus did not call down legions of his angels to destroy the violent and conquer evil.

He keeps to his own programme.

He too is happy in his meekness and knows he will conquer through meekness.

Time is on his side.

The last word has not yet been said on the choice man will make at the end of his earthly life.

And the meekness of God awaits man at that moment.

It is therefore a question of faith. But, as he did in the beatitude of meekness, Jesus asks us to look beyond the contingent, beyond history, to the real beyond.

We make history without concerning ourselves about who will write that history and what they will say of the men who are caught up in it. We make history, keeping an eye all the while on the kingdom of which the beatitudes are the fundamental law, and to which Jesus bears eternal witness.

If Jesus has said to me : 'Blessed are the meek for they shall inherit the earth', then I must possess the earth with meekness. Do not tell me it is difficult; I know it is, terribly difficult, because we sin through our lack of faith in the words of Christ and the absence in us of the childlike heart that would gives us the courage to fulfil totally the demands of the Gospel.

That is the reason why we are not happy, why our nights are tormented by fear, and our actions characterized by indecison and cowardice.

Meekness achieves its first victory by not multiplying corpses, and already this is in itself a considerable victory. The joy that comes from not having harmed one's brother far surpasses the joy given by some object that has been obtained at the cost of a mountain of corpses.

To end one's earthly existence in the certain knowledge that one has never caused blood to flow constitutes one aspect of one's happiness. But it is not enough. To move among men without a knife or a gun, to enter the meeting place unarmed and without preconceived fears indicates belief in a better world, it indicates the presence of confidence in the spiritual inheritance of man as he journeys towards perfection.

Have we not repeated it so often : that we believe in man, that we are at one with him?

Have we not fought for his freedom and his progress?

If so, the moment has now come for us to give proof of this confidence of ours and not to be discouraged by difficulties as they crop up.

Christ believed in man.

Gandhi believed in man.

Martin Luther King believed in man.

Why should we not believe in him ourselves? I can almost hear the reply : 'But we do believe in him, and we want to free people from the slavery of possessions, we want the poor of Latin America to achieve their liberation from the few hundred families who now hold them in bondage, we want the whites to stop treating the negroes as outcasts . . .

And so we come back to where we began. The idea that we might solve the problems that bother us by cutting off a few hundred heads does not bring us peace. We still have the impression that you get more immediate results by getting the better of someone else. Basically, we are in a hurry and do not want to accept the patience of God.

Yet Gandhi proved that he had lost no time.

I do not believe that Martin Luther King, had he resorted to methods of violence, would have obtained results any greater than those he obtained through love.

Deep inside me, I feel that all this haste is deceptive.

And if it is not, this is not something that can be readily proved from the actual effects of peace and the attempt to build on the rock of a people's patience.

I remember a story that made the rounds among the negroes

of the southern United States, part of the literature that is born of the struggle for freedom. Listen.

'It was hot, terribly hot. The cicadas were singing on the branches of the trees along the deserted street in the early hours of the afternoon. Tom, the young negro boy, had gone to the newspaper depot after school, as he always did, to collect his great bundle of papers. He had to deliver them to the distributors before going home to eat. But he always ran, and earned himself a few dollars each week without much effort. And anyway, he liked his work.

'But that day, dash it, he kept needing to spend a penny. Perhaps it was the fault of some exercise that had been set him in school and made him a bit anxious; perhaps it was the turnips he had eaten the night before. At all events, there he was out in the street with the cicadas singing, and he with his pack on his back, desperately wanting to spend a penny. But there was not a single public convenience for negroes in the whole area. There was indeed one splendid one, but that was for whites, and Tom had walked past it many times before, sorely tempted to go in; but he was terrified of meeting some great Jim on his way out, buttoning his flies.

'This time he tried it. The street is deserted. All the great Jims are taking their siestas, lying on their hammocks in the shade. Tom dumps the papers at the foot of an enormous plane tree. Then he looks round : not a soul in sight.

'His bare feet feel the freshness of the floor of this fine, white-man's toilet.

'What pleasure to relieve oneself in these cool, white-tiled surroundings! Then an enormous poster catches Tom's attention, making him forget his fear. He wants to work out what it says. Strange how a boy's curiosity is aroused by forbidden things!

'Then suddenly Tom jumps.

'He hears the sound of a pair of shoes close by on the pavement, the shoes of some great Jim.

'No chance now to escape; you are caught, Tom; prepare yourself for a thrashing. You dared to go into a public toilet for whites. You know the law of Alabama, you must go to a toilet for blacks, people of your own race.

'Jim is blocking your escape route, his eyes icy with rage. Poor Tom, your agility is of no use to you now. Jim is strong and used to wild-boar hunting.

'One kick sends you to the ground, and then, little Alabama negro, you slip and fall till you end up with your face in your own urine.

'That is how they punish transgressors of the law, which means "their" law.

'Get up now, little Alabama negro.

'You have two choices before you, and I will tell you what they are, because I have suffered a lot myself for the cause of negro liberation. The first choice is that you should get up from the ground, clean yourself, and then, adopting a docile, submissive attitude, step out of the trap. But once outside, bearing in mind your sturdy legs, you suddenly turn round with a stone in your hand and you hurl it at Jim. Then you run off, nursing your hatred which you will describe at home to your family and intensify tomorrow among your friends of your own race. The day will come when we will destroy Jim!

'But there is also another choice, a more difficult one, and I, Martin Luther King, draw your attention to it in the name of our revolution of love. Get up, Tom, and recognize in the smell of that filth, which is the common filth of humanity, the smell of Christ's blood, defiled with spittle on the way to Calvary.

'Jim is more ignorant than cruel. He is not aware of the evil he is doing, but he will one day.

'Forgive him, Tom, in the name of Jesus, forgive him.

'It is so much simpler to take revenge. The difficult thing is to love, and you must love.

'The society we are building for tomorrow needs the binding

cement of love. We cannot go on living with a knife in our belt for ever. Tomorrow we will have to live with Jim, and Jim will understand us then as we understand him.

'It is too easy to take revenge and destroy.

'You, Tom, must build your tomorrow with the power and the violence of love.'

This is no fable that I have just recounted; it is a page of the Gospel lived out in the flesh of an insignificant negro educated by a great prophet of peace, Martin Luther King.

He was convinced that, with a people who believed in love, it was possible to carry out all the revolutions of history. And with one advantage.

If you engage in a revolution of love you will be able to sustain it, it will be lasting. If you trust in arms you will have to be on the look-out continually for someone who might want to start a counter-revolution.

A man who loves no longer needs to protect himself against anyone, since he already contemplates the face of God.

I am aware that many people will smile at this observation, just as they smiled condescendingly when they heard Jesus talk, and listened to the beatitudes.

But truth and history will not change on that account.

Gandhi would say : 'Give me a people who believe in love, and you will see happiness on earth.' And Martin Luther King would add : 'Teach a people to control their instinct for vengeance, and to accept adversity, like young Tom, and you will have a genuine nation of free men, not a population of well-dressed gorillas armed with sub-machine guns.'

But here, too, it is a question of faith, and as St Paul says, it is faith that will conquer the world.

And in spite of everything, faith gives grounds for confidence – as in the words Isaiah used when he prophesied the universal reign of peace :

'The wolf lives with the lamb,
the panther lies down with the kid,
calf and lion cub feed together
with a little boy to lead them . . .
The lion eats straw like the ox.
The infant plays over the cobra's hole;
into the viper's lair
the young child puts his hand'

(Is 11 :6–8).

Chapter Sixteen

BLESSED ARE THE MERCIFUL

When we reach the gates of paradise, after a suitable number of years of regular purgatory, and find ourselves thronging round the entrance, along with our friends, relatives and acquaintances, and an angel of God appears in our midst crying out: 'Into your places!' I am quite certain that, to a man, we will all make for the last place, and the crowd will not be near the entrance but in the farthest corner, especially if there is a bit of shadow.

In other words, what happens then will be exactly the opposite of what happens here on earth when one is trying to catch a bus in the city, and all the Christians, sisters included, elbow their way to the front of the queue.

The fact is that during our long, patient wait in that place of prayer and peace which goes by the ugly and unsympathetic name of purgatory, we will have had plenty of time to realize, deep within ourselves, that we are proud good-for-nothings, and if at last we manage to arrive, still limping, at the longed-for gate of salvation, we will, without any doubt, owe it to the mercy of God.

And then something will happen, so unique and so great will be our joy at being pardoned, that we will no longer have any desire to argue with anyone, least of all with those closest to us, about our supposed earthly merits; rather, we will be seized by a great longing to move among the crowd, searching for someone who we once genuinely believed, before we departed from the now far-distant earth, was a source of suffering for us.

And should we chance to meet the head clerk who overloaded us with work, or the mother-in-law who took pleasure in making us suffer the agonies of death long before the moment came, they will be the first we embrace, because at that moment they will give us the chance to say in our hearts: 'God has forgiven me great sins, but I too have something to forgive them. And by doing so, I hope to be quits.'

All the same, it is sad that we will only understand these matters up there, and down here we will go on using our elbows to get ahead of other people; go on tossing angrily in our beds because we have missed out on promotion; go on nursing an unvoiced resentment in our heart against the imprudent husband who dared to say: 'Don't you realize you're a bore?' If we were to expose our hearts to the light of day and break into their innermost recesses, what trash would emerge! What a squalid series of thoughts and feelings, of animosity, hatred and bitter judgments, would come to light.

And not against the Chinese or the far-off inhabitants of Papua, but against the brother who recites the Office with me in choir; against my wife with whom I share my life; against the mother who bore me; against my colleague at work, with whom I struggle to earn my daily bread.

Which of us has nothing to do or say 'against' someone?

And that is why we are not happy.

Because happiness begins at the moment in which we overcome ourselves for mercy's sake pardoning the brother who offended us, and thus acquiring a pledge of God's mercy towards ourselves.

Blessed are the merciful; they shall obtain mercy.

Jesus himself had difficulty in explaining what this meant, and nowhere is it said that he has been particularly successful: our poor hearts are so sick.

He said some terrible things to convince us, but his efforts were as good as wasted.

I have come across religious sisters who would have been

prepared to die as martyrs to preserve their virginity, but who were not prepared to expend one ounce of goodwill to establish good working relations with a nearby convent.

I have known parents who made extreme sacrifices to provide their children with food but who could not manage to make even the smallest effort to reach agreement between themselves and stop abusing one another.

I have seen bishops spend themselves to the point of exhaustion in the service of the Church, but who could not bring themselves to go out of their 'palaces' in search of the lost sheep, their primary concern being to prop up their own undisputed authority and the dignity of the Church. It might well appear from this that the Gospel is no longer read, and that we have replaced it with a thousand and one other ways of interpreting our relationship with God and with our fellow men.

Each one of us has some object of adoration, some subject he sets up on his altar: for one it will be chastity, for another authority, for another the honour of the Church, and for others it will be work or economy or a good name, canon law or a moral treatise, an old catechism or a new one, but few, all too few, are prepared to adore the loving will of Jesus, which was spelled out for us so carefully in the Father's name.

For it was Jesus himself who said to us: ' "But I say this to you who are listening: love your enemies, do good to those who hate you, bless those who curse you, pray for those who treat you badly. To the man who slaps you on one cheek, present the other cheek too; to the man who takes your cloak from you, do not refuse your tunic. Give to everyone who asks you, and do not ask for your property back from the man who robs you. Treat others as you would like them to treat you. If you love those who love you, what thanks can you expect? Even sinners do that much. And if you lend to those from whom you hope to receive, what thanks can you expect? Even sinners lend to sinners to get back the same amount. Instead, love your enemies and do good, and lend without any hope of return. You will have a great reward, and you will be sons of the Most High, for he himself is kind to the ungrateful and the wicked.

' "Be compassionate as your Father is compassionate. Do not judge, and you will not be judged yourselves; do not condemn, and you will not be condemned yourselves; grant pardon, and you will be pardoned. Give, and there will be gifts for you: a full measure, pressed down, shaken together, and running over, will be poured into your lap; because the amount you measure out is the amount you will be given back" ' (Lk 6: 27–38).

Could any words express more clearly what Jesus wants of us; speak to us of the way in which God wishes us to live out our religious commitment; or explain what is God's true and innermost purpose in establishing his Church here on earth? I hardly think so . . . and yet?

As if that were not enough, he, normally so gentle, went on to threaten us, telling us we were hypocrites as long as we went on noticing the speck in our brother's eye while there was a beam in our own, and came finally to the point of confronting us with the dilemma of eternal salvation: 'There is nothing for it: either you forgive or I cannot save you; either you overcome your resentment or you wait for the sentence . . .'

' "And so the kingdom of heaven may be compared to a king who decided to settle his accounts with his servants. When the reckoning began, they brought him a man who owed ten thousand talents; but he had no means of paying, so his master's gave orders that he should be sold, together with his wife and children and all his possessions, to meet the debt. At this, the servant threw himself down at his master's feet. 'Give me time,' he said, 'and I will pay the whole sum.' And the servant's master felt so sorry for him that he let him go and cancelled the debt. Now as this servant went out, he happened to meet a fellow servant who owed him one hundred denarii;

and he seized him by the throat and began to throttle him. 'Pay what you owe me,' he said. His fellow servant fell at his feet and implored him, saying, 'Give me time and I will pay you.' But the other would not agree; on the contrary, he had him thrown into prison till he should pay the debt. His fellow servants were deeply distressed when they saw what had happened, and they went to their master and reported the whole affair to him. Then the master sent for him. 'You wicked servant,' he said. 'I cancelled all that debt of yours when you appealed to me. Were you not bound, then, to have pity on your fellow servant just as I had pity on you? And in his anger the master handed him over to the torturers till he should pay all his debts. And that is how my heavenly Father will deal with you unless you each forgive your brother from your heart" ' (Mt 18:23–34).

In this parable we are all included; no one is left out.

He told it for our benefit. We are the debtor who owed ten thousand talents to the king. Anyone who remains unconvinced of this can stop reading this book and (a far graver thing) the Gospel. Life will explain things to him, old age above all, if he has the patience to get there.

For no one, not even God, has power to change anything in a soul that looks on itself as 'light', 'virginity', 'strength', 'balance', 'religion'. I have already pointed out that Jesus was killed by a group of those 'respectable pharisees' because they were not waiting for salvation; they thought they were saved already.

There was nothing more to be done for them, because everything was done already, wrapped up, catalogued, signed and sealed. But the terrible thing is that each one of us carries in his heart a trace of the same disease, that sense of security and self-sufficiency, of being better and more capable than others. In short, we are Pharisees. And this is the source of all our troubles in our dealing with our fellow men, of our malicious judgments and our sins against charity.

We are not happy because we are unforgiving, and we are unforgiving because we feel superior to others.

Mercy is the fruit of the highest degree of love, because love creates equals, and a greater love makes us inferior.

First let us establish three premises :

Those who do not love feel superior to everyone else.

Those who love feel equal to everyone else.

Those who love much gladly take the lower place.

Each one of us can identify his position somewhere along this spectrum, which comprises the three degrees of the spiritual life here on earth :

Death for those who do not love.

Life for those who love.

Holiness for those who love much.

The beatitude of the merciful relates, like all the beatitudes, to the realm of holiness and we have to admit that Jesus set his sights high when he had the courage and confidence to place this lofty ideal before us. It is the beatitude that he himself lived to the full, stooping, out of love, to the lowest place, even to the extent of being rejected as a common criminal, fit only to be hung on a gibbet.

St Paul sums it up so well in his letter to the Philippians : 'His state was divine, yet he did not cling to his equality with God but emptied himself to assume the condition of a slave, and became as men are; and being as all men are, he was humbler yet, even to accepting death, death on a cross' (Ph 2 :6–7).

Rather than remaining in one or other of the three positions, which is very rare, we find ourselves straining towards the beatitude of Jesus, moving onwards towards perfection, in a continual oscillation between death and life, between life and holiness; experiencing the struggle between nature and grace, the fatigue that comes from rowing with the oars of virtue, and the unexpected joy of the wind that brings us the gifts of the Spirit.

Anyone who is living in grace will know what I mean.

But at this point a word of advice might be useful, and it follows the same line as Pascal's teaching on faith, 'act as if'.

There will be moments when you will come up against almost insurmountable difficulties in your efforts, however great they may be, to love your neighbour.

Difficulties caused by his sin, his unkindness or his superficiality. When this happens, remember that to know how to love, when we read nothing but evil, deceit and slovenliness in our brother's face, is beyond our human powers – yet we are so deeply immersed in what is human. It is then that you have to 'act as if' you loved him with the very love of Jesus dying on the cross.

It is not a question of trying to alter your feelings. You will not succeed in doing that. You have to prove yourself by your actions.

The feelings follow rather than precede rational and supernatural truths. It would be unreasonable to expect feelings of love from a heart smarting under the hurt of some pain received, or of anything worse.

But we can always perform actions which will affect our decisions and our prayer.

I will give two examples to explain what I mean.

You have been offended by a relative, or at least you think you have. A fundamental misunderstanding has developed between you. You are sure you are right, and I am not disputing that. I too believe that you are in the right, that he said what he said to you out of egotism, to gain his own ends, perhaps to hurt you. I accept all that. But precisely because you are in the right, I say that it is up to you to overcome your feelings, to take the first step, to offer him your forgiveness from the depths of your heart.

Do not aggravate the wound; do not allow your attitude to harden in silence. Do not run through the catalogue of your own virtues – it will only make you suffer more. Help yourself, as far as you can humanly speaking, by concentrating on his positive side, on the good qualities you will find there in spite of the defects, on all he has done for you in the past. But above all let your soul overflow with forgiving love; feel that you are less than him, lowlier, more needing of forgiveness. See him and the offences he has committed against you with the eye of Jesus, veiled in death on the cross.

Then, with your new-found peace of soul, you will understand what the beatitude of mercy means, and you will be, as Jesus said, 'sons of your Father in heaven, for he causes his sun to rise on bad men as well as good, and his rain to fall on honest and dishonest men alike' (Mt 5 :45).

And now another example.

You are a religious, living in one of the many convents of the world. You try to get along with everyone, to live according to the Gospel. And yet you are surrounded by people who do not live according to the Gospel, who do not believe in your vocation, who take advantage of you and steal from you.

Of course, but the moment has now come when you can prove evidence for their abuses and their acts of theft.

You could accuse them, take them to court, see to it that they are sentenced.

Of course, but the moment has now come when you can prove to the world and to yourself whether or not you believe in the Gospel. It is no use consulting your feelings. It would not be difficult to guess that they are in turmoil, doing their best to sweep your charity away, like a torrent in flood.

At that moment, 'act as if' you had all the charity on your side.

Perform some concrete actions.

Do not accuse them.

Jesus asks this of you, and to put his Gospel into practice is perfect love.

Later, when it is humanly possible, you can put your feelings in order.

But meanwhile you have laid solid and true foundations for your forgiveness : concrete actions.

They make you 'sons of the Most High, for he himself is kind to the ungrateful and the wicked' (Lk 6 :35).

Here lies the solution to the difficult problem of human relations, here we find the strength to acquire the self-mastery that is necessary if we are to pass through the 'narrow gate of the beatitudes', and become 'sons of the Most High who is kind to the ungrateful and the wicked'.

Ultimately, we have to remember one thing, which is that, in moments of conflict, we must absolutely avoid appealing either to truth or to justice alone. If we do, we shall very soon find our way blocked by that same truth or justice.

Let me explain. Faced with the brother who wrongs me, who wounds, insults and deceives me, I cannot help saying, 'I am in the right.' I cannot shut my eyes and try to find excuses. The fact is that he *is* wronging me, he *is* insulting me, he *is* stealing from me. And I think and say so objectively, for the truth is the truth. But, quite as objectively, I continue : Although I can see clearly that you are in the wrong and I am in the right, I am not going to appeal either to reason or to justice, but instead follow the difficult path of love. If I do not, I will never escape from the dilemma, because my brother will counter my arguments with his own, and so on *ad infinitum.*

And here let us remind ourselves of something else. Wars are fought in the name of justice and men cut each other's throats in defence of truth, because each one has his own truth to defend.

But Jesus's attitude is completely different, and in the end we will simply have to come to terms with it, especially since he has given us such an uncompromising example. Jesus went beyond justice through love, overrode the truth by his own self-sacrifice.

He knew 'what was in man'. There was little to hide about the inner reality. It was no secret that man is a 'scoundrel', a 'cheat', a 'good-for-nothing'.

Jesus, in the presence of the adultress, the prostitute or the thief, did not beat about the bush by saying that these men and women were without sin.

Briefly, he did not deny the truth, but he did not stop at the truth. He went beyond it . . . possibly forgetting it for a moment. He pretended not to notice, he feigned ignorance like Isaac when he felt the rascal Jacob, who had come in disguise, covered with kid's skin, his clothes smelling of his brother Esau, in order to snatch the birthright from him.

'Yes, the smell of my son,' exclaimed the father, 'is like the smell of a fertile field blessed by Yahweh. May God give you dew from heaven, and the richness of the earth, abundance of grain and wine !'

But it was not his son Esau, it was Jacob who carried off the father's blessing.

What a moving 'stratagem' of love !

If God had not found the way of love when confronted with sinful man, and if he had only invoked justice and truth, how would he have overcome the great divide in order to save us? As he died on the cross, Jesus closed the chapter of mere justice and inaugurated on earth the authentic chapter of 'mercy'.

And as the mantle of his blood falls on us, it will yield an unparalleled fragrance, making us acceptable to the Father's embrace.

And so it is up to us now to use the same 'ploy', the same methods, with those brothers whose gross behaviour would otherwise make it impossible for us to forgive.

From now on, whenever we encounter a thief, or a Magdalene or a Peter, whose cowardice or deception or evil living requires our forgiveness, we will know what to do.

Instead of casting stones, and doing what the Jews suggested Jesus should do with the adultress, it will be for us to say: ' "Woman, where are they? Has no one condemned you?" "No one, sir," she replied. "Neither do I condemn you," said Jesus. "Go away and do not sin any more" ' (Jn 8:11).

If we reject this way of looking at life and of interpreting the facts, we fall back on the 'juridical', 'inward-looking', 'dead' Church, which is not in Rome, although we have become accustomed to saying so rather too glibly in order to shelve our personal responsibility, but in our own miserable hearts which, instead of listening to Jesus, go on hating, like the Pharisees of all the temples and holy places of this world.

Chapter Seventeen

BLESSED ARE THE PURE IN HEART

When Teilhard de Chardin wrote his *Hymn of the Universe* and sang, 'Blessed are you, harsh matter', he certainly did not err on the side of pessimism. And it may be that the secret of the enthusiasm which this Jesuit poet and mystic has succeeded in arousing all over the contemporary world lies in the fact that he looked on the world with serene, optimistic eyes. What is more, if, as some would have it, there is something sinful in this, Vatican II was guilty of the same lapse when it decided to express its confident attitude towards the world and to state that the Church, from then on, fully accepted involvement in the dialogue, and still more in the life, the expectations and the conflicts of the world.

Naturally not everyone agreed with this, especially not the prudent. Indeed, what opinions is a prudent man not capable of expressing? He even went so far as to say that it would take at least fifty years to redress the errors perpetrated by that good-natured optimist, known as John XXIII, who made the mistake of calling the Council.

But if this were true, and the prudent man, that faithful champion of orthodoxy, were right, I would become a Muslim immediately. I would argue that if in the Church of God, the Church of the Spirit, the Church which is defined as the 'people of God', people can make such a glaring mistake, giving unprecedented and world-wide recognition to a man like this simple peasant from Bergamo, and so prepare the ground for a spiritual harvest of proportions hitherto unknown, at least in our generation, it must mean either that the Spirit is not at work or people do not understand; therefore the Church does not exist, or if it does it is dead. But the Church is alive, more alive, indeed, than ever before; the people of God are listening and have grasped what is going on within. They have acclaimed Pope John and the Council and applauded the optimism of the fathers, and they suffer because of all the cynics, the prophets of doom and the fearful, who, today as always, reveal by their fear that they have no faith.

Because it is faith that overcomes the world, not fear.

Because it is faith that tells me the Church is not in my hands, even if I happen to be a cardinal, but in the hands of the all-powerful God, and therefore, as Pope Pius XI used to say, in good hands.

But let us forget the outbursts of criticism, and turn our attention to the optimism of the Council; and to the optimism of Teilhard, who wrote :

'Blessed be you, universal matter, immeasurable time, boundless ether, triple abyss of stars and atoms and generations : you who by dissolving our narrow standards of measurement reveal to us the dimensions of God.

'Blessed be you, impenetrable matter : you who, interposed between our minds and the world of essences, cause us to languish with the desire to pierce through the seamless veil of phenomena.

'Blessed be you, immortal matter; you who one day will undergo the process of dissolution within us and will thereby take us forcibly into the very heart of that which exists.

'Without you, without your onslaughts, without your uprootings of us we should remain all our lives inert, stagnant, puerile, ignorant both of ourselves and of God. . . .

'You I acclaim as the inexhaustible potentiality for existence and transformation . . .

'I acclaim you as the universal power which brings together

and unites, through which the multitudinous nomads are bound together and in which they all converge on the way of the spirit.

'I acclaim you as the melodious fountain of water whence spring the souls of men and as the limpid crystal whereof is fashioned the new Jerusalem.

'I acclaim you as the divine "milieu", charged with creative power, as the ocean stirred by the Spirit, as the clay moulded and infused with life by the Incarnate Word.

'Sometimes, thinking they are responding to your irresistible appeal, men will hurl themselves for love of you into the exterior abyss of selfish pleasure-seeking : they are deceived by a reflection or by an echo.

'This I now understand.

'If we are ever to reach you, matter, we must, having first established contact with the totality of all that lives and moves here below, come little by little to feel that the individual shapes of all we have laid hold on are melting away in our hands, until finally we are at grips with the *single essence* of all subsistencies and all unions.

'If we are ever to possess you, having taken you rapturously in our arms, we must then go on to sublimate you through sorrow.

'Your realm comprises those serene heights where saints think to avoid you – but where your flesh is so transparent and so agile as to be no longer distinguishable from spirit.

'Raise me up then, matter, to those heights, through struggle and separation and death; raise me up until, at long last, it becomes possible for me in perfect chastity to embrace the universe.'

In these wonderful pages of Teilhard there are two key sentences, which indicate fully and unequivocally that the optimism of this great thinker was tempered by his sense of the cross and his full consciousness of the reality of sin.

The first runs : 'If we are ever to possess you, having taken you rapturously into our arms, we must then go on to sublimate you through sorrow.'

And the second : 'Sometimes, thinking they are responding to your irresistible appeal, men will hurl themselves for love of you into the exterior abyss of selfish pleasure-seeking : they are deceived by a reflection or by an echo.'

One could not express more clearly or more immediately the reality of the evil of sin, and it is precisely on the basis of this consideration that Teilhard begs God to deliver him from the hold of matter, so capable of deceiving him, and bear him upwards into complete freedom, the freedom of grace: 'Raise me up until, at long last, it becomes possible for me in perfect chastity to embrace the universe.'

I do not know where one could find a more beautiful way of expressing the beatitude of purity.

Today I would translate Jesus's words, 'Blessed are the pure in heart' as, 'Blessed is he who knows how to embrace chastely the entire universe.'

Jesus did not come in order to add to our burdens, he came to set us free; he did not come to deprive us of that embrace, but to make it chaste.

To be pure is to embrace things chastely; to be impure is to embrace them in a lustful way, defiling them, violating them and prostituting them in the process. Is that not true?

A man embraces his own wife chastely, but not the woman he buys by exerting his male superiority.

We embrace our work chastely, and our house acquired honestly, our toil and our friendships, but not our thefts, our arrogance, our blasphemies, our insincerity or our intolerance.

There is a vast difference between a husband's creative embrace, and the functional embrace of the soldier of fortune who breaks in the doors of the vanquished and rapes the first woman he meets.

As soon as we really understand that Jesus did not come to

deny us love and union, but to raise them to a new level for us, making them even more beautiful, more human, more joyful, more authentic, we will have taken a great step forward in our understanding of the Gospel. But often, only too often, we want to try things out in our own way, and nine times out of ten, our misfortunes stem from this desire of ours to 'try', from this practical if not theoretical denial of the law which God gave us out of love.

If only those who have refused to listen to the beatitudes of Jesus could turn back! Those who have preferred to walk the way of 'possession' of material things, and who, with each new step, have sunk deeper into the quicksands of vice and guilt! Let doctors and lawyers speak up at this point; let them tell us of the painful loom on which man weaves the fabric of his sin! There is no limit to the suffering, the mistakes, the depravity and the wickedness.

And how bitter is the path of guilt! How many tears have been shed as a result of the illicit possession of things, of the violence of the strong man who wishes to become stronger, of the covetousness of the man who had and wants more, of the lust that is falsely labelled love, and the prostitution that poses as '*la dolce vita*'.

But can man really be so blind?

Can it really be that Jesus's word is only to be fulfilled in the midst of these bitter contradictions and that the ideal we glimpse through the beatitude of purity must spring from an ocean of mud and refuse?

This is the one point at which we might legitimately give in to pessimism, when those who smile condescendingly at the optimism of the Council fathers seem to be right.

Poor things! Surely you know the world better than to try and re-establish its contact with the Church?

Has your experience of history not taught you to abandon all hope and rule out the possibility of any sort of union with this 'curse', this 'world of sin' as St Paul would have it?

Are you actually planning to try again?

The thing is that in this optimistic determination to try again there is a radically new element. When they defined the Church as the 'people of God', the fathers of the Council said in effect that they, the hierarchy, were united with the people of God and therefore with those who sin. They too are on the other side, for on this side, that of the pure, the sinless, Jesus is alone, with the one exception of Mary.

They said that good and evil men cannot be separated one from another, that the Church does not contain all the good men and the world all the evil; that we are all enmeshed in sin and guilty of a covetous approach to material things.

So the hope of saving even one person from the ruin of sin is identical with the hope, given us by Christ, of saving all men, of saving the Church, his bride.

In short, it is not the 'others' who find it difficult to possess the world chastely. We all do. The bishop who is in danger of becoming a miser does; and the priest who keeps three mistresses; and the president of the Christian men's organisation who may become a notorious usurer; we all do whenever we forget to pray or depart from our God even briefly.

I can no longer delude myself, thinking that I am immune, 'saved' by preferential treatment, chaste once and for all because I have received one sacrament or a series of sacraments.

I too am a poor wretch, obliged to struggle in order to free myself from the shackles of sin; to call on the grace of God in order not to lose my faith; to remain continually on the watch so as not to be damned. This is why the fathers were right to be optimistic in spite of everything. Being optimists, they hoped for my salvation, and in hoping for my salvation they hoped for that of my fellow men.

But happiness does not simply consist in ridding myself of the hell within me, it involves establishing heaven there.

Happiness is heaven!

The 'blessed are the pure in heart' stands for something positive and expresses a profound conviction; it means living here and now in the happiness of that 'chaste possession of the universe', experiencing joy, even within the limits of the moral law and the discipline that charity imposes on me.

That is why Jesus said : 'Blessed are the pure in heart : they shall see God.'

This is the positive aspect of the beatitude, the recompense for the gigantic effort of accepting the moral commitment involved, the response to my attempts to strip myself of my sensuality, my wealth and my pride.

They shall see God! Purity of heart leads me to the vision of God. By embracing things chastely, I learn to discern in the depths of those things the features of God's face.

And do you think you are asking for something of small consequence? If the world knew how great is the joy of seeing God, it would burn the worthless bits and pieces of its riches in horror and make haste along the path that leads to him.

But it does not know, and who can tell it? Who is going to proclaim in this valley of dry bones the great hope that we will see God? Certainly not he who has nothing but words to offer.

We need to convince ourselves that today we carry out our apostolate simply by living, that the Good News is communicated by people's lives. Do you want to pass on the message of the beatitudes? Then be happy yourself.

Do you want to proclaim the happiness of the pure in heart? Then be pure in heart yourself.

Because you yourself see God through eyes that have become accustomed to the struggle to embrace things chastely, you will instil in your fellow men a longing for purity and hope for the great vision.

Chapter Eighteen

BLESSED ARE THE PEACEMAKERS

I do not know what your experience is, but I know how it is with me. When I think of my soul, I sometimes imagine it as a small boat on the high seas, but more often as a nomad's tent on the edge of the desert.

Sea or desert, either is the unbounded domain of my solitude. It is within the powers of all men to get there, but they will have to make an effort to do so.

But then I have to make an effort to get there myself; I need to sail far or walk hard in order to reach the centre of my being where I have learnt to experience peace.

I find the image of the tent particularly appealing, especially now that I know the tent from experience, and how to pitch it in the most favourable position for passing the night.

The evening search for somewhere to camp has proved an enormous source of joy!

During the day I have never had any difficulties about associating with other people and spending time on their camping sites; indeed, I have even sought them out.

But in the evening – yes, in the evening I have always contrived to place my tent as far away as possible in order to enjoy a little recollection, to savour the 'great silence', as we call it, which begins after the recitation of Compline.

In the desert, when the sun sets after the toil and trouble of the day, the wind drops and with it the burning heat and life seems to begin afresh. It is the hour of peace. On a stretch of level but not too sandy ground, beside the hillock which provides your shelter, gather up the dry brushwood of which there is no lack, even in the most deserted places, and make a fire.

That is the first thing you need to do so as to boil the water for the broth in which to break the bread you are going to bake under the sand by the heat from the embers of the fire.

An hour later everything is finished, and, restored by the hot broth and a few dates, you can throw whatever remains of the wood on to the fire and leave it to cast its fantastic lights into your chapel under the star-lit sky.

After that, move away a little and settle down in a sand-dune or sit on some hospitable rock, and then, without haste, with no watch and no definite programme, begin to pray.

I will never be able to find words strong enough to express what it means to stay with God like this, hour after hour, in the vastness of the night.

Do not deprive yourself of the experience even if the initial effort costs you something and you have to break through a certain element of coldness in the first encounter with the focus of your faith.

You will not be entering the lists alone.

Sometimes I have had to go for three-quarters of an hour or an hour before making contact with my inner self, before entering into my prayer in any real sense. I too have learned what it means to wrestle with the Angel, as Jacob did that night at the ford.

I have learned to appreciate how necessary purification is for our prayer, and that we should not be discouraged by our early difficulties. But I have also learned to savour what follows after the initial coldness, to recognize the first signs of the peace of God, to experience the presence of God and rejoice in his revelation.

There is no predictable limit set on the delights of prayer, just as there is no limit set on its dryness. These are the two unmistakable signs of God's action within us; you will never be able to control them yourself and you will never be able to foresee what is going to happen next. The action is always in the hands of God.

But that does not matter. He is God and I am his creature; he knows and I do not.

It is only right that he should sometimes stand in the way of my haste, or change some plan that I had concocted myself.

He, not I, must lay down terms for the dialogue.

In the darkest night he is the one who can see the path along which to lead me.

Meanwhile, the one thing that gives me strength to pray, or at least to want to pray, is the peace it brings.

Try it and you will see.

The resistance you put up to boredom, distractions and the life of nature round about you, your efforts to control your feelings, your imagination, and above all your desire to escape, will slowly but surely bring you into a state of true peace, a peace that is different, not of this world.

And then you will begin to acquire a taste for the reality which is forming in the deepest centre of your being; you will learn how better to recognize the least signs of its presence and to sense its unique value. Naturally you will sometimes have this experience after you have altered your own judgment about something, professed your love, renewed your desire to change your way of life, or promised to make this or that act of detachment. But ultimately it is God who brings you to understand that there is no peace where there is disorder, that it is not adoration when we make idols of creatures.

Not without reason has peace been defined as 'tranquillity in order'.

It is difficult to feel the peace of God unless one has first resolved seriously to be faithful to one wife, to pardon those who may have offended one, to live by one's own work, to discipline one's instincts and desires a little.

That a unity exists between life and prayer, day and night, thought and action, God and our neighbour, is beyond doubt, and God points it out to us so delicately, and yet so firmly. Once this order has been established, however, even if it remains a relative order, like the satchel of an untidy child who nevertheless loves his home : quite beyond our weaknesses and our problems, he gives us the joy of peace and of intimacy with himself.

So do not be in a hurry to leave your place of prayer.

Do not become obsessed with time.

Enjoy that peace as much as you can.

It will begin to shine like a light in your face. And that will be the light your fellow men will be needing when you return to them. The apostolate consists in passing on that light, not the hollow sound of your own words.

The peace of God is a light which shines in the faces of those whom the Gospel calls the 'sons of God'.

'Happy the peacemakers : they shall be called sons of God' (Mt 5 :9). I do not wish to sound presumptuous, but I can definitely claim to have seen that light. Let me explain.

Because of the damage done to my leg as the the result of an accident in the desert, my superiors have assigned me the less heavy work. I had entered the fraternity with the idea of becoming a mountain guide or at least of working with the miners in Belgium or Kenya, and instead I found myself cooking and carrying meals to those of my brethren who were doing a stint 'in the desert'. Such are the ironies of God's dealings with us !

This work, that of ministering to my brothers who were praying alone on the mountain, pleased me greatly, because there is always something more I can learn about the mystery that lies closest to my heart : prayer.

It involved taking provisions every three or four days to those

Little Brothers who had decided to make a forty-day retreat in imitation of the forty days spent by Jesus in the desert.

The Little Brothers are obliged to do this during their sabbatical year, three or four times, that is, during their lives, and it provides the occasion for a kind of spiritual renewal, a second or third noviceship. Normally speaking they spend these periods in the desert, or else on Monte Subasio, where a number of hermitages have been set up.

As I was saying, it was my task to prepare a basketful of provisions and carry it up. Naturally, when I go and find them, I look my brethren in the face and . . . well.

Solitude is a serious, demanding affair and no one succeeds in overcoming the difficulties all at once. But in general Little Brothers are used to it, and the teaching of Père de Foucauld has helped them to endure the struggle that is involved in being alone with God.

On the other hand, it is no trifling matter. For anyone who stays alone on the mountainside for forty days the alternatives are clear-cut : either one finds God and therefore happiness, or else one runs away, seized by fear and boredom. Most of the brethren I come across are among those who find God.

And so, I have discovered what light means in the face of a man who stands face to face with the Transcendent.

That this is so should be no cause for surprise – rather the contrary would be surprising – since God is God, and not a wall or a star. What, then, did the sight of this light shining in my brother's face do to me? I will tell you. It gave me a great longing to stay with him, not to go away, to speak of the things of God, and above all to listen, and to go on listening. To look into his eyes, and at his skin which had assumed a transparent quality, and to hear his voice.

Heaven does indeed exist, for here was heaven. It exists already within each one of us when we exist in God.

Enthralled by the light which irradiates from the man of peace,

I wanted to spread it. Meanwhile, experience taught me one thing: that it is not virtue which creates prayer, but prayer that creates virtue. It is very important to grasp this, because generally speaking we are inclined to approach the question from the wrong end. That is to say, we think the results depend on our own efforts, when in fact they depend far more on our long hours of patient and courageous prayer. Whenever a married couple comes to me nowadays in my cell, saying: We are having problems; we do not love one another as we used to; we quarrel frequently. I answer without hesitation: Pray more; improve your relationship with God and you will find that you own relationship becomes easier.

If a young man comes to tell me that he seems to be so weak-willed and feels humiliated by his moral failures, I try to persuade him not to pin his hopes on physical exercise, or yoga, or human considerations, but on grace, on the presence of God, on the Eucharist, and above all on the benefit to be drawn from spending at least some time each day in humble prayer, prayer that is patient and as free as possible from feelings and human imaginings.

In very serious cases of drug addiction, sexual immorality or alcoholism, I have come to have such faith in the efficacy of grace and the transforming power of prayer that I say with complete conviction: Have faith, and if you want to get better, go in for the sun cure . . . !

Yes, Jesus is the divine sun who broke through to heal the world with the supernatural power of the Sacrament.

If you want to be cured, spend one hour every day for an entire year in a quiet chapel, before the exposed Sacrament if possible, stay there like a poor man, repeating slowly: 'Jesus, have mercy on me, a sinner.'

Choose a good priest to be your guide. Make use of this time to study the Bible and the liturgy, but above all stay in the sun; let the presence of Jesus penetrate you through and through, wherever there is rottenness and wounds.

Normally the cures take place before the end of the predicted time.

Some people may smile at this, and for anyone who is unfamiliar with the power of Christ that would be natural, but I can assure you that the difficulty of effecting such miracles of healing has nothing to do with the power of Jesus which is always fully available; rather, it almost always stems from the failure to believe that a cure is possible, or simply from the refusal to be cured at all.

But in order to do this, you will tell me next, one needs faith, and I have so little or none at all. Well, I have a secret I would like to share with you. Only a few will accept what I say, of course, but it is is all the same of the utmost importance. The thought comes from Pascal, and I have put it to the test time and time again.

It goes like this : 'act as if'. I will explain. Are you in trouble, and yet have the feeling that you have not sufficient faith to cope with it? All right then, 'act as if' you did have faith, organize the details of your life as if you lived by faith. You will find that everything will work out in occordance with your desire for faith.

Take another example. You go to pray, and you feel so empty and arid that you ask yourself whether you believe in anything or anybody at all. You feel the urge to get up and go. But no, stay there, 'act as if' you were filled with fervour, live through your prayer with the same determination as if it were a moment of enthusiasm. Above all do not shorten it, do not cut back on the time. Rather prolong it, endeavouring to understand that faith relies on the will and the will on faith, not on taste or feeling. When you finally do get up from your prayer, you will find I have given you good advice.

One more example : you are involved in a sexual relationship which worries you because it has no solid foundations : either you have fallen for someone who is already married, or for someone who has messed up your life and made you the slave of your senses; or, worse still, you have been unfaithful to your consecration to God or have caused someone else to be so, and you feel continually uneasy about it. To mention peace in the context of situations like these which are, unfortunately, by no means few and far between, is like talking about a calm sea when the wind is blowing a force ten gale.

There is nothing to be done.

But there is. There is something you can do to recover your peace and along with your peace the fulness of God. 'Act as if' you possessed utter faith, unbounded hope and endless charity and cast yourself into the fray, not relying on yourself but on the strength that comes to you from your trust in God. 'Act as if . . . '

You will not overcome yourself in a day, but eventually you will succeed in doing so if you rely on deeds rather than words and if you have patience, untiring patience.

If only you could believe! Jesus would say to you.

If only you could stand before me, I, who am the life; beside me, who am the way.

'If anyone believe in me, even though he dies he will live' (Jn 11:25).

Blessed are the peacemakers, for they shall be called sons of God.

That is what the gift of peace means: sonship of God, the authentic and profoundly interior awareness that one has become part of a family which has God for its Father and which already lives 'in heaven'.

I believe this is the ultimate gift that can be made to man while he lives here on earth, his surmounting of the terrible obstacle of fear and death, his definitive victory over the anguish of being, and of dying, alone.

Not for nothing does this truth find its place in the one prayer Jesus himself taught us to say:

'Our Father, who art in heaven,
hallowed be thy name;
thy kingdom come;
thy will be done on earth, as it is in heaven.'

And at the same time it unequivocally stamps out the subtle heresy regarding faith which would separate the Transcendence of God from his Immanence in this world.

Experienced in practical terms this heresy is perennial, but it is particularly prevalent amongst the present generation of Christians.

Either because they have penetrated more deeply the secrets of certain laws of nature and the cosmos, or because they have studied more attentively or with greater awareness the intimate bond that exists between all created things, they end up by denying the direct action of God on those things themselves.

What has God to do with the winds and the sea?

What has God to do with men's physical health, with the fruitfulness of the earth?

They have tended to imagine that, by correcting once and for all certain exaggerations or puerilities of their ancestors, they would thereby discover at least the exact point of insertion of the divine into the cosmos.

They have set about desacralising the universe and 'secularizing' the Church with such enthusiasm! And with great passion they have demolished walls which admittedly were tottering, but which none the less possessed some hidden structures that were still valid.

Take care not to exaggerate and so pass from one extreme to another. In the process of purging the uninstructed old women, who were the last frequenters of so many country churches, of their superstition and childish fideism, do not fall prey to the far greater danger of being unable to recite the Our Father and of ending up, involuntarily perhaps, outside the Church itself.

For how can you possibly repeat the words Jesus addressed to the Father, 'give us this day our daily bread', if you no longer believe that God has anything to do with the productivity of the fields and the rhythm of the seasons.

And as you go into hospital for a serious operation, how will you be able to repeat, painfully but sincerely, the prayer he himself placed on our lips, 'deliver us from evil', when you have become accustomed to thinking and believing that all will depend on the skill of the surgeon alone. Gradually you will stop praying, you will no longer be capable of praying, and even if you have not yet acquired the terrible courage to say that there is no *beyond*, you will certainly no longer be receptive to the message Jesus came to give us, the 'good news' he preached to us, his own poor, and which provides the living inspiration of the entire Gospel.

God is my father!

And if he is my father, he intervenes continually in the affairs of his son.

He concerns himself with the small things as well as the great, he is concerned with bread as much as with health, with my vocation as much as with my death. This is precisely what St Matthew is telling us in the sixth chapter of his Gospel.

'That is why I am telling you not to worry about your life and what you are to eat, nor about your body and how you are to clothe it. Surely life means more than food, and the body more than clothing! Look at the birds in the sky. They do not sow or reap or gather into barns; yet your heavenly Father feeds them. Are you not worth much more than they are? Can any of you, for all his worrying, add one single cubit to his span of life? And why worry about clothing? Think of the flowers growing in the fields; they never have to work or spin; yet I assure you that not even Solomon in all his regalia was robed like one of these. Now if that is how God clothes the grass in the field which is there today and thrown into the furnace tomorrow, will he not much more look after you, you men of little faith? So do not worry; do not say, "What are we to eat? What are we to drink? How are we to be clothed?" It is the pagans who set their hearts on all these things. Your heavenly Father knows you need them all. Set your hearts on his kingdom first, and on his righteousness, and all these other things will be given you as well. So do not worry about tomorrow: tomorrow will take care of itself. Each day has enough trouble of its own' (Mt 6:25–34).

Peace comes from the conviction that these things are true.

Carlo Carretto

Love is for Living

CONTENTS

FOREWORD

When I was about twenty, I had the great fortune to discover the Bible, and I have ever since set this down as one of the greatest moments of my life.

It was to this discovery, I am quite certain, that I owe that spark of spiritual fervour which led me first to an apostolate in the world and then to the contemplative life of the Little Brothers of Father de Foucauld.

The Bible has never let me down. It has given me everything I have needed, stage by stage. It has been with me as my faith has grown from the ardent enthusiasm of youth to the crucible of the desert, in which the soul, deprived of all external help and a prey to the most painful dryness, is twisted and shaken like a leaf in the storm of the Spirit. It is the only book I have always carried with me, and it is the book I wish my brothers to place on my breast with the crucifix and rosary when I am let down into the grave.

But before then – if I have time and if God my Lord wills it – I should like to read it over with those who do not know it, either because they have never bought it or because they have bought it but have been discouraged by the first difficulties. I should like to read it with the simple, the poor, with those who, like myself, have no formal exegetical training but who possess the one thing necessary: the desire to know the book of God.

I confess that this has always been my wish, and I have often dreamed of sitting beside someone and saying: let's start here, and then go on to there, and there, and there; and the pupil learns to walk alone on the path to his discovery of God's word.

Unfortunately little help comes to us from the past.

The Bible was almost a forbidden book. The Church experienced a dark age in which not even Christian families had a love for the Bible and the vast majority of Catholics had almost no knowledge of Scripture.

Happily things have changed, and the strong wind of the Spirit, which blew through the Church at Vatican II, is sweeping against the walls of ancient convents, battering the sacristies of a Christianity reduced to the miserable light of our own shortsightedness and shaking the laity who have remained ignorant of Christ because they were not allowed to read the Bible.

The terrible phrase is not mine, but I have experienced its truth like St Augustine its author: *Ignorantia Scipturarum ignorantia Christi* (He who has no knowledge of Scripture has no knowledge of Christ).

How true it is!

It is even truer in our own day, when so many Christians are forced to reconsider their position with regard to the faith. Taken off-guard by the recent rapid changes in the world, many find themselves asking: 'Do I still believe?' or 'Who is the God of my faith?' The reply is not always easy, especially for someone intent on demolishing the sentimental superstructures of his own religious past, the altars cluttered with saints but empty of sacrifices.

Even when a reply is given, the difficulties do not disappear.

There is widespread anxiety, particularly amongst those who felt they were free from unbelief and who in the past were convinced they had totally resolved the problem of God. 'Do I still believe?' And 'Who is the God of my faith?'

Yes, each of us nas to ask himself in which God he believes: an unmysterious God, the product of his own wishful thinking and need for security, or the God of Abraham who leads us by paths not of our own choosing?

A miracle-working God who keeps us safe and comfortable, or the God of the crucified Jesus?

And if my God is the God of Abraham and the God of Jesus, where have I learnt to look for Him, to know Him, and to love Him?

Have I been satisfied with substitutes, or have I consulted the *real* book, the inspired book, the book which tells me what He is like, what He thinks and says and does? That book is the Bible, God's authentic word.

This is the truth which is daily gaining ground, the conviction Christians are acquiring under the guidance of the Spirit.

I am convinced that because of it we shall enjoy a glorious post-conciliar spring, a feature of which will be the return of Christians to the Bible.

The movement is irreversible, like the liturgical movement, like the rediscovery of love as the soul and fulness of the Christian message to the world.

Assured of the truth of this, I have tried in prayer to walk the paths where the divine wind is most felt. I have tried – if I may change the image – to collect in my little bowl as much of this saving grace raining down on the Church as I can.

How I long to describe God's action in souls, pitiful though my pen is!

How I should like to help even one young person who felt lost in his or her search for the God of Abraham, the God of Jesus. I should say to that young person: Trust the Book that God wrote for our instruction. Take the Bible, put it on your desk, say to yourself, 'From now on I shall make this book my very own; I shall keep it beside me, I shall never stop reading it, I shall try and understand everything God tells me.'

This in fact is the incalculable and irreplaceable value of the Bible: it is God who speaks, it is God who reveals Himself to the soul when the soul in humility and openness scans its pages for God's eternal will.

We must add one last word on the plan of the present work, which might well seem strange to some readers.

Writing a book is extremely simple: all one has to do is put one word after another. The difficulty is to get the book read: times are unsuitable.

It is not that most people are distracted or that Welfare State citizens prefer to look at the television or go to a concert.

The simple fact is that we bore people, we cannot present the things of God satisfyingly.

That is the real reason, and I admit I have no solution.

In the present case, dealing with the Bible, I should have been systematic, profound. But I had a shock. I discovered I was not a theologian, or a philosopher, or an exegete, I was nothing at all, and I should undoubtedly have given up the idea if I had not seen one good trump in my hand: the experience of a life of faith, *my* life of faith. So I thought I would start from there and offer the reader, in the form of daily meditations, what the Bible has told me in faith and continues to tell me in life.

The men of today believe in the value of existence, in the testimony of life, partly because, sometimes without knowing it, they look to the existential experience of others for a reflection of their own. In this they are not mistaken, and the proof is the Bible itself.

The Bible relates the history of God's People on their pilgrimage to the Promised Land. This journey is surely the exemplar of all the journeys of all men. In recounting our own history, we recount that of others: 'There is nothing new under the sun' (Qo 1:9).

But sometimes, reading human history, we conceive a wish to discover what makes it all tick, what lies behind the veil of our existence.

Then is the moment to go in search of it, to leave the guidance of human books behind and commit oneself totally to God's Book.

That is all there is to it.

The following biblical meditations are intended to be like the self-starter in a car. When the reader has come to an end of them, he will have only to engage the right gear, let the clutch in and set off on his journey of discovery into the Bible.

May the Spirit of the Lord give you and me the grace to feel the sweetness of His presence.

CARLO CARRETTO

INTRODUCTION

I wrote *Letters from the Desert** sitting on the arid dunes of the Sahara. They cost me ten years of suffering, and I love them for that. I tried to place myself, naked, poor and alone, in the presence of God's eternal Majesty, totally committed to penetrating the logic of the Gospels, which is inexhaustible. I tried to imagine myself in mind and heart beyond time, to visualize the Last Day, when He the Supreme Judge will come to separate the chaff from the wheat. I felt I was chaff. I could not deceive myself: I did not know what it meant to love.

In the face of Love's judgement I felt enclosed in my own infinite and omnipotent egoism, a freshly-cut log still full of sap, refusing to burn, merely smoking and sizzling.

This was why.

One evening, in the desert, I had met an old man shivering with cold. It might seem odd to call the desert cold, but cold it is: the Sahara has been defined as 'a cold country which is extremely hot when the sun shines'.

Anyway, the sun had set, and the old man was shivering.

I had two blankets with me – indispensable for warmth on a night in the open. Giving him one meant going cold myself.

I was afraid, and I kept both blankets for myself.

I did not shiver with the cold that night, but I trembled before God's judgement on the following day.

* London and Maryknoll, New York 1972.

I dreamt I had been killed in an accident, crushed by the weight under which I had gone to sleep.

With my body trapped under tons of granite but still alive – very much so! – I was judged.

The two blankets, nothing else, were the subject of the judgement.

I was declared unfit for the Kingdom, and I could see why.

I who had denied my brother a blanket for fear of the cold had failed to observe the commandment of God: 'You shall love your neighbour as yourself' (Lv 19:18). I had set greater store by my own skin than by his.

And there was more: I who, having accepted to imitate Jesus in becoming a Little Brother, had received the revelation of Christ, who loved His neighbour not only *as Himself* but, infinitely more, *to death on the cross*, had failed to observe my duty as His disciple.

How could I enter the Kingdom of Love in these conditions? I was rightly judged unfit and requested to remain outside until I had mended my ways. That was how my purgatory began.

In meditation and suffering I had to undergo the two stages of man's religious life on earth: the Old and the New Testaments, the former to convince to me of the truth of the first commandment, 'You shall love your neighbour as yourself', and the latter to impress on me the force of Jesus's words, 'Just as I have loved you, you also must love one another' (Jn 13:34), to the ultimate sacrifice.

In short, I had to learn to give both blankets, the first to show that I loved the old man as myself, the second to prove that, in imitation of Jesus, I was able to carry the sorrows of others.

Stripped of my blankets, shivering with the cold while my brother went warm, I should have entered the Kingdom of Love. But not until then!

I must confess that I was not prepared to do this, I was unfit. I had to start again from scratch, retrace the entire path, trying to understand Jesus's lesson better, trying to see the essence and not just the details of the Law, its spirit, not its letter.

But doing the journey again is no easy matter when one is old and tired and the road long, rough and difficult.

It is so much easier to stay put, or better still to die and so avoid all need to set out. 'Lord, I have had enough. Take my life; I am no better than my ancestors' (1 K 19:4), said Elijah sitting down under a furze bush.

The realization that we are as weak as others, 'no better than our ancestors', is such a shock to our pride that we prefer to die than attempt the difficult path of renewal.

But it is also the discovery of our true poverty, and this, ultimately, is a good and precious thing.

Once we realize we are poor, weak and empty, we can start again and give our lives a new direction.

This is precisely what Elijah did. Strengthened not by his own efforts but by the food left by God's angel, he 'walked for forty days and forty nights until he reached Horeb, the mountain of God' (1 K 19:8).

How I too should like to reach the mountain of God! That is now my only aspiration, my only dream: the mountain of God, the Horeb of contemplation, inner joy, deep endless peace, infinite love.

When I was a novice in the Sahara, the novice-master would occasionally invite us to undertake a period of 'real desert life'. With some bread, a few dates and the Bible in our knapsacks, we left for one of the many caves hollowed out from time immemorial in the spurs of the mountain. We had to live alone with God as far as possible, accepting the suffering of loneliness, the nausea of putting up with one's own company, the effort of arid and often painful prayer.

We had only one book with us, the Bible, because it is the only book worthy to stand open when God is present in naked faith and the soul struggles with him as Jacob struggled at Peniel (Gn 32:23–33).

I should like to set out once more in the same way, with no more than the Bible and some bread in my knapsack. I shall look for solitude for forty days, and I shall travel alone. I shall go beyond time, but without trying to escape that dreadful judgement of Love when I had refused the poor man my blankets: the lesson had to stay with me. It is in any case a journey I shall have to make sooner or later, and it is better to start it now, because *love is for living*.

PART I

If, like Elijah, we wish to cross the desert in search of God's revelation, we cannot afford to wander aimlessly. We have to follow a well-trodden path and commit ourselves with all the strength of nature and grace.

Faith, hope and charity are the shortest and safest path.

Our first seven meditations will be devoted to them.

Chapter One

IMMERSED IN THE LIGHT

Half way on my journey through life
I found myself in a dark wood
Far from the path.

This is how Dante described himself at the age of thirty-five.

Alas, I did not wait so long to enter the dark wood of sin. I was there long before the poet, when I was only eighteen.

But then half way through life I was bathed in God's light, a full searching light which penetrated every corner of my being and filtered through it like sun through the leaves of a forest.

I feel immersed in God like a drop in the ocean, like a star in the immensity of night; like a lark in the summer sun or a fish in the sea.

More: in God I feel like a child in its mother's lap, and my finite freedom everywhere touches His Being which wraps me round tenderly; my need to grow and expand and my thirst for fulfilment are sated every minute by His living Presence.

I can do nothing without Him, I can see nothing except through Him.

There is no creature, thing, thought or idea which does not speak to me of Him and which is not a message from Him. 'Up, up to the outermost point of the universe and down, down to the utter limits of my own nothingness, I see Him.'

The entire universe is a Sacred Host which contains Him, speaks to me of Him and in which I adore Him as both immanent and transcendent, the root of my being, my beginning, support and final end: as *He Who Is*.

God is the sea in which I swim, the atmosphere in which I breathe, the reality in which I move.

I cannot find the tiniest thing which does not speak to me of Him, which is not somehow His image, His message, His call, His smile, His reproach, His word.

> The heavens declare the glory of God,
> the vault of heaven proclaims his handiwork;
> day discourses of it to day,
> night to night hands on the message.
>
> No utterance at all, no speech,
> no sound that anyone can hear;
> yet their voice goes out through all the earth,
> and their message to the ends of the world.
>
> (Ps 19:1–4)

And I feel like singing:

> Bless Yahweh, my soul.
> Yahweh my God, how great you are!
> Clothed in majesty and glory,
> wrapped in a robe of light!
>
> You stretch the heavens out like a tent,
> you build your palace on the waters above;
> using the clouds as your chariot,
> you advance on the wings of the wind;
> you use the winds as messengers
> and fiery flames as servants.
>
> (Ps 104:1–4)

I close my eyes and see God who 'shakes the earth':

> The sun, at his command, forbears to rise,
> and on the stars he sets a seal.

He and no other stretched out the skies,
    and trampled on the Sea's tall waves.
The Bear, Orion too, are of his making,
    the Pleiades and the Mansions of the South.
His works are great, beyond all reckoning,
    his marvels, beyond all counting.
Were he to pass me, I should not see him,
    nor detect his stealthy movement.
Were he to snatch a prize, who could prevent him,
    or dare to say, 'What are you doing?'

(Jb 9:7–12)

How I tremble to talk with Him! I think the world must leap at the sound of his voice. As I contemplate His greatness, I think to myself:

Who was it measured the water of the sea in the hollow of his hand
and calculated the dimensions of the heavens,
gauged the whole earth to the bushel,
weighed the mountains in scales,
the hills in a balance?

Who could have advised the spirit of Yahweh,
what counsellor could have instructed him?
Whom has he consulted to enlighten him,
and to learn the path of justice
and discover the most skilful ways?

(Is 40:12–14)

Everything disappears in comparison with the eternal God, and the greatest things become as nothing:

See, the nations are like a drop on the pail's rim,
they count as a grain of dust on the scales.
See, the islands weigh no more than fine powder.

All the nations are as nothing in his presence,
for him they count as nothingness and emptiness.
(Is 40:15, 17)

Man's littleness is terrifying; and yet since the moment love bridged the gap I desire nothing more than to feel how small I am.

I am Yahweh, unrivalled;
there is no other God besides me.
Though you do not know me, I arm you
that men may know from the rising to the setting of the sun
that apart from me all is nothing.
I am Yahweh, unrivalled,
I form the light and create the dark.
I make good fortune and create calamity,
it is I, Yahweh, who do all this.
(Is 45:5–7)

How odd doubt looks in these moments of light! How could I ever doubt God?

Can it argue with the man who fashioned it,
one vessel among earthen vessels?
Does the clay say to its fashioner, 'What are you making?'
Woe to him who says to a father, 'What have you begotten?'
or to a woman, 'To what have you given birth?'
(Is 45:9–10)

And such greatness is so close to us! Not only close, but in us, around us, because in Him 'we live, and move, and exist' (Ac 17:28).

For your great strength is always at your call;
who can withstand the might of your arm?
In your sight the whole world is like a grain of
dust that tips the scales,
like a drop of morning dew falling on the ground.
Yet you are merciful to all, because you can do all
things
and overlook men's sins so that they can repent.
Yes, you love all that exists, you hold nothing of
what you have made in abhorrence,
for had you hated anything, you would not have
formed it.
And how, had you not willed it, could a thing
persist,
how be conserved if not called forth by you?
You spare all things because all things are yours,
Lord, lover of life,
you whose imperishable spirit is in all.
(Ws 11:21–6)

So much light!

And how easy it is to witness to the light! It is the priestly function of man as man. Upright on earth, I feel that the creatures turn to me so that I can voice their silent adoration of God.

The wind, the fire, the dew and the frost, the ice and the snow, the mountains and the hills, the springs and the seas press on me from all sides. They seem to say: You must not fail in your vocation to speak for us all in the sight of God.

And I pray:

All things the Lord has made, bless the Lord:
give glory and eternal praise to him.
Heavens! bless the Lord:
give glory and eternal praise to him.
Sun and moon! bless the Lord:

give glory and eternal praise to him.
Showers and dews! all bless the Lord:
give glory and eternal praise to him.

(Dn 3:57, 59, 62, 64)

The more I sing God's praises, the more I feel that creatures thank me for having helped them express themselves and that they smile in happiness at my kingship.

I know that by adoring God I am performing a fundamental, eternal act, an act which is an end in itself and part and parcel of my being. It brings me happiness, total, lasting happiness. Nothing is left now but my promise for tomorrow:

I will remind you of the works of the Lord,
and tell of what I have seen.
By the words of the Lord his works come into being
and all creation obeys his will.
As the sun in shining looks on all things,
so the work of the Lord is full of his glory.
He has fathomed the deep and the heart,
and seen into their devious ways;
for the Most High knows all the knowledge there is,
and has observed the signs of the times.
He declares what is past and what will be,
and uncovers the traces of hidden things.
Not a thought escapes him,
not a single word is hidden from him.
He has imposed an order on the magnificent
works of his wisdom,
he is from everlasting to everlasting,
nothing can be added to him, nothing taken away,
he needs no one's advice.
How desirable are all his works,
how dazzling to the eye!
Who could ever be sated with gazing at his glory?

(Si 42:15–16, 18–22, 26b)

Chapter Two

FAITH

It is odd, but none the less true, that too much light can seem like darkness.

If I try and look at the sun, everything goes black.

Nothing could be truer, nothing more opaque, than the existence of God. Nothing could be clearer, more rational, more tangible than the creation of the universe by God, nothing more mysterious. Nothing could be more evident than the eternity of the soul, nothing more painfully dark at the moment of death.

In our relationship with the transcendent God we enter the regions of faith, and faith is dark, obscure, naked and often painful.

Whether we like it or not that is how the matter stands, and as we progress we see it must be so.

'At present we are looking at a confused reflection in a mirror', says St Paul (1 Co 13:12), and no amount of reasoning, however acute, can change that.

Because he is a creature, man is immersed in darkness, in the 'mystery' which is not a lack of light but the reflection of a light which far exceeds him. That light is so 'new' that he is obliged to undergo a gradual education and revelation which will engage his entire existence.

God could add nothing to what He has already done – and does – to explain things better, to make our relationship with Him easier, to convince us more of His existence and Providence.

What could He add to the immensity of the universe to express His own infinity? What would He achieve by making even more splendid the splendour of nature's beauty, or by improving the already staggering perfection of our nervous system and the laws which govern the universe?

Nothing at all.

The beauty, greatness and perfection in which we are immersed cannot exempt us from the act of faith, they cannot substitute for it.

Immersed in the light, we have to cry out, 'I believe in the light'; moved by the perfection of creation, we have to proclaim, 'I believe in Perfection'.

But that is not enough.

The gap between believing in a God who is immanent in His creation, in a God who is, as it were, visible to the naked eye, and believing in a God who transcends His creation is so great that we are forced to accept, in faith, that the transcendent God is unknown, that He is darkness to our human eyes.

He is and will always be – even in Heaven, when we shall see Him 'face to face', as Scripture says – the great Mystery.

However, this God has willed and wills to reveal Himself to man, to make Himself known: life on earth is given to us for this purpose, so is purgatory, so is Heaven. God discloses himself to man in time and in eternity, and this loving gift of Himself to us in the knowledge we can have of Him and in the love with which we shall possess Him will never come to an end. But there will always be something of His *Mystery*, and we shall never tire of contemplating it, of nourishing ourselves on His gradual revelation, of plunging into the sea of His hidden love and luxuriating in the possession of it.

The path and the hour of this knowledge both begin here on earth, firstly in the symbols and signs of creation, then in the lines and veils of Scripture, then in the existential experience of ourselves and the whole world, and finally in the contemplation and transforming union of the mystical life.

All of it takes place under the guidance of faith.

Seen in this context, faith is the certainty and guarantee of this gradual divine revelation; it is the bandage protecting man's sick, immature eyes from the pain of too much light; it is the patient teacher of the infant soul learning to walk without support; it is the instrument of God who knows all and who respects the gradual, logical development of man who knows nothing.

It is the testimony God gives us in Christ to the 'things that are above'; there is no testimony other than this.

Has anyone ever thought of communicating with the transcendence of God by human means? Has anyone ever thought there could be a voice or presence clarifying the Mystery without the need for faith? Yes. Jesus Himself tells us in the parable of Dives and Lazarus (Lk 16:19–31).

For denying the poor man the scraps from his table, the rich man, who 'used to dress in purple and fine linen and feast magnificently every day', went to hell when he died and was there tormented.

In his agony he bethought himself of his five brothers at home and begged Abraham 'to send Lazarus to his father's house to give them warning so that they did not come to this place of torment too'.

Abraham replied that it would serve no purpose: 'They have Moses and the prophets, let them listen to them.'

The rich man insisted: 'They will repent', he said, 'if someone comes to them from the dead.'

'If they will not listen to Moses or to the prophets', retorted Abraham, 'they will not be convinced even if someone should rise from the dead.'

How many times, especially in our younger days, have we thought like the rich man? 'If someone comes from the dead' – no, says Jesus, it would be useless, 'you would not be convinced even if someone should rise from the dead.'

Just imagine what would happen if Lazarus came down

from Abraham's bosom and addressed you from beyond the grave. Imagine he came to you one night, while you were lying alone in bed. Imagine his talking to you, telling you what you should do, etc.

Even before dawn, once you had recovered from your surprise, you would probably be saying to yourselves: 'I had indigestion last night. It gave me bad dreams.'

And after a good breakfast you would carry on living just as before, no better, no worse. And so should I. It would be Father Malachy's miracle all over again.

No, there is no human substitute for *faith*. We cannot avoid *believing*. There is no way round the enormous effort of 'living by faith', not even miracles.

Crowds witnessed the multiplication of the loaves by the lake and 'had enough to eat', but few believed in Jesus, and at the first difficulty in the so-called Discourse on the Bread of Life (Jn 6:32–66) many of His disciples 'left him and stopped going with him'.

Crowds saw the resurrection of Lazarus (Jn 11), but few believed in the Man who had done it. Some even decided to do away with Him because He was an obstacle to their plans.

No, not even miracles exempt us from living by faith, from walking in the faith. They can do no more than help us by witnessing.

Is this assistance rare? Surely it fills the space surrounding us? Is there any creature which does not speak to us of *Him*? which is not His photograph and symbol? which is not an invitation from Him?

Are we not immersed in the sublime, in the immense, in the beautiful, in the perfect, dreaming the most extraordinary dream? Are we not part of an infinite multiplicity continually being reduced to the most fantastic unity? If we look through creation, do we not see *God*?

Is not the immensity of the universe an image of *His* immensity?

Is not He, and only He, the reply to all our questions?

Yes, He is, most definitely!

The problem, however, remains: our relationship or dialogue with God, our discovery of God, takes place in faith and only in faith.

Chapter Three

THE CALL TO FAITH

The paradigm of every call to faith, the most impressive model of every human story about faith, the most stirring pages of man's epic struggle in his dialogue with God are contained in chapters 12 to 25 of the Book of Genesis.

It is the story of Abraham.

> Yahweh said to Abraham, 'Leave your country, your family and your father's house, for the land I will show you. I will make you a great nation; I will bless you and make your name so famous that it will be used as a blessing.
>
> I will bless those who bless you:
> I will curse those who slight you.
> All the tribes of the earth
> shall bless themselves by you.'
>
> (Gn 12:1–3)

This is the mystery of God's 'call', the mystery of our 'vocation'.

It takes place in the darkness of faith, and all human reasoning is powerless to penetrate it.

How did Abraham 'pick up' the divine message? How did John XXIII hear at fourteen the voice which told him he would be a priest? How did each one of us find his path in life?

The answer is: by faith, and that is a new dimension at work in us, one which does not start from reason, one which, while not contradicting reason, surpasses it infinitely because it can reach God: in faith, the soul is invited to establish a living relationship with God, to see Him, listen to Him and speak with Him.

Abraham is the ancestral head of all men of faith, of all those whose lives enjoy this new dimension, who accept the risks and the consequences. He is the founder of the family of believers, he stands at the head of the 'people of God', those mysterious folk who puncture reality and carry on beyond things, who hear the voices coming from the other side, who travel beyond time into eternity, looking for the Absolute, the Infinite, who consider themselves to be exiles on earth, perpetual nomads, who are not satisfied with what they can see but look for the invisible God, who learn to find Him everywhere and who obey Him as a King, as a Tremendous Lover.

In short, Abraham is the model of those who respond to God's call.

That call never ceases: God is always calling, but there are special moments which we record in our memories or perhaps in a note-book and which we never forget.

Abraham did not forget that first summons: 'Leave your country, your family and your father's house, for the land I will show you.' Abram (as he then was) left his country and followed the voice.

> Abram was seventy-five years old when he left Haran. He took his wife Sarai, his nephew Lot, all the possessions they had amassed and the people they had acquired in Haran. They set off for the land of Canaan.
>
> (Gn 12:4–5)

Man's vocation or call is a moment of light, an unexpected gleam in the darkness, a gap in the fog, a star among the clouds, a lighthouse in a storm at sea.

Once the call has sounded, there is no doubt as to which way to go. Some people worry about how the Lord spoke to Abram or St Francis. Such worry is useless as we shall never know. God appears to each individual in the most suitable way to make him understand what is wanted of him, and God is not short of means. To Mary He sent an angel; to Joseph He spoke in a dream, to Moses in a burning bush, to Elijah in the sound of a gentle breeze.

The important thing is that God speaks and the soul listens and understands.

If God did not speak, what other voice could ever reach into our frightful solitude? If God did not call, who would ever rescue us from our nothingness? Our faith rests on the certainty that God is looking for us, that He breaks through our isolation to lead us where He wills, to create our happiness, bring us to our final end, quench our thirst for ever.

Abraham's vocation took place in three stages: a call to detachment; an eternal promise; a severe test.

We have already mentioned the first of these. Abram was asked to leave his country, his people, his paternal roof and travel to a land God would show him. The first thing therefore that God asked of Abram was an act of trust, a gesture of personal commitment.

If it was true for Abraham, it is equally true for us.

We must leave something to follow God, detach ourselves from someone to respond to our call; we must go; and this runs counter to our idle ways and lazy habits.

It is not easy to go when we do not know where we are going, and it is painful to leave loved ones behind. But go we must if we are to respond fittingly to a God who says: Trust Me and Me only.

After that comes the promise:

> 'I will make a Covenant between myself and you and increase your numbers greatly.' Abram bowed to the ground and God said this to him: 'Here now is my covenant with you: you shall become the father of a multitude of nations. You shall no longer be called Abram; your name

shall be Abraham, for I make you father of a multitude of nations. I will make you most fruitful. I will make you into nations, and your issue shall be kings. I will establish my Covenant between myself and you, and your ancestors after you, generation after generation, a Covenant in perpetuity, to be your God and the God of your descendants after you. I will give to you and to your descendants after you the land you are living in, the whole land of Canaan, to own in perpetuity, and I will be your God.'

(Gn 17:2–8)

A promise like this would have meant little to me. I have never wished to be the father of peoples. But to Abram, who so much wanted a son, the promise meant everything, it was the answer to his deepest longings.

How true it is that God creates in us the desire and the satisfaction, the thirst and the quenching stream!

Yahweh dealt kindly with Sarah as he had said and did what he had promised her. So Sarah conceived and bore a son to Abraham in his old age, at the time God had promised. Abraham named the son born to him Isaac, the son to whom Sarah had given birth.

(Gn 21:1–3)

Isaac, son of the promise, grew up among the tents and flocks of the old patriarch. This father's joy, this fruit of his power for love, was as beautiful as a new-born lamb, as pure as milk, and Abraham was moved when he thought of him, his heart jumped for joy. When the great test came, the terrible trial to Abraham's faith, God had only to choose that flimsy piece of flesh.

There was nothing Abraham held dearer than that. God asked for it as the supreme treasure.

It happened some time later that God put Abraham to the

test. 'Abraham, Abraham,' he called. 'Here I am,' he replied. 'Take your son,' God said, 'your only child Isaac, whom you love, and go to the land of Moriah. There you shall offer him as a burnt offering, on a mountain I will point out to you.'

(Gn 22:1–2)

Everything is clear to the believer, everything logical to the man who loves God; a person who is used to listening to 'the voice' has only to obey. Abraham did. We must.

There will be a moment in our vocation when we shall be put to the test, when each of us will undergo, with mortal risk, an extreme trial which engages the whole man to the roots of his being.

Never is a man more of a man than at that moment, never more in God's hands than in that test. To lose that chance of loving is to lose almost all life's value. The very universe is agog to know how man will answer his eternal God.

Rising early next morning Abraham saddled his ass and took with him two of his servants and his son Isaac. He chopped wood for the burnt offering and started on his journey to the place God had pointed out to him. On the third day Abraham looked up and saw the place in the distance. Then Abraham said to his servants, 'Stay here with the donkey. The boy and I will go over there; we will worship and come back to you.'

Abraham took the wood for the burnt offering, loaded it on Isaac, and carried in his own hands the fire and the knife. Then the two of them set out together. Isaac spoke to his father Abraham, 'Father,' he said. 'Yes, my son,' he replied. 'Look,' he said, 'here are the fire and wood, but where is the lamb for the burnt offering?' Abraham answered, 'My son, God himself will provide the lamb for the burnt offering.' Then the two of them went on together.

When they arrived at the place God had pointed out to him, Abraham built an altar there and arranged the wood.

Then he bound his son Isaac and put him on the altar on top of the wood. Abraham stretched out his hand and seized the knife to kill his son.

But the angel of Yahweh called to him from heaven. 'Abraham, Abraham,' he said. 'I am here,' he replied. 'Do not raise your hand against the boy,' the angel said. 'Do not harm him, for now I know you fear God. You have not refused me your son, your only son.'

(Gn 22:3–12)

I cannot think of a more beautiful scene than this.

For all time it remains the image and symbol of Calvary, that other hill on which, carrying the wood of His sacrifice, climbed the One whom the Father's love had given for the salvation of men: Jesus.

And it remains the model for all our trials and victories in faith. Sooner or later we too shall have our supreme hour in which God will ask for our reply to His love and will place us naked on the hill of sacrifice.

It will be the most important moment of our existence; it will sum up all the other moments lived in search of our vocation and in the tension of our faith.

Then will come joy, true and lasting peace, the stability of our relationship with God, the fulness of our earthly experiences, the fitting reply to His loving initiative.

Chapter Four

HOPE

If we have found our vocation in faith, we can begin to live it in hope.

Elijah 'walked for forty days and forty nights until he reached Horeb, the mountain of God' (1 K 19:8), just as Israel had wandered for forty years in the desert before gaining access to the Promised Land.

'Forty' in biblical language, does not refer to a specific length of time; it indicates just a long period. We have a long way to go to fulfil our vocation; the end comes only after a period of effort in which we shall need determination, courage and perseverance. As Scripture says: 'Your endurance will win you your lives' (Lk 21:19).

We can, of course, walk without a vocation and therefore without hope, but that is something quite different. If we are walking without hope, our 'sacred history' has not yet begun. Heraclitus said that 'everything is in motion', and the image of history is the river.

However, it is one thing to be swept away by the current, quite another to swim with it. Best of all one can take a boat. Realizing that one is on the river, discovering the purpose of the journey, letting oneself be carried along and rowing against the current are all quite different things.

Birth, life, work, love, death can be regarded as a meaningless fate, or they can become free and joyful acceptance, ecstatic contemplation, a hymn to joy.

The passage from one to the other is brought about by one's

vocation. That is why faith is important. Without faith there are no answers to the questions of life.

Hope continues in time that initial intuition of faith; it is faithfulness to one's vocation, the strength to live it out day by day, the steady gaze on the distant goal right up to the last day of all.

Hope scrutinizes the horizon, fixes in the heart the features and landmarks of the land to be reached. It is faith's memory.

While blind faith contemplates the incomprehensible God and scrutinizes His will in order to fulfil it, hope brings it into time, and to do this it peers as far as the eye can see, way beyond the edge of the desert, beyond the hills of Moab, beyond Mount Nebo from the top of which God showed Moses the Promised Land (Dt 34:1). And if faith is rare and difficult, hope is no less so.

When the people of Israel left Egypt, things were not easy. Moses found himself with the dramatic, frightful and unenviable task of leading through a parched and unknown country a multitude of about 600,000 men, not counting their families (Ex 12:37), who lost heart at each new obstacle, could not understand Moses and his mania for freedom and would have preferred to stay peacefully behind in Egypt where the pots of steaming meat and the rich aroma of roasting onions assailed the nostrils of men who were slaves at heart as well as in fact.

No, it was not easy.

And as it turned out only two men survived the test: Joshua and Caleb. Not even Moses won through: he was buried outside the Promised Land. Two is not many out of 600,000!

The Exodus is the story of a people chosen by God for Himself, and to some extent it serves as the model for all men and therefore for ourselves. Its stages are the stages of our life, its difficulties our difficulties, its hope our hope.

The main obstacle to the hope of the Israelites as they left Egypt was the Sea of Reeds.

It is not easy to trust an invisible and distant God when over one's shoulder, visible and all too near, is the enemy's army and in front an impassable sea.

That the sea would open up was the unlikeliest idea to occur to the people; but that the sea would then close in on the Egyptian army at the exact moment of their crossing – that was something to talk about.

> 'Then the angel of Yahweh, who marched at the front of the army of Israel, changed station and moved to the rear. The pillar of cloud changed station from the front to the rear of them, and remained there. It came between the camp of the Egyptians and the camp of Israel. The cloud was dark and the night passed without the armies drawing any closer the whole night long. Moses stretched out his hand over the sea. Yahweh drove back the sea with a strong easterly wind all night, and he made dry land of the sea. The waters parted and the sons of Israel went on dry ground right into the sea, walls of water to right and to left of them. The Egyptians gave chase: after them they went, right into the sea, all Pharaoh's horses, his chariots, and his horsemen. In the morning watch Yahweh looked down on the army of the Egyptians from the pillar of fire and of cloud, and threw the army into confusion. He so clogged their chariot wheels that they could scarcely make headway. 'Let us flee from the Israelites,' the Egyptians cried, 'Yahweh is fighting for them against the Egyptians!' 'Stretch out your hand over the sea,' Yahweh said to Moses, 'that the waters may flow back on the Egyptians and their chariots and their horsemen.' Moses stretched out his hand over the sea and, as day broke, the sea returned to its bed. The fleeing Egyptians marched right into it, and Yahweh overthrew the Egyptians in the very middle of the sea. The returning waters overwhelmed the chariots and the horsemen of Pharaoh's whole army, which had followed the Israelites into the sea; not a single one of them was left. But the sons of Israel had marched through the sea on dry ground, walls of water to right and to left of

them. That day, Yahweh rescued Israel from the Egyptians, and Israel saw the Egyptians lying dead on the shore. Israel witnessed the great act that Yahweh had performed against the Egyptians, and the people venerated Yahweh; they put their faith in Yahweh and in Moses, his servant.'

(Ex 14:19–31)

It does not need many such episodes to show the believer what God can and does do for His people. One is enough, and the soul can go back to it in meditation any time it needs to.

Our difficulty is not that we find it hard to believe in such a striking and distant fact. Without going so far as to reject it as absurd and impossible – that would take some courage – we can happily consign it to the limbo of religious memories which have nothing to say to our daily life *here and now*.

No, our difficulty is to hope that similar things – on a smaller scale, perhaps! – can still happen in *our* lives, at a moment of particular difficulty.

For example . . .

But then every one of us can furnish examples.

Sooner or later God leads us to our Sea of Reeds. At first He let us play like patriarchal children under the peaceful tents of youth. The spiritual life was easy, we thought we could do anything, we had only to command and our will obeyed.

Then one day . . . like David we saw Bathsheba bathing, like Solomon we were tempted by wealth, like Samson we yielded to Delilah, like Saul we became jealous, like Judas we fell for the purse.

At that moment we discover our true identity; we realize our radical impotence, our infinite illogicality and confusion. We stand on the shores of our Sea of Reeds.

Shattered by temptation, our peace gone, divided in ourselves as if there were two people and two wills instead of one, we suffer all the reverses our arrogance and limitless presumption deserved. And the Sea of Reeds does not open up. Blows fall in quick succession, eating away the very fabric of our humanity; the noble virtues of which we were so proud disintegrate one by one.

> 'I thank you, God, that I am not like the rest of mankind. I fast twice a week; I pay tithes on all I get . . .'
>
> (Lk 18:11–12)

But now we know we *are* like the rest of mankind, all of them.

It is one of the hardest, most humiliating experiences for the person who thinks himself religious to discover how full of wind, how lacking in substance, his religiousness is.

Isaiah, who was not deceived by the religious observances of his people, had some pertinent things to say:

> We were all like men unclean,
> all that integrity of ours like filthy clothing.
> We have all withered like leaves
> and our sins blew us away like the wind.
> You hid your face from us
> and gave us up to the power of our sins.
>
> (64:6–7)

We recognize the truth of these words – in our own lives. And if God did not continually intervene in man's history, the wind of our sinfulness would blow all humanity away like leaves and destroy it in a few generations.

If the Sea of Reeds is a fact and a symbol in the history of our salvation, each of us can find on its banks not just a symbol or a distant fact but a living reality, Jesus Christ, who came to save humanity from its sins.

He is the 'crossing', the 'miracle', the 'strength', the 'sacrament', the 'life', the 'victory', of that Exodus. As man lies gasping on the banks of his own impotence in the chains of his slavery to sin, Christ comes with a cry of hope: 'I have conquered the world' (Jn 16:33).

'I am the Life' (Jn 14:6).
'If any man is thirsty, let him come to me' (Jn 7:38).
'If any one believes in me, even though he dies he will live' (Jn 11:26).

And if man lets the Saviour touch him and has hope, the miracle happens: the sea parts to disclose dry land.

The impossible becomes possible. David sings his Miserere, Samson pays for his sin in tears, Solomon writes his Song of Songs.

Only Judas does nothing; in the mystery of human abjection, he has not allowed the Saviour to heal him.

He hanged himself and died without hope.

Chapter Five

WALKING IN HOPE

Christ is our hope in the fullest sense of that word. When He comes to us in the Sacrament at the fervent wish of our faith, the impossible comes true, impurity vanishes, violence becomes meekness, madness beatitude, death life.

With Jesus charity starts to flow again in the veins of the selfish man trapped in his horrible frozen cave.

From the moment our lives cross His, the thing is done. He is there on all our 'crossings', He Himself becomes our 'crossing', the continuing passover. This is more easily said than done; so much depends on our faith. And without faith . . .

Some people stay on the banks of the Reed Sea all their lives, unable to believe they can ever get across. Enclosed in their own impotence, they cannot believe in God's omnipotence. All they have to do is believe, and they are paralysed by disbelief.

Faith would smash the waters apart, but without it even God's omnipotence is powerless.

How universal this scene is!

No wonder Jesus cried out against men's lack of faith; no wonder He grieved for their obstinacy of heart.

It is difficult to have faith, it is difficult to walk in hope. The Exodus lasted forty years because the people of God found themselves unable to respond to God's love. They preferred to wander in the desert, frightened victims of their own contradictions and fears. God has constantly to ask: 'Is my hand too short to redeem? Have I not strength to save?' (Is 50:2).

He puts this question not only to those who are afraid to take the first step of faith, the crossing from sin to grace, but also to those who have crossed the Reed Sea, who have witnessed the spectacular miracle, who have tasted the joy of liberation, who have looked behind them and seen 'the pick of Pharaoh's horsemen sinking to the bottom of the sea like a stone' (Ex 15:4–5).

In their minds the memory of that crossing has faded. Faced with the need for another act of faith, another act of hope, they are once more in the grip of fear and hope falters.

They are only a few yards from their Lord, but they refuse to feel His healing touch.

If faith does not bubble up, if hope fails, not even Jesus can complete our crossing.

This will go on for forty years, and it is the story of our contradictions.

What a life we make for ourselves!

Why are we so reluctant to believe? Why are we so afraid of trusting in God?

There seem to me to be two main reasons.

1) We have lost our spiritual infancy.

To believe, to be rich in hope, we must be small, as small as infants in their father's arms. Instead we have grown up, become sophisticated, learnt to judge God by the standards of our own essential weakness.

Jesus tells us that unless we change and become like little children we shall never enter the Kingdom of Heaven (Mt 18:3). It is a solemn thought.

This is why spiritual infancy is the secret of making the jump. If we can make ourselves small again we shall be able to believe and hope, and our lives will become simple, unswerving, full.

We must make ourselves small before God, as small as possible, as small as David who believed absolutely that he could not be beaten by Goliath, as small as Joseph who never disputed the angel's orders, as small as Mary who accepted with unswerving simplicity the improbable betrothal of herself and the Spirit of God, the incredible conception within her of Jesus the Christ. 'Blessed is she who believed' (Lk 1:45): therein lies Mary's greatness – and ours too if we learn to believe and hope.

There is no other test of greatness.

Looking at a piece of bread on the altar and saying, 'That is Christ' is pure faith. Noting and listing all the sins of the people of God and its leaders and still letting oneself be guided by the mystery of the Church and its infallibility is a formidable thing; knowing that our bodies rot in the grave and yet believing in the resurrection of the body is a tremendous last test of life.

The successful candidate is the one who has made himself small and does not treat God's mysteries as though they were coins in his pocket.

2) We spend too much time looking backwards; we make no progress on the path of faith because we are too busy looking over our shoulders.

We are thinking of the fleshpots of Egypt, dreaming of the past. Ezechiel reproached the Israelites with hankering after the slavery of Egypt and failing to follow paths laid down by God on Sinai (23:21–31; cf Hos 11:5). We prefer to stay where we are; we are not quite sure God is to be trusted.

His tastes are not to our liking: He gives us manna instead of solid meat, but we do not learn from the experience of the Israelites who were punished for their greed (Nb 11). Our tastes are sensual. We will happily sell our birthright for a plate of soup (Gn 25:29–34); we ask God for wisdom, as Solomon did, but then wallow in lust (1 K 3:8–9; 11:4); we jockey for positions of trust and leadership, but then sell our souls for a vineyard (1 K 21).

It is the same old story. If only we learnt from it that we are no better than others, that we are too happy to drink the water that poisoned our fathers and listen to the Sirens that betrayed our ancestors! God had other things in store for us; He invited us on quite a different adventure:

'I will betroth you to myself for ever,
betroth you with integrity and justice,
with tenderness and love.'

(Hos 2:21)

It is God who speaks here in words which express the grandeur of His call, the fulness of His love for us.

If only the Virgin of Israel, of whom Jeremiah speaks (18:13) and whom we may take to represent the human soul, would place her hand in God's and, light-footed as a doe and free as a lark, allow God to lead her where He would!

The desert would be crossed in the twinkling of an eye; its solitude would become the ideal place for this infinite love, the bower of a living joy-filled union, the pleasance of the indescribable adventure of love, of our relationship with the eternal, true and infinite God, of our soul's marriage to its gracious Lord!

Instead, what do we find?

Betrayal, adultery, fumbling and hesitation, idolatry, compromises with hell: these lead the soul to the limits of its resistance. Sometimes it looks as if the end has come, and we abandon ourselves to the filthy embrace of Giant Despair.

Hope seems to have been exhausted, only hell is left to listen to our ravings.

Suddenly from the abyss of human misery a force arises which we thought was spent.

It seems to have its origin in the mere instinct for survival, not in a conscious personal act: who can tell where it comes from?

It is a thread of hope!

We start again on the road to the Promised Land.

Chapter Six

LOVE

We are now on the threshold of the great mystery, the source of life, the answer to end all answers: love.

Of what use would faith be on its own? What would be the point of a life lived in hope? What would justify the Exodus, with its discomfort, its long marches, the weariness, thirst and bitter water (Ex 15:22–5), the plague of snakes (Nb 21: 6) and the continual striking camp for new horizons? Love, nothing else.

I set out for love; I am on the move because I am in search of love; I cling to faith and hope because of love.

As St Paul says, 'There are three things that last: faith, hope and love, and the greatest of these is love' (1 Co 13:13).

With light and life love is man's final end and so is identified with God. In John God has defined Himself as Love, and we can therefore confidently assert that our end is love just as we say that our end is God.

And if we look carefully, we shall soon realize that love is a mystery no one can ever define, just like the mystery of God.

We feel love, we experience it, look for it, possess it, but we do not know what it is. Understanding it is beyond us. And yet it 'makes the world go round'! Love is the hinge on which the universe revolves.

Nature comes to life in spring, the flowers burgeon, the animals move, mankind walks – all for love. If it were not for love, the earth would be a lifeless desert, birds would not mate, vegetables would not reproduce, man would remain a lonely being. Without love the universe is unthinkable!

We human beings, however, who share in the life of the created world and therefore in all the different kinds of mineral, vegetable and animal love, are also called to share the life of the uncreated world, the divine life.

While here below we live through our earthly spring and smile at the seasons of time, fulfilling ourselves, urged on by the created love which moves us to food or war, to human kindness, to created good, the divine generosity is at work and the movement towards uncreated love – God – begins. In theological language this movement is called 'charity'; it is the supernatural love for God which begins on earth and is completed in total, eternal union with God hereafter. From birth to death man the microcosm experiences all the degrees of created love, but they cannot ever satisfy him. He knows they are not enough. There is an emptiness in him which cannot be filled by earthly love alone. There is a divinely established tension or drive to a love which is not created, which like God is infinite, eternal, transcendent.

Man thus constituted lives on earth but yearns for heaven; he chooses a wife and is still alone, gives life to children and moves through life unaccompanied. There is something in him which remains unsatisfied, which makes him restless, a perpetual seeker.

He is like a pole looking for the other pole, an abyss in search of another abyss.

Augustine said that the heart was restless until it rested in God (*Confessions* I, I, I). This uncreated Love, this Lover distant but near, this reality which is unknown and yet known already is the goal of man's aspirations, searchings and desires. It is God.

Man gropes for God, and God is a love worthy of man. God is repletion, fulness, satiety, peace, joy, happiness – man's last end and total fulfilment.

Whether it is created or uncreated, every kind of love accomplishes a union or marriage and at that moment gives satisfaction, joy, peace, possession – of a kind. The hungry man looks for food, becomes one with the food and his physical life is satisfied; one heart looks for another and friendship results, one body looks for another and gives birth to life, the mind looks for the truth, finds it and experiences joy; man looks for God, unites himself with God and enters eternal life.

The love of a man and his wife is the clearest image of a universal phenomenon, from chemical reactions to the rotation of the stars, from the life of flowers to the nesting of birds, from the mystic's prayer to the uncreated Trinity.

The Bible calls the history of salvation, Israel's journey from slavery in Egypt to freedom in the Promised Land, a sort of betrothal between the Chosen People and the God of Abraham, the mystical marriage of Israel and Yahweh. The prophets are full of it: Isaiah (54:4–8), Jeremiah (2:2), Ezechiel (16:8), Hosea (2:21) all call God Israel's Spouse. The Song of Songs is the wonderful account of the love between God and His people and, ultimately, since the people is an abstract entity, between God and the human soul. God is the soul's Spouse and says to it:

> How beautiful you are, my love,
> how beautiful you are!
> Your eyes, behind your veil,
> are doves;
> your hair is like a flock of goats
> frisking down the slopes of Gilead.
>
> (Sg 4:1)

He adds:

> You ravish my heart,
> my sister, my promised bride,
> you ravish my heart
> with a single one of your glances,
> with one single pearl of your necklace.
>
> (Sg 4:9)

And the soul replies:

Let him kiss me with the kisses of his mouth.
Your love is more delightful than wine;
delicate is the fragrance of your perfume,
your name is an oil poured out,
and that is why the maidens love you.
Draw me in your footsteps and let us run.

(Sg 1:2–4a)

If only the world knew these things! If only it knew that the search for God is the greatest adventure of love!

If only it could see that the saint is not an escapist but someone who has realized where true love is and will not rest until he has found it!

Yes, the saint has understood before anyone else. He takes a decision, forges ahead towards his goal, impatient with delay: he wants to anticipate Heaven here on earth!

Then after him comes everybody else, including ourselves – at least I hope so, because there is no other way, there is no other goal.

Most people need a longer apprenticeship. They find difficulty in believing that God is right, they wish to see for themselves and in the process get burnt, dirtied, poisoned and discouraged.

Many begin to see the light at the end of their earthly pilgrimage; many more do not begin to until they are in purgatory, the Kingdom of Silence, meditating on their lives, accepting expiation or purification for their errors and cowardice, undergoing the slow and penetrating fire of charity which rids the soul of all disordered attachments, egoism, pride, falsehood, idols.

There is no other possibility . . . unless . . . no, I cannot bear to think of it, let me contemplate love, let me imagine that all of us will believe in love in the end.

All roads lead to God, to contemplation of the Divine Majesty, to possession of the divine goodness. God is waiting for us; He has been longing for the return of His prodigal son.

Chapter Seven

THE PATH OF LOVE

If there had been no sin, things would have been simple, or so at least we limited mortals, victims of sin, like to think.

Man would have steered the course of his life, from the dawn to the twilight of his earthly existence, straight towards God, confidently, without being led astray by will-o'-the-wisps.

The seasons of life, the possession of creatures, the partial vision of things in time would not have obstructed the eternal season of God, the possession of the Absolute and the contemplation of the Transcendent.

Facts are facts, however. There was a break, and nothing has turned out as it might have done.

Here is not the place to embark on the how and why of sin. I am not a theologian, and the theologians have not fully convinced me: there is always something which exceeds our ability to understand . . .

I simply accept the matter. There has been a break, and none of us can doubt it; no one can fail to taste its bitter reality.

Is there anyone who does not feel that *within himself* all is not well?

That there is something wrong, unmanageable, disordered, evil, sick? Who among us does not feel that from the chasm of our being a pestilential miasma rises up, that – to change the image – a twisted, barren root, which withstands the axe of our will and proliferates in our stony field after a single night of inactivity or an hour of inattentiveness on our part, emerges triumphantly from the impoverished soil?

Evil is real, fearfully real, and our existential experience of life is more than enough to convince us of this, certainly more than theological considerations, even though these are accurate (if partial because of our limitations). It is in living and growing old that we perceive the truth about sin, that first calamitous break with God, and feel its seriousness and constant presence.

There is no cancer, however malignant, no septicaemia, no leprosy however frightful which can compare with the gravity and horror of evil.

The people who have had the clearest insight into it are not the hardened sinners filthy with sin but the saints, after years of struggle with it. They blanched merely to think of the obscenities, revolts, blasphemies, violence, evil and perversion it could cover. But even their view was limited.

The face of Jesus – the authentic, unique Saint – went as white as a corpse in the Garden of Olives and then 'his sweat fell to the ground like great drops of blood' (Lk 22:44).

Jesus suffered an agony of soul to see evil – sin, a thick and horrifying crust covering Him – as the Just Judge, the Father of eternal love, saw it at the divine Tribunal.

What a terrible thing sin is, man's rebellion against God, saying no to Love! We cannot really understand it; and therefore we cannot properly understand hell. Hell baffles us: we cannot conceive or express it, our minds are not big enough.

Jesus, however, *could* understand it, and that is why He suffered all a man can suffer and did not flinch from flinging into the scales the whole weight and value of His sacrifice. Our bitter experience of sin's consequences in our life, our many betrayals will perhaps have helped to give us some understanding.

What a tragic vision we should then have of human reality in history: from the Hiroshima bomb to the hunger of the Third World, from populations uprooted by hate and immured in concentration camps to the racial and social turpitude of all centuries, from the Pharisaism of the rich to the debasement of the poor, from the disintegration of the family to the boredom of wealth, from the fading smiles of children to the desperation of the old!

Do not tell me that war is inevitable, or that the world cannot produce enough food for everybody, or that certain races are destined to dominate and others to serve, or that life is life and man cannot escape the law of the jungle.

No, evil is evil, sin is sin, and the biblical image of a forbidden fruit wrenched from the grasp of a loving God in disobedience to His will is the prototype of a reality none of us can dispute because we experience it for ourselves in the depths of our own being.

Yes, I am capable of treating my brothers as Hitler treated the Jews, of dropping not one but a thousand atomic bombs, of committing any sin. I know, because experience has told me.

There is no sin in the world that I have not committed or am incapable of committing, and so we are all one in Adam, and the tragic tree of Eden is the tree of reality under which we rest from the noonday sun while the devil prowls around like a roaring lion looking for someone to eat (1 P 5:8). How true the Bible is!

Our only course is to accept things as they are and start again at the foot of the slope.

Step by step we must retrace the path. Expelled from Paradise for disobeying love, we must return by loving.

Love is the surest guide. This time, you see, Jesus is our leader.

Just as human nature fell in an act of disobedience, so salvation came in Christ's act of obedience. It was not Jesus's sufferings which redeemed humanity so much as His inner attitude of love and obedience to the Father, which was obedience to Light, Love and Being.

We must climb the slope again even though it will not be easy and even though at every corner there is a wild beast to chase us back.

With our hand in Jesus's hand and our eyes on His, we must walk towards the Promised Land as members of God's people.

When I say that it is love that must guide us, I mean all of love.

We must not make the mistake of separating love into human and divine and then concentrating on the latter to the neglect of the former. That would be mistaken zeal.

Jesus Himself told us that the second commandment, which is like the first, enjoins us to love our neighbour as ourself and that the whole Law hangs on these two commandments (Mt 22:39–40). Too often people deceive themselves that they can separate love of God from love of one's neighbour. We are all familiar with the 'disembodied' religious zealot who looks for God and is harsh with his fellows, who takes refuge in prayer and lets his neighbour die of starvation.

He is deluding himself!

Love cannot be divided. If it is genuine it serves God *and* the neighbour in the same act. Or better, it sees God in the neighbour and the neighbour in the heart of God.

This proper balance or identity is not easy to achieve; it is extremely uncomfortable for one thing. But today perhaps more than ever before, when we are more aware of the world's unity and reject with vigour and disgust a Christianity which separates adoration of God from His presence in suffering humanity, the effort must be made.

God is in the man to be saved, and the man to be saved is in God's thoughts. The commandment of love embraces both poles of this relationship.

> Anyone who says, 'I love God',
> and hates his brother,
> is a liar.
>
> (1 Jn 4:20)

If a man who was rich enough in this world's goods
saw that one of his brothers was in need,

> but closed his heart to him,
> how could the love of God be living in him?
>
> (1 Jn 3:17)

Love of God goes hand in hand with love of one's fellow men. We love God in our neighbour and our neighbour in God. And if we do, we are moving towards our full realization as persons in Jesus Christ.

There is a story which I particularly like because it expresses all this so wonderfully. It is the story of St Christopher.

St Christopher – so this story goes – was a giant of a man, a pagan, converted by a hermit. He had great difficulties in prayer: he could not convince himself that God was really there. He became discouraged with the hours of fasting and psalms and kept on asking his mentor when he would see the face of God. The hermit realized that it was premature to force his new pupil to undergo the dryness of prayer and so suggested an easier, more 'human', programme. He asked him whether he knew of a river not far away which travellers found very difficult to cross.

> 'Because thou art noble and high of stature and strong in thy members thou shalt be resident by that river, and thou shalt bear over all them that shall pass there.'

This was equivalent to saying that the face of God was still not clear to Christopher in naked faith and that he would therefore find it in the people he served.

So, equipped with a massive staff, Christopher set to work, day after day, bearing pilgrims across the river . . . until one day he carried over Jesus in the form of a small child. At that moment the pagan giant became Christ-Bearer and discovered the face of God.

Our situation is like that of Christopher. Working and loving our work, building up our family, being part of society and trying to make it happier and juster, loving things, all things, as messages of God, we gradually climb the steps of love to reach up to God.

And when we manage to break through the human, earthly wrapping of life, when we finally succeed in puncturing the appearances that surround us, we shall understand that our efforts to be faithful to love, our patience in bearing ourselves and others have been instrumental in drawing us up to the pure and eternal love of God.

PART II

As we said in the first part, we should not draw any distinction between love for God and love for our neighbour. Both these loves must be lived out together and welded into a single whole.

There are two schools, both created by God for our benefit, which, with steady training, can help us to do this: the family and work.

In the following seven meditations we shall be thinking about these two things.

Chapter Eight

IT IS NOT GOOD THAT THE MAN SHOULD BE ALONE

God is not 'alone', because He is a Trinity. If there were only one Person in God, He would be a solitary figure. God is not solitary: He is Love, and Love is the opposite of solitude.

God is Three in One, and this is a beautiful thing to be able to say; if it were not so, we should understand nothing of God. Perfection does not consist in being one Person in one nature; perfection consists in being three Persons in the unity of a single nature, and God is this perfection.

The mystery of the Trinity is the most beautiful thing we can contemplate and with the mystery of the Incarnation of the Word gives us more than enough to sustain us on our long journey towards Love.

I spend hours on end contemplating these two mysteries, and I never tire of it. I often weep with love and experience an inexpressible longing.

I think of the Father's face, I am enraptured by Jesus's face, I contemplate the face of the Holy Spirit: I believe they are the same thing, but that is a revelation only He can give and He gives it to the creature who asks in love: 'O Lord, reveal Yourself to me.'

The three divine Persons wrapped in the mystery of Their incomprehensibility reveal themselves to me in prayer, and I have no more passionate wish than to deepen my knowledge of Them.

This is eternal life, which we already possess here on earth if we do the Father's will. 'Eternal life is this', said Jesus, 'to know you, the only true God, and Jesus Christ whom you have sent' (Jn 17:3).

A single Person in God would be inconceivable. He would not be God because He would be sad, and God is joy, supreme joy.

God explodes from within the explosive heart of love: He cannot be contained. The person who loves knows what I mean by this and will bear me out. The created universe is under the sign of this explosiveness, this growth, this expansion. They say that it is growing and that new stars are continually being born.

I do not know what God could add which would explain His explosive, loving, creative nature better to us.

Everything speaks to me of this love, this gift, this diffusion of Himself.

From the stars to the flowers, from chemical reactions to the beasts of the field, from the cosmos to man, the command to 'be fruitful and multiply' is stamped into the nature of things, it is the rhythm of the universe, it is the hymn of the galaxies and of young couples going to the altar.

When God looked at the man He had just created, He said: 'It is not good for the man to be alone', and He provided a companion: woman. The creation of woman is beautifully told in Genesis:

> Yahweh God made the man fall into a deep sleep. And while he slept, he took one of his ribs and enclosed it in flesh. Yahweh God built the rib he had taken from the man into a woman, and brought her to the man.
>
> (Gn 2:21–2)

As always in the Bible, the truth is concealed beneath symbols and the signs of words. Adam's sleep is like an ecstasy in which the man sees and loves and desires the creature for whom he searches and whom God Himself offers, the creature who suits him, who will complete him, who will gladden him, who will help him to make the most of himself.

And waking up he sees this creature and exclaims: 'This at last is bone from my bones, and flesh from my flesh' (Gn 2:23).

The biblical account of the creation of woman reads almost like a children's story. It is one, in fact, because basically man will always be 'God's child', and here it is God talking. But it has such a ring of truth about it that beyond the signs of the words there lies the mystery of the deep, unbreakable union of man and woman.

It is God's intention that they should be 'chips off the same block', so that metaphysically a man will not be able to say to a woman: 'Go away, I don't know you, you and I don't belong together.'

No, he will always have to say: 'Bone from my bones, flesh from my flesh' and remain with her; as long as life lasts, he cannot separate himself from his own flesh.

Man therefore must be united with his wife: God wanted it to be like this, and so should we.

'It is not good for the man to be alone': these are strong words. If God says so, there can be no doubt: 'It is not good.'

To live his life properly man must marry. He cannot say too lightly, 'No, I shan't get married, I'll stay on my own.' He would commit a sin if he did, because sin is disobedience to God, to God's will.

Except for higher motives (to which we shall return shortly) or because of some evident impediment (incapacity, illness, destitution), man on earth must obey God's invitation and bear those clear words constantly in mind: 'It is not good . . . it is not good . . . it is not good.'

Why do I put so much emphasis on this?

Because it is necessary to do so. Some men believe they can renounce marriage for no good reason; some suffer from the erroneous conviction that marriage is not one of the most important things in life.

Some even exclude marriage simply because it is not convenient, others for trivial reasons such as not wishing to share their property.

No, to live his life properly a man must marry.

Woman completes man, and man woman. Love fulfils them, makes them better, introduces them more easily into the divine stream of charity, forces them to become open, transforms them.

And it also makes them fruitful. We have said that fecundity is stamped into the nature of things as a sign of God's creativeness, and man is no exception.

Marriage makes man a father and woman a mother, and so sublime is this miracle that we should kneel when we speak of it.

When a father gazes into the innocent eyes of his son, he will, if he looks carefully, see the mystery of the infinite, of the unfathomable, of the ungraspable. He will feel that even though this little body belongs to him, because it was born from his blood, it comes from a distant world, from infinity, from God. God created him at the very moment when man desired a son and in the unity of love saw him as it were issuing forth from the chaos of non-being.

For an instant man has shared in God's creative joy and has touched the infinite. Whenever love is lived to the full, man feels he is touching God, and this is the sole moment in which man on earth can say exultantly, 'For ever'.

People often talk of children as if they were encumbrances, matrimonial 'accidents', undesirable.

Of course, if we are wrapped up in ourselves we shall understand nothing of the fulness of love. We shall look only for the pleasure, and the marriage is organized and calculated with a view to excluding children.

Birth control can be a virtue, a noble sacrifice, a real necessity, but when it is motivated by the egoism of the rich and healthy – who are its main practitioners – it becomes a perversion.

The person who decides to have no more children has left the trajectory of God's explosiveness and is like a rotten branch waiting to consummate its uselessness on the bonfire.

I can understand that a young couple may be obliged to limit the size of their family because of the wife's health, for example, or because they are destitute, or for some other perfectly valid reason arising out of the difficulties of life today, but I cannot see how they could possibly do so with a smile, happy in the knowledge that they have found a means of deceiving life.

No, it is a great sorrow, a sadness, not to see the face of a child that should have been born but now will never be.

A normal, healthy, decent man who still retains some feeling for God should want children, a lot of children. A woman even more so.

Pharisaism, which has been with us in every age, urges us, almost unconsciously, to put a higher value on the sexual act than on the intention, and in some people's morality the only worry is to avoid contravening the law.

Because everything has been done according to the letter of the law, with a calendar in hand, some couples manage to have no children without offending morality; but the result is an unfruitful life.

And if their lives are unfruitful, who will save them from judgement?

Will God analyse their acts and overlook their lives?

Will he not rather call them 'hypocrites', as Jesus called the Pharisees, or better still, 'whitened sepulchres'?

Chapter Nine

LIFE TOGETHER

The purpose of marriage, however, is not only to give birth to children – although that on its own is a thing of divine beauty. It is also designed to fulfil the marriage partners. The matrimonial union does not concern only the generation to come: it should also be seen as a divinely willed means to fulfil, reconcile, cheer, sustain, improve the man and the woman.

This fulfilment is brought by love, it is realized in love.

Here we could apply Augustine's famous 'love and do what you like', in the certainty that if the partners really love each other they will find in their mutual relationship the path, the pointer, the ladder to another love which should develop in every creature on earth and take it later to perfect union with God. I should say that matrimonial love – for those whose vocation is marriage, that is, for most of mankind – is the beginning, the pattern, the blueprint, of love for the Absolute in which, beyond time, we shall all be absorbed.

Marriage partners who love each other find that love synthesizes their relationship. Life together becomes easy in love; it becomes easy to understand, bear with and excuse each other. It even becomes easy to sacrifice oneself for the other.

Love in marriage ultimately helps a man to leave the dark cave of his egoism and the constant danger of returning to himself and to become open to creation and so to God. I have seen impossible youths – timid, introvert, unmanageable – suddenly become gentle, open, altruist in the warmth of a girlfriend's love. It is like seeing a dead branch fill with sap and bud at the approach of spring.

Love is an all-the-year-round spring!

We can never sufficiently express the benefits of love, especially on the sick, the timid, pessimists, egoists, difficult cases.

No medicine is so powerful as genuine love.

Everything mends and comes to life; and instead of lapsing into an empty, sterile melancholy, we set off with enthusiasm as if life had started to flow through our veins again.

Saved by love, we find in it the joy of life, application to our work, dedication to an ideal, and under its inspiration we can at last devote our lives to something worthwhile!

Love, truth, is God's finger laid on man's heart.

Furthermore, such an intimate and radical life for two as marriage imposes sets man on the path to self-discovery. In his partner's eyes he sees himself as in a mirror, with all his mystery and unfathomable depth.

It is fatal if love does not survive this discovery. We have to realize that in ourselves we find not only positive aspects but negative aspects too. We uncover weakness, limitation, mediocrity and even, unfortunately, evil. At this moment a new love, more mature, more realistic, more subtle, must come to the fore: we mean *mercy*, *compassion*, a degree of love which should fill the waning years of our life on earth.

It is all too easy to love one's partner when she is young and wrapped in mystery; much more difficult when one discovers her ugliness, limitations, slovenliness, egoism. If a man cannot survive the crisis precipitated by this discovery with the love of mercy, he is sowing the seeds of future difficulties; he is entering a tragic stage in his marriage.

If, on the other hand, he remains true to his love and sees his own sin and weakness in his partner's, he becomes accustomed to facing the truth, and his life enters a new phase animated no longer by feeling or emotion but by true and genuine love.

Then, when the family has grown to three or more, the school of love takes on an unsuspected, almost total plenitude. There are times – unfortunately rare because original sin is an ever-present reality – when we begin to wonder whether Heaven has not come down to earth.

The father-mother-child relationship approaches the summit of love.

It is a competition to feel others' lives more precious than one's own, and, to be faithful to this stimulus, we can – albeit still on a natural plane – approach the degree of love Jesus showed and which He called in the Gospel 'His commandment'.

'Just as I have loved you, you also must love one another' (Jn 13:34), that is, to the point of sacrificing one's life, which is the highest degree of love. And here I must make my confession: I was unprepared under the great rock when I dreamt I was dead and was being judged by God. As I told the reader earlier, I had abandoned the world and my affairs to look for God alone. I had gone into the desert to strip myself and to learn to love those poorer than myself. And yet on the night it was cold, I denied a poor old man a blanket. I was afraid of shivering in the night.

Would you believe it? To show me my own insignificance and to coax me into the ways of that truth which we call humility, God lay in wait for me.

Some months after the episode of the blanket which I had refused to give to Kadà – the poor man in the desert – a medical lieutenant of the Foreign Legion said to me: 'Brother Carlo, if you are going to Tazrouk, visit the camps at Uksem: there you will see some really poor people.' Without thinking that God was trying to teach me something new, I set out to visit the camps as soon as an opportunity presented itself.

I arrived at dawn one morning and it was still cold. I was taken near a tent apart from the others in which a woman was dying.

She was a black slave, unmarried but with a tiny little boy.

I went into the tent and stood aghast at the indescribable squalor.

The poor woman was lying on a mat of dried grass, shivering. Her only bedclothing was a piece of blue cotton cloth (blue being the typical colour of the Tuareg tribe who 'employed' her). It was in tatters and could have afforded her no warmth. At her side lay the child in half a woollen blanket.

Even in the face of death, this poor woman had preferred to go cold while her child had all the warmth she could offer.

She was not a Christian, her 'employers' forced her into prostitution, she counted as absolutely nothing, she was dying as the real poor of the Third World die. But she had expressed perfect love for her son: she had loved him to the point of sacrifice and with such simplicity as if it had been a matter of course, a thing of no importance.

I felt as dry as the sand in the desert, humiliated by a divine sublimity which this woman had lived in unadorned nature but which I had not learnt in the superiority of grace.

God was there in that infinitely poor tent. He had managed to persuade that person, loved and respected by no one, to accept an act worthy of Jesus's love on Calvary: the simple, unprotesting gift of self.

Chapter Ten

THIS IS WEAKNESS, NOT LOVE!

It is evening, any one of countless typical evenings.

Dad has come home from work and is now happily reading his newspaper comfortably ensconced in an armchair. Mum is in the kitchen preparing the evening meal, and every so often, taking care not to interrupt unnecessarily, she asks how the day went or gives her own small items of daily news from the neighbourhood.

The atmosphere is peaceful and relaxed.

Until . . .

An intruder enters the camp.

Two feet high and still uncertain whether to be a biped or a quadruped, he leaves his corner where he has been engrossed in smashing the last of the toys showered on him by doting parents, crawls over to his father's chair and with a wild snatch rips the paper from his father's grasp.

The room is charged with tension. Mum interrupts her work to remove the little nuisance and take him back to his toy (thrown to the wild beast, dedicated to the sacrifice, for love of peace). 'Come on, you naughty little thing,' says Mum in a vague tone, 'leave Daddy's paper alone.'

Dad patiently gathers up the bits, looks at his wife as if to say that it is all her fault for not training the child properly and then resumes his reading.

Not many minutes go by – just enough for the toddler to summon up strength again – and here he is crawling towards the evening's prey: Daddy's paper.

There comes another tug, more eyes raised in exasperation, another quick lift back to the corner.

It is evident that the peace is ended and war declared, no holds barred. On one side there is a combatant who wants to win and knows he can, on the other two combatants who are at their wits' end and wish just to establish a truce.

This time the attack recommences immediately, without even a pause for breath. It being such fun to pull, the little horror tugs on the end of the tablecloth.

The result: three broken glasses, a lot of noise and, much more serious, the shattering of that fragile peace.

'Can't you control that child . . . I come home after a hard day's work and all you can do . . .'

'Now look here, I have him all day long, you don't help, and instead of taking an interest in the child you simply go out in the evening.'

'Right, I'm going.'

And he has a snack in a café.

My only wish is for that young couple, victims of an age like our own in which the institution of authority has crumbled, in which parents bring their children up like savages for fear of creating complexes, in which, out of a mistaken concept of love, they no longer have the courage to administer punishment, to read quietly to themselves this passage from the Bible:

> A man who loves his son will beat him frequently
> so that in after years the son may be his comfort.
> A man who is strict with his son will reap the benefit,
> and be able to boast of him to his acquaintances.
> A man who educates his son will be the envy of his enemy,
> and will be proud of him among his friends.
> A horse badly broken-in turns out stubborn,
> an uncontrolled son turns out headstrong.
> Pamper your child, and he will give you a fright,
> play with him, and he will bring you sorrow.

Allow him no independence in childhood,
  and do not wink at his mistakes.
Bend his neck in youth,
  bruise his ribs while he is a child,
or else he will grow stubborn and disobedient,
  and hurt you very deeply.
Be strict with your son, and persevere with him,
  or you will rue his insolence.

(Si 30:1–3, 8–9, 11–13)

These are the words of Eternal Wisdom, because the Bible is the word of God, and even if we have to interpret them, bring them down to our level, which is not high, and apply them to our situation, which is always unstable and mutable, we cannot fail to find in this passage a clear, precise exposition of the educational relationship that should exist between parents and their children.

The mentality that has grown up in the last decades, which have been an age of transition from a past that is still not dead to a future that is not yet mature, is decidedly incorrect, or better, unbalanced.

Just as democracy has replaced absolute rule 'from above', an education of 'love' has replaced the authoritarianism of the past.

But since man is by nature unbalanced, he has simply substituted one exaggeration for another. Excessive intransigence has given way to licence; instead of commands there are invitations, instead of punishments caresses.

It was once said that democracy is an appropriate gift to mature peoples, just as freedom is a proper bequest to responsible people.

The mistake, however, is to think that I can offer democracy to the immature, freedom to irresponsible children. The parent has a *duty* to educate, lead by the hand, guide and punish because the child is not mature, he cannot yet do things for himself. His mother and father supply the strength he lacks, the judgement he lacks, the light he has yet to acquire.

The child has a *right* to be educated, supported, corrected, punished. Otherwise there is chaos – for the parents and, worse still, for the child himself.

In the episode with which we began this meditation, what went wrong? In my opinion the mistake lay in the fact that the parents were afraid to make the child suffer; they could not bring themselves to punish him; they were terrified of seeing him cry. It is not that they did not know what to do. Nothing is simpler, especially when the child is three or four. Stay where you are without being a nuisance – play properly as you should do – don't touch this or that – get up, sit down, like this – don't interrupt when others are speaking – and so on.

The trouble starts when parents fail to apply their educational programme: they yield in the face of disobedience, they give in to tantrums, they accept the child's point of view. In short, they adopt the child's programme, which is irrational and arbitrary.

In particular they have no idea how to punish. From a mistaken idea of love, they cannot bear to hear the child cry, they are afraid that punishment is harmful, they think the child should be always smiling and satisfied.

Their mistake here is colossal. The child needs to cry; he longs to be punished, to be bent, to be put right.

Punishment is a solid and nourishing food which he cannot do without: the sense of justice deep in his nature demands it.

Punishment liberates him. It releases the pus from the boils. It makes the child laugh when all is over and the operation is successful.

Listen to the Bible again:

> Do not be chary of correcting a child,
>   a stroke of the cane is not likely to kill him.
> A stroke of the cane
>   and you save him from hell.

(Pr 23:13)

Parents should have the strength to bend their child's sick will because of the love they have for him. It is for love that they must be the masters, he the subject.

Out of love for him they will make him cry.

If they accept the child's will, what are they doing in fact? They are accepting a fatuous, senseless thing, something Scripture calls 'folly':

> Innate in the heart of a child is folly,
> judicious beating will rid him of it.
>
> (Pr 22:15)

How angry I get when I see parents laughing at the stupidities of their children! How can they go along with such senselessness? How can they tolerate such obstinacy and capriciousness? I have witnessed evenings poisoned by the presence of one or two horrible children who, appreciating their parents' weakness, rampage like unchained beasts with the sole purpose of asserting their nascent personalities, vain and empty even at this early stage.

I have seen families in a state of war simply because the children have not been fortunate enough to have a mother or father with an iron fist – or at least a determination and ability to make for a goal which must be reached at all costs.

Let us be quite clear that it is not just a question of punishing, of hitting out, as if education were like rearing cows or mules.

The parents have to achieve what must be achieved, whatever the price.

Some children need only one good hiding all their lives; others might need only a stern look.

The important thing is that the child knows that he and not his parents must give in. This is especially true in infancy, which should be the most favourable age for laying the foundations of a proper education. The French call it the years of *dressage*.

Later, as the child grows, he will be given more responsibility and invited to cooperate instead of just undergoing education – this is particularly true of the crisis of adolescence – but the duties of those who have received from God and nature the mission of leading him to the threshold of maturity are indispensable to the end.

These observations affect not only the education of the children but also the unity and affection of the parents.

Too often the marriage begins to crack, harsh words to be bandied about, simply because of the partners' inability to bring up their children properly or because of their disagreement over how to do so.

'It's up to you.'

'You're just weak.'

'What are you doing while I shout myself hoarse?'

'It's too easy to give orders to us women while you men go off without ever lending a hand.'

And because we are basically sinful, we always end up by blaming the other person.

And in blaming the other person we do not realize that we are digging the first spadefuls of that bottomless pit of evil: lack of love.

Chapter Eleven

MAN AND WORK

As the bird is made to fly and the fish to swim, man is made to work.

Work is man's natural element, and his life on earth would be inconceivable without it. In work he fulfils, completes and expresses himself as well as expressing, fulfilling and completing creation.

We could say that God created a world that was unfinished. He intended to invite man to cooperate with Him in His work of completing creation: man would become God's associate in realizing the divine plan, in making the divine will effective.

By his work man puts the finishing touch to creation, he improves and adorns it.

Take an uncultivated hillside: nothing but brambles, thorn-bushes, twisted trees. There is a wild olive-grove: the leaves are small, dry, the fruit desiccated.

Along comes man.

He seems to caress the trees with his work. He cuts them back, tidies them up, grafts on new stock, manures the ground. After a time the olive leaves have softened, the berries have become succulent, the very branches seem to stretch out at peace, more harmoniously, more truly themselves.

The wild hillside is transformed into a rich olive-yard: the 'after' is better than the 'before'.

We could say that man is not 'alone' in his work, that God Himself works through him: and that is true.

God, immanent in creation, works with creation to effect His plan and makes use of everything, including man.

How mysterious God's work in the world is!

Too often we have an anthropomorphic concept of God; we think of Him in crude physical terms. We imagine Him to be detached from creation, whereas the catechism's phrase to the effect that 'God is immense' should draw our attention to the reality of the situation. God is here, He is there, He is everywhere; He is in me, in the olive-tree, in everything. He is the root of Being, He is the Being in which everything shares.

What a stupendous mystery!

However, returning to our main theme, we can say that God thought and willed man like this and in calling him to life called him to work.

Seen in this 'theological' light, work is indispensable to man because God's plan incorporates it.

God's hand calls to beauty in the hand of the artist; desires the unity of the human family in the hand of the technologue; desires bread for His children in the hand of the workman.

God is in all men's work and in all people of goodwill. No discovery of man's is absent from God's mind, no technological achievement is possible without His divine will for good.

Yes, work is indispensable for man.

It could be objected that prayer, not work, is 'indispensable'. We are made to pray, not to work, it is urged. The objector would like to be thought pious, but in fact he does not realize what he is saying.

His idea of prayer is too abstract, too angelic. The Benedictines, who were great contemplatives, and the Trappists, who are familiar with the strenuous efforts required by prayer, divide the day into three sections: seven hours of work, seven of prayer, seven of sleep.

The rest is devoted to cementing these three sections together.

If a person says that 'we are made for prayer', he is obviously unaware, perhaps because he has never tried it, that one cannot pray for twenty-four hours on end – not, that is, without going mad.

The person who prays, particularly if he prays a lot, needs

work to give balance to his day and rest to restore energy to his hours of prayer.

No one can spend all day in church – unless, of course, we wish to produce sick and unbalanced minds.

In the first chapters of Genesis we read: 'The Lord God took the man and settled him in the garden of Eden to cultivate and take care of it' (Gn 2:15).

This brief biblical text is extraordinarily instructive and should be engraved in everyone's thoughts.

A question springs spontaneously to mind: is man obliged to work? The answer is clear and applies universally. Except for very special reasons, man is obliged to work. God gave man work before sin, when the earth was still a 'garden of Eden' and Adam was still at peace with himself and with God.

God's original plan was for man 'to cultivate and take care of' the land. In His Wisdom He decreed at the very beginning: 'Let us make man in our own image . . . let them be masters of the fish of the sea, the birds of heaven, the cattle, all the wild beasts and all the reptiles that crawl upon the earth' (Gn 1:26).

The command is unmistakable, and ignorance of the texts is no excuse for excluding it from our lives.

If someone says, 'My father has left me a considerable fortune; I've enough to live on for the rest of my life and so I needn't work; in fact I shan't work, I shall live a life of total ease', is he justified? No, he is not. He is in a state of sin, continual sin. Work is not merely a means of earning bread and butter with which one may dispense if there are alternative sources of income, it is much more: it is a divine commandment, a service to humanity, a duty of man on earth and finally, as we shall see, a redemption from sin.

Our puritan and bourgeois education is a funny thing: we're terrified of seeing our daughter come home pregnant.

But we rarely ask her: are you working? have you made yourself useful today? are you an idle little teenager spending God's hours listening to records on the bed, just killing time?

In this we have to admit that we are the heirs of an age in which Christianity itself was infected by pagan culture and a pagan mentality.

The nobles, even Christian nobles, considered work unworthy of their lineage, and the rich bourgeoisie regarded it as no more than an instrument for accumulating wealth.

Of course they never wondered whether they were free not to work because they had no need of money; whether they could live on private income and be obligated to no one!

I have to say that I have never heard a sermon in church against those who live on private means even though they are young and fit!

But I was saying that even the Christians' way of life has been infected by the pagan attitudes of previous eras.

Let me give you an example which caused me much grief during the critical period of the worker-priest experiment. With my own ears I heard from informed Christians phrases such as 'The priest should not be working. It will damage his dignity.' Sentiments like this reveal the extent to which the mentality of the pagan world has infiltrated the Christian ranks and the extent to which we have departed from the evangelical spirit.

How could someone with the effrontery to speak like this never have paused to consider that Jesus, the Eternal Priest, spent thirty years doing manual work? Was that beneath His dignity?

What does dignity depend on anyway? Expensive clothes? A fat bank balance?

My Jesus, how far have Your followers wandered from Your example!

They forget that You, Son of the Most High, bridge between heaven and earth, the most extraordinary Man who has ever lived on earth, eternal judge, Incarnate Word, did work with Your hands which they would consider beneath Your priestly dignity!

What a terrible thought!

Chapter Twelve

WITH SWEAT ON YOUR BROW SHALL YOU EAT YOUR BREAD

An aspect of work we have yet to consider is that it is *redemptive*.

If it is true that work is the means by which man participates in God's creative work, an instrument of harmony and beauty, the fulfilment of wonderful plans all contributing to the unity and happiness of the human family, it is also, and will remain so until the end of time, 'redemptive'.

Not for nothing did God tell Adam after his sin: 'With sweat on your brow shall you eat your bread' (Gn 3:19).

Before the disorder introduced by sin, work was a joy; sin brought effort, suffering, toil. From then on work has been redemptive, helping man to free himself from evil, to pay his debts with justice, to be responsible and useful, to collaborate day after day in his own salvation. And here I am not talking to those whose work is governed by the harsh necessity of procuring 'daily bread', especially when it is scarce and uncertain.

I feel unworthy to do so, especially now that I witness the daily drama of poverty as a Little Brother among the poorest of the poor. I have seen people who have had no choice (and that is perhaps the most painful part of it) but are forced by penury to take any work left on the market: heavy, dirty, badly paid, brutalizing. I have seen men at the bottom of mines crucified by the dust that corrodes the lungs and the continual damp which swells the joints and leads to old age at forty! men bent under the African and Asian sun, on the roads or in shipyards, with picks and shovels which hour by hour become instruments of torture, under-nourished, dirty, joyless, living in lonely huts at night far from their wives and children. How you redeem the world, you poor workers! How you bear the heavy privilege of the cross!

No, I shall not speak to you. I am lost in admiration, and I kneel before such suffering! I shall speak instead, in your name, to those who are not forced to work for their daily bread, either because they have enough money in the bank or because they receive enough charity, and I should like to remind them, in the name of the others, that the Lord's command to work applies to everyone, including them.

You cannot exempt yourselves merely because you have no need of food. Blood corroded and poisoned by sin flows in *your* veins too, and nothing is more harmful to virtue and Christian asceticism than idleness and ease, nothing more hurtful to holiness than sloth. If you do not make an effort, if your brow does not sweat, you cannot live the Gospel: do not delude yourselves! Do not try to escape the cross: you cannot!

In many Catholic circles today, there is a sort of panic in the face of the difficulties of the young to fulfil their vocation or resist temptation or live in charity. The young sit for hours on end with their bottoms glued to a chair in front of the television, they get up as late as possible in the morning, they live lives which lack nothing and from which sacrifice is totally absent, and they expect the problems of the evangelical life to be solved! How can they be? Is Jesus's teaching no longer applicable today? 'Anyone who does not carry his cross and come after me cannot be my disciple' (Lk 14:27) – does this not apply to the Christians of wealthy countries? of the well-off continents? I have no hesitation in asserting that consumer society is a far greater danger to the Christianity of our time than communism, which is much deprecated and combated. Even though communism might impose its hard cross on men and deprive them of their freedom, it might do less harm to a way of life which, because it is based on hedonism and opulence and banishes the cross completely from people's homes and from the streets, threatens to deaden Christians' wills and turn Christians into baptized pagans.

We must keep watch and be vigilant. This means respecting God's word.

Only God's word does not pass!

And if God tells us that we must eat with 'sweat on our brow', well, we have to make sure we do.

Can an athlete hope to breast the tape without effort? Can a champion hope to win if he is not prepared to sweat for it? And is virtue easier than a race? charity more easily attainable than an athletic prize?

Modern civilization has taken away the sweat of previous centuries with its scientific advances. The car enables us to avoid tiring journeys on foot, the washing-machine the drudgery of scrubbing clothes, the aeroplane tedious journeys by train or boat: we no longer raise a sweat.

The Christian, however, who knows he must sweat, looks for new ways of doing so, so as not to escape the Lord's warning.

Why should cleaners and domestics be employed in colleges and seminaries and religious houses to sweep, wash and serve?

Even in novitiates I have seen the novices waited on by poor people who are often very badly paid. It is anti-Christian and a scandal.

Would it not be much better to share the work out among the young men themselves, accustom them to tidying their own rooms, keeping the house clean, organizing their meals, peeling potatoes?

Of course they would lose out on aesthetics, but they would gain in humility and charity.

A religious community has to find work for its members to keep the spirit in training and preserve humility. It should return to the rule of the first monks whose *ora et labora* expressed a proper emphasis and who could show the world rough hands soiled with hard work.

It seems to me that at meal times the religious should ask

himself, like any other man: 'Have I earned this bread? or am I living off other people's work – or worse, off the alms of the poor?' Things would certainly change then, and the world would learn from us the value of work and its importance in the economy of salvation.

Manual work, of course, as it is commonly understood, is not the only way of raising a sweat. When I returned to Europe from the Sahara, I found two young couples in Paris who had decided to work in the Sahara: a doctor and a social worker, a teacher and a nurse.

Instead of working in Paris they had decided to work together in Third World countries. They will undoubtedly 'sweat' more than in France, but it is equally certain that their Christian way of life will be a lot easier and happier.

People are already worrying about the time, now not far off, when our mechanical civilization can offer everyone not just one day off a week but two or even three. What shall we do with so much free time?

Congress follows congress, and apocalyptic voices are raised in warning as if we had reached the world's end – when not knowing what to do men will go mad or at least collapse into a state of nervous exhaustion. I hope only that amongst the multitudes of pagans who add to their cars a private yacht or plane there will still be some Christians capable of occupying their spare time in working for others. Nothing to do? Then I suggest you take a look at the outskirts of our cities.

That is where the refuse of life's great sea ends up, even in our prosperous consumer states. It is difficult to know where to begin, there is so much to be done, so many wounds to soothe.

Where do ex-prisoners go? How do ex-prostitutes live? Where are the rivers of subnormal people hidden? Have you ever visited mental hospitals, old folks' homes?

Have you never gone into the slums? Or into deserted country hamlets where only the old peasants are left, most of them incapable of work in the fields? Time on your hands?

Have you never thought, out of love for Christ, of spending a day – just a day – with an old peasant to help him cut his corn on the hillside because he cannot afford a mechanical mower? Time on your hands?

Has it never occurred to you to spend a day in the dirtiest house in some village helping the poor woman get a bit straight and giving her a chance to catch her breath?

What is that in comparison with the ocean of evils washing over humanity? Nothing, practically nothing. But it is an act of love like Jesus's death on Calvary, and an act of love can achieve a lot. If nothing else, it can give you a bit of true peace and the world the impression that hope is still possible.

Not much?

I think it is.

Chapter Thirteen

LOVE EVERY CREATURE

Bless Yahweh, my soul.
Yahweh my God, how great you are!
Clothed in majesty and glory,
wrapped in a robe of light!

You stretch the heavens out like a tent,
you build your palace on the waters above;
using the clouds as your chariot,
you advance on the wings of the wind;
you use the winds as messengers
and fiery flames as servants.

You fixed the earth on its foundations,
unshakeable for ever and ever;
you wrapped it with the deep as with a robe,
the waters overtopping the mountains.

At your reproof the waters took to flight,
they fled at the sound of your thunder,
cascading over the mountains, into the valleys,
down to the reservoir you made for them;
you imposed the limits they must never cross again,
or they would once more flood the land.

You set springs gushing in ravines,
running down between the mountains,

supplying water for wild animals,
attracting the thirsty wild donkeys;
near there the birds of the air make their nests
and sing among the branches.

From your palace you water the uplands
until the ground has had all that your heavens have to offer;
you make fresh grass grow for cattle,
and those plants made use of by man,
for them to get food from the soil:
wine to make them cheerful,
oil to make them happy
and bread to make them strong.

(Ps 104:1–15)

This psalm is the poem of creation and one of the most beautiful poems. We should sing it often and add so many other verses of our own: what our eyes have discovered, what our love has fixed on. The poem should never end.

If only our hearts were always tender and our souls fresh when we look at creation! What a source of joy it would be on our pilgrimage!

We can pass by and see, or we can pass by and not see: it depends on us.

Creation is like a message written on things, a story told in symbol, a source of conversation for our souls.

But we have to learn how to read, listen and converse.

We are in constant danger of our hearts turning to stone, either with old age or with the petrifaction of sin: and then it is goodbye to our hymn, goodbye to our conversation!

We become the deaf mutes of the Gospel, and in that case only Jesus can cure us.

Loving nature, conversing with nature, is not something extraneous to our love for God: it is a part of it, an essential ingredient.

God speaks to us, teaches us, gives us His first revelation, in the symbols of the created world. Later we shall receive the revelation in word and later still a direct, personal revelation from God, but things still continue to reveal God, as God Himself intended, and we cannot forget it.

Not to look at nature, not to love it to the full, is to refuse to read a document God has specifically composed for us in His love.

St Francis thoroughly understood this truth and made it his own, very particularly his own, and he managed to write that masterpiece of love, the *Canticle of Creatures*: 'My Lord be blessed for all His creatures.'

There is more, however, much more, and it is perhaps our own time which is discovering it. The universe is not only a means whereby God reveals Himself to us, a sort of document in which the Creator explains things to man, but a reality which contains Him. I can even say that it is a kind of Host concealing God Himself under a mysterious veil.

God is *immanent* in His creatures, He is *immense*, He is everywhere. I used to think this was only a catechism answer.

But now I feel it for myself, much more deeply, much more intensely.

God is in nature, God is in matter: matter is divinized, vivified, by God's presence. Now that I know these things I no longer kick stones about as I used to as a child; I have a greater understanding of the Orientals who wish never to do violence to nature because they respect it too much as mediating God's presence.

Perhaps the medievals' love of and attachment to the divine Transcendence has helped us forget that God is also immanent, that He is everywhere. It has created in the past a western religious concept which takes little or no account of natural realities, sees no connection between God and plants, between God and the animals around us.

I shall never forget a group of schoolboys waiting at a station in May sunshine throwing stones at the lizards and throwing the lizards with a laugh on the fire. Such things are relics of a time when a supposed love of God saw no connection with a love of nature and created people, even religious, who saw nothing wrong with hunting, and by that I mean not catching a hare or pheasant for the family to eat, but the brutal joy of seeing game twitch under the shower of lead.

These times have gone, but they are still a very recent thing. And here, if the reader will allow me, I should like to say something about a great prophet of our time and his message to the modern world: Teilhard de Chardin.

This priest, this Jesuit, this scholar was years ahead of his time and did much to force us Christians to resume our dialogue with the cosmos in its physical and metaphysical reality.

It is difficult to limit oneself when talking about him, so versatile and impressive is his thought. The Church is right to say that he must be read with caution and prudence and that some points in his grandiose vision of things are imprecise and vague.

I personally should not choose him as my professor of theology, but I feel that his role – which will pass because he worked alone in such a vast area that future generations will easily go far beyond him – is still of value to us in our change-over from our usual vision of an almost Mediterranean God to God the Creator, Ruler and Soul of the Universe.

Teilhard has helped us rediscover almost physically the presence of God in matter and evolution. Do not tell me he is a pantheist because he sees God in rocks and atoms. His whole life as a priest and a Christian, with its obedience to his vocation and the Church, is there to show us how totally he believed in the Transcendence of God, the Incarnation of the Word, the tragedy of sin and death.

No, like Francis, Teilhard celebrates the Cosmos in song in its new modern dimensions, and I am not afraid of exaggerating when I say that his *Hymn to the Universe* matches the height and depth of the *Canticle of Creatures* and has the same mystical impact. It comes from our own time, and a student of engineering or chemistry will perhaps make it his own with greater joy and not forget it so easily.

It reads like this.

'You are blessed, naked Matter, dry earth, hard rock, you who yield only to violence and oblige us to work if we wish to procure our bread.

You are blessed, dangerous Matter, terrible mother, you who swallow us if we do not chain you.

You are blessed, universal Matter, unlimited duration, bankless river, triple abyss of stars, atoms and generations, you who in breaking down our narrow scale of measurement reveal the very dimensions of God.

You are blessed, impenetrable Matter, stretched everywhere between our souls and the world of absences, you make us long to pierce the seamless veil of phenomena.

You are blessed, immortal Matter, you who one day in dissolving in us will necessarily bring us to the very heart of what is. Without you, without your attacks, without your jerks, we should live inert, puerile, ignorant of ourselves and God.

You who wound and heal, you who bend and restore, you who destroy and build, you who fetter and liberate, lymph of our souls, hand of God, flesh of Christ, Matter I bless you.

Matter I bless and greet you not as the pontiffs of science or the preachers of virtue describe or rather disfigure you, a complex of brutal forces and base appetites, but as you appear to me today in all your truth.

I greet you, inexhaustible capacity for being and becoming.

I greet you, universal power for coupling and union through which the multitude of monads pass in their convergence on the path of the Spirit.

I greet you, harmonious spring of souls, limpid crystal from which the New Jerusalem will be cut.

I greet you, 'divine milieu' full of creative power, agitated ocean of the Spirit, clay kneaded and vivified by the Incarnate Word.

In the belief that they are obeying your irresistible call, men often throw themselves out of love for you into the external abyss of selfish pleasure; they are deceived by a reflection.

To seize you, Matter, starting from a universal contact with everything that moves we must gradually feel the various particular forms of what we hold crumble in our hands until we stand firm grasping what is consistent and unified.

If we wish to possess you we must sublimate you in suffering, having joyfully embraced you.

You reign, Matter, in the serene heights where saints think they can avoid you – flesh so transparent and mobile that we cannot distinguish you any more from the Spirit.

Take me up there, Matter, for strain, separation and death, take me where I can at last chastely embrace the Universe.'

Chapter Fourteen

YOU SHALL NOT MAKE YOURSELF A CARVED IMAGE

The reader of the Bible is impressed by its insistence on the dangers of idolatry and the vehemence with which this sin is attacked.

The thinking developed by the People of God on their journey through the desert is like a symphonic treatment of the theme of Yahweh's spiritual and transcendent nature.

Moses told the people: 'Yahweh spoke to you from the midst of the fire; you heard the sound of words but saw no shape' (Dt 4:12).

> 'Take great care what you do, therefore: since you saw no shape on that day at Horeb when Yahweh spoke to you from the midst of the fire, see that you do not act perversely, making yourselves a carved image in the shape of anything at all: whether it be in the likeness of man or of woman, or of any beast on the earth, or of any bird that flies in the heavens, or of any reptile that crawls on the ground, or of any fish in the waters under the earth. When you raise your eyes to heaven, when you see the sun, the moon, the stars, all the array of heaven, do not be tempted to worship them and serve them. Yahweh your God has allotted them to all the peoples under heaven, but as for you, Yahweh has taken you, and brought you out from the furnace of iron, from Egypt, to be a people all his own, as you still are today.
>
> Yahweh has been angry with me on your account; he has

sworn that I shall not cross the Jordan or enter the prosperous land which Yahweh your God is giving you as your heritage. Yes, I am to die in this country; I shall not go across this Jordan; you will go over and take possession of that rich land. Take care therefore not to forget the covenant which Yahweh your God has made with you, by making a carved image of anything that Yahweh your God has forbidden you.'

(Dt 4:15–23)

Yes, the idea and belief of God's transcendence are at the root of all biblical thinking, and it is understandable that the legislator should take precautions to prevent the people from turning God into something material.

'I am Yahweh your God who brought you out of the land of Egypt, out of the house of slavery.

You shall have no gods except me.

You shall not make yourself a carved image or any likeness of anything in heaven or on earth beneath or in the waters under the earth; you shall not bow down to them or serve them. For I, Yahweh your God, am a jealous God and I punish the father's fault in the sons, the grandsons and the great-grandsons of those who hate me; but I show kindness to thousands of those who love me and keep my commandments.'

(Ex 20:2–6)

I have often wondered where the danger of idolatry comes from.

Is it in us or outside us? Does it affect the ancient Hebrews or also us moderns who claim to have put the ancient attitudes behind us? I have come to the conclusion that the danger is in us and that the sin of idolatry affects all ages. The people of the Old Testament were tempted to make idols of wood, ivory or silver to hang from their camels' saddles, while the people of the New Testament carry saints' medals in their pockets instead of God in their hearts.

The motive is more or less the same. We are too idle to make the effort to think of God as beyond time and space, in His Transcendence and Mystery – it is so much more convenient to give Him a cheap face in order to replace His remoteness with something tangible, something close to us, something above all which will heal us when we are ill, enrich us when we are poor.

Now I must make it quite clear that I am not criticizing devotion to the saints. Devotion to the saints is commendable when it is properly integrated into one's central worship: the adoration of God.

No, I am talking about belief not in a witness of the Church triumphant but in pieces of wood with supposedly magic powers, all too frequent in the undergrowth of post-Christian piety.

Originally the articles were Christian objects which served a useful purpose, but in the hands of idolaters they have become idols, idols in the form of medals, holy pictures and crucifixes. In my view the more a people's faith declines – real, strong, enlightened, virile faith – the more piety-stalls proliferate; the more superficial piety becomes and the more it approximates to a fear of becoming ill or the hope of winning the pools, the greater need man feels to build altars to his own idols.

I have found these altars of modern idolatry everywhere, even in church. Imagine what it must be like outside!

I remember a self-styled atheist who could not end his day without a sign of the cross.

I have met many lorry-drivers in the Sahara who live as if God did not take care of them and who have pictures of St Rita or St Anthony as charms on their windscreens!

That is idolatry.

This is not to say that the question is an easy one. What is ever clear in the muddled human heart? What significance are we to attribute, for example, to a cross round somebody's neck?

Is it a reminder of his parents' faith or a kind of totem or charm? One can never tell. Who is to say that it has no mysterious and hidden power of protection? Idolatry and superstition are still religious forms, certainly, however unsophisticated, and they frequently occur in people who have lost the true faith – the dying ashes of a lost inheritance.

The Bible is really biting, however, when it tries to convince people that an idol is an idol, a thing of no value, a god who neither sees, feels nor moves, a god who is powerless to help.

Jeremiah says in his celebrated letter to Baruch on idolatry:

> Plated with gold and silver, their tongues polished smooth by a craftsman, they are counterfeit and have no power to speak. As though for a girl fond of finery, these pagans take gold and make crowns for the heads of their gods. Sometimes, the priests actually filch gold and silver from their gods to spend themselves, even using it on presents for the temple prostitutes. They dress up these gods of silver, gold and wood, in clothes, like human beings, although they cannot protect themselves either from tarnish or woodworm, in spite of the purple cloaks they drape them in. Their faces even have to be dusted, owing to the dust of the temple which settles thick on them. One holds a sceptre like the governor of a province, yet is powerless to put anyone who offends him to death; another holds sword and axe in his right hand, yet is powerless to defend himself against war or thieves. From this it is evident that they are not gods; do not be afraid of them.
>
> However much was paid for them, there is still no breath of life in them. Being unable to walk, they have to be carried on men's shoulders, which shows how futile they are. It is humiliating for their worshippers too, who have to stand them up again if they fall over. Once they have been stood

up, they cannot move on their own; if they tilt askew, they cannot right themselves; offerings made to them might as well be made to dead men. Whatever is sacrificed to them, the priests re-sell and pocket the profit; while their wives salt down part of it, but give nothing to the poor or to the helpless. As to the sacrifices themselves, why, women during their periods and women in childbed are not afraid to touch them! As you can see from these examples that they are not gods, do not be afraid of them.

(Ba 6:7–14, 24–8)

People have been tempted since time immemorial to ascribe magic power to things and places. To the Samaritan woman at the well trying to defend herself by engaging him in a religious dispute, Jesus uttered that magnificent phrase: 'The hour has come when true worshippers will worship the Father in spirit and truth' (Jn 4:23).

Worshipping God 'in spirit and truth' is the way to purify the soul of the tendency to adore idols, to protect it from the constant danger of worshipping human values, of believing in what is perishable, of according excessive importance to power and riches. 'True worshippers worship the Father in spirit and truth.' That is how we can escape the tangled undergrowth of spiritist magic, the confusing fog of mysterious beliefs, faith in amulets, powers ascribed to bits of wood . . . and holy water.

Do not be scandalized. In some places where faith in Christ is no more than a memory and sacramental life has disappeared, I have seen people put great value on the annual blessing of the house. Their idea seems to be that the water is something magic, a panacea against illness, a means of driving out evil spirits and powers. Young people increasingly react against this type of piety and, so they say, prefer atheism. I am not at all sure they really understand the problem.

A high proportion of what the young call atheism is probably only the need to be free of this fog of superstition and to rid themselves of a traditional piety they no longer find convincing.

Many young people are casting down the idols of the past and rebelling against a way of thinking about God which offends their modern cultural sensibilities.

The moderns may have many faults, but at least they have the merit of wanting to understand. And given that the house inherited from their grandmothers is awash with a piety based on oleographs in bad taste, they prefer to consign the lot to the cellar and leave the walls of their soul bare and uncluttered.

Bare walls?

Would to God this were true! It would be the finest preparation for the future religious development of their souls.

But . . . when the picture of St Anthony and the oleograph of the Holy Family have been removed, they are soon replaced by photos of idolized football teams and then a long series of modern idols: cinema stars, dancers, pop singers, guitarists.

Alas! Idolatry begins on another level because the soul, this poor soul deprived of its God, cannot do without Him and so looks for substitutes, even fourth rate ones. But at least these do not perform miracles, and that says something for their manufacturers!

And what about people too old to play soccer and jive, who are scandalized at the frivolity of youth's idols and tell them so?

What do they put in place of St Joseph when they have thrown his picture away?

The autographed photo of some influential VIP; letters of recommendation; people who can offer promotion, career opportunities, transfers long dreamed of.

Candles are lit as our grandparents lit them in church – but now they are candles of adulation, and the incense is flattery.

And let us not talk of the tricks resorted to to reach these idols, the acts of prostitution to receive their favours: they would be worthy of the cleverest harlequin.

PART III

Apart from the family and work as schools created by God for our training in His eternal love, there is another essential human-divine activity as continuous as breathing and the beating of the heart: prayer.

Prayer, from childlike invocation to infused contemplation, accompanies the development of the soul in its increasing maturity and guides it to the peak of union with God. This is the subject of the following seven meditations.

Chapter Fifteen

PRAISE OF GOD

When the soul opens itself to the love of God, the first word it utters is a word of praise, a cry of exultation.

> I love Yahweh, my strength,
> my stronghold and my refuge.
>
> (Ps 18:1–2)

It is like a need bottled up in our inmost heart which at last finds an outlet:

> My heart is ready, God
> – I mean to sing and play.
>   Awake, my muse,
> awake, lyre and harp,
>   I mean to wake the Dawn!
>
> (Ps 108:1–2)

It is like a spring which travels miles underground and then finally gushes out in a silver stream:

> God, you are my God, I am seeking you,
> my soul is thirsting for you,
> my flesh is longing for you,
> a land parched, weary and waterless.
>
> (Ps 63:1–2)

Prayer is above all a reply. Later it will include requests, many of them, but basically it is a reply.

This is because God makes the first request.

If He did not speak first, all our talking would be in vain.

If He did not leave His isolation, nobody could liberate us from ours; if He did not call to us from the abysses of being, nobody would dream of replying. Yes, to have love you need two people, and man is the passive partner in love.

God is the first, the active partner.

Jesus said:

> 'No one can come to me
> unless he is drawn by the Father who sent me.'
>
> (Jn 6:44)

It is the Father who takes the initiative. He comes to us from the silence of His Transcendence and calls us by name.

And man replies.

That is how the conversation of prayer begins.

When we become aware that He is calling us, when we hear resounding in the emptiness of our poverty the deep echo of the petition He Himself has placed in our being, we are disposed to prayer, we have placed ourselves in a position in which prayer is possible.

And as we said earlier, the first reply is a 'thank you'.

It could not be otherwise. We are creatures by nature, He the Creator.

Unless we establish ourselves in that particular relationship, we are not living in truth and we cannot pray.

As he discovers his creatureliness, man says to his Creator:

Lord, you have been
our refuge age after age.

Before the mountains were born,
before the earth or the world came to birth,
you were God from all eternity and for ever.

You can turn man back into dust
by saying, 'Back to what you were, you sons of men!'
To you, a thousand years are a single day,
a yesterday now over, an hour of the night.

(Ps 90:1–4)

And again:

Come, let us praise Yahweh joyfully,
acclaiming the Rock of our safety;
let us come into his presence with thanksgiving,
acclaiming him with music.

For Yahweh is a great God,
a greater King than all other gods;
from depths of earth to mountain top
everything comes under his rule;
the sea belongs to him, he made it,
so does the land, he shaped this too.

(Ps 95:1–5)

This is our response to God's call.

To any gift however great or small the creature who opens his eyes and heart to life responds with praise.

It must be so.

To gasp with wonder at the beauty of a sunset and to shout with joy at the sight of a new-born child is to pray, and our prayer is a gasp of admiration.

Yahweh, our Lord,
how great your name throughout the earth!

Above the heavens is your majesty chanted
by the mouths of children, babes in arms.

(Ps 8:1–2)

Yes, how true that is: God's majesty is chanted 'by the mouths of children'.

We must be children if we wish to pray, or at least become children.

The great of this world are too sceptical, too 'experienced', too 'clever'; they remain in their silence, closed to the prayer of adoration.

But if we are small by nature or have become small by grace we can offer praise and sing in ecstasy:

I look up at your heavens, made by your fingers,
at the moon and stars you set in place –
ah, what is man that you should spare a thought for
  him,
the son of man that you should care for him?

Yet you have made him little less than a god,
you have crowned him with glory and splendour,
made him lord over the work of your hands,
set all things under his feet,

sheep and oxen, all these,
yes, wild animals too,
birds in the air, fish in the sea
travelling the paths of the ocean.

(Ps 8:3–8)

Now this is quite something! But only the small man discovers he is big, king of creation, 'little less than a god'. The 'great', the 'wise', the 'powerful' cannot see or understand – or sing. They do not pray, and this is the severest possible defect, the most wretched state to which a man can sink.

How vital it is to become small if we wish to learn how to pray!

How vital it is to feel insignificant if we wish to say:

Send out your light and your truth,
  let these be my guide,
to lead me to your holy mountain
  and to the place where you live.

Then I shall go to the altar of God,
  to the God of my joy.

(Ps 43: 3–4a)

to respect the truth of humility if we wish to pray:

Blessed be Yahweh, my rock,
who trains my hands for war
and my fingers for battle,
my love, my bastion,
my citadel, my saviour,
I shelter behind him, my shield.

(Ps 144:1–2)

Yes, humility is truth, and truth is humility.

It is true that man is 'little less than a god', but we must be little to understand it. It is true that God is our God and that everything we have comes from Him, but how hard it is to understand for someone who is not spiritually a child! Our Lady understood it, and she put it into words in a prayer that is and will always be the pattern of every prayer of adoration, the perfect response to all God's requests:

'My soul proclaims the greatness of the Lord
and my spirit exults in God my saviour;
because he has looked upon his lowly handmaid.
Yes, from this day forward all generations will call
me blessed,
for the Almighty has done great things for me.
Holy is his name,
and his mercy reaches from age to age for those
who fear him.

He has shown the power of his arm,
he has routed the proud of heart.
He has pulled down princes from their thrones and
exalted the lowly.
The hungry he has filled with good things, the rich
sent empty away.
He has come to the help of Israel his servant,
mindful of his mercy
– according to the promise he made to our
ancestors –
of his mercy to Abraham and to his descendents
for ever.'
(Lk 1:46–55)

It was her answer to God's eternal request for the Incarnation of His Son.

Chapter Sixteen

PETITION

Prayer is not only a reply but frequently – very frequently – a petition.

> Take pity on me, God, take pity on me.
> I call on God the Most High,
> on God who has done everything for me.
>
> (Ps 57:1–2)

One does not have to go very far in life to learn to call, shout, beseech. How fragile and weak and little man is on earth! How brittle his stability, which the merest trifle can upset.

> Save me, God! The water
> is already up to my neck!
>
> I am sinking in the deepest swamp,
> there is no foothold;
> I have stepped into deep water
> and the waves are washing over me.
>
> (Ps 69:1–2)

This is how the prayer of petition arises, a prayer so great and all-pervading that for many people it is synonymous with prayer. For many people praying means asking, and often they are unaware of other forms of conversing with God.

Worn out with calling, my throat is hoarse,
my eyes are strained, looking for my God.

God, you know how foolish I have been,
my offences are not hidden from you.

(Ps 69:3, 5)

And again:

My soul is all troubled,
my life is on the brink of Sheol.

(Ps 88:3)

From the depths I call to you, Yahweh,
Lord, listen to my cry for help!
Listen compassionately
to my pleading!

If you never overlooked our sins, Yahweh,
Lord, could anyone survive?

(Ps 130:1–3)

Sometimes when our distress is exceptionally intense, we feel that God Himself is against us:

Pity me, Yahweh, I have no strength left,
heal me, my bones are in torment,
my soul is in utter torment..
Yahweh, how long will you be?

(Ps 6:2–3)

Your own hands shaped me, modelled me;
and would you now have second thoughts and destroy me?

(Jb 10:8)

You have plunged me to the bottom of the Pit,
to its darkest, deepest place,
weighted down by your anger,
drowned beneath your waves.

(Ps 88:6–7)

The fact is that the person now has a deeper awareness of sin, and his relationship with God has consequently been radically upset.

To the person who really loves, sin is the betrayal of a friend, infidelity to a spouse, the desertion of a father. And God is this Friend, this Spouse, this Father.

When the soul realizes the horrible thing it has done, it cannot help crying out and weeping for sorrow.

Have mercy on me, O God, in your goodness,
in your great tenderness wipe away my faults;
wash me clean of my guilt,
purify me from my sin.

For I am well aware of my faults,
I have my sin constantly in mind,
having sinned against none other than you,
having done what you regard as wrong.

You are just when you pass sentence on me,
blameless when you give judgement.
You know I was born guilty,
a sinner from the moment of conception.

God, create a clean heart in me,
put into me a new and constant spirit,
do not banish me from your presence,
do not deprive me of your holy spirit.

(Ps 51:1–5, 10–11)

I think this Miserere psalm could be recited every day of our lives and still not be sufficient. And many of us – those who have not managed to reach a state of perfect love in this life – will have to recite it for aeons on end in purgatory.

I do not need to imagine a purgatory of fire; I can think of a place like my cell when I am alone or a dry desert landscape where only God and I are present.

Charity becomes the fire which burns the fibres of the soul. The memory of what our poor life has actually been compared with what it should have been is enough to instil in us the desire for repentance. The sight of our love for God betrayed, derided, despised, sold down the river, prostituted, will plunge the sword of pain to the centre of our being and make us pine with sorrow.

I am memorizing Psalm 88, which I regard as the prayer of purgatory, partly because it contains some phrases which to be true and genuine in myself would need the night of the soul.

Yahweh my God, I call for help all day,
I weep to you all night;
may my prayer reach you
hear my cries for help;

for my soul is all troubled,
my life is on the brink of Sheol;
I am numbered among those who go down to the Pit,
a man bereft of strength:

a man alone, down among the dead,
among the slaughtered in their graves,
among those you have forgotten,
those deprived of your protecting hand.

You have plunged me to the bottom of the Pit,
to its darkest, deepest place,
weighted down by your anger,
drowned beneath your waves.

You have turned my friends against me
and made me repulsive to them;
in prison and unable to escape,
my eyes are worn out with suffering.

Yahweh, I invoke you all day,
I stretch out my hands to you:
are your marvels meant for the dead,
can ghosts rise up to praise you?

Who talks of your love in the grave,
of your faithfulness in the place of perdition?
Do they hear about your marvels in the dark,
about your righteousness in the land of oblivion?

But I am here, calling for your help,
praying to you every morning:
why do you reject me?
Why do you hide your face from me?

Wretched, slowly dying since my youth,
I bore your terrors – now I am exhausted;
your anger overwhelmed me,
you destroyed me with your terrors
which, like a flood, were round me, all day long,
all together closing in on me.
You have turned my friends and neighbours against me,
now darkness is my one companion left.

(Ps 88)

Purgatory will be like this if I have not learnt to live love to the full in this life, and when I think of it I am afraid.

In the end who deserves hell, who deserves Heaven? After all, are our lives any more than systematized mediocrity?

Do we not belong to the army of the lukewarm – those afraid of going too far?

Was not Christ condemned to death because of people who did not sufficiently care? In the praetorium and on Calvary, was not the crowd, with a few exceptions, a collection of people who 'couldn't really care less'? Was not Jesus condemned in ridicule?

He was in earnest, but were most of the other people there? Were they really interested in Him? Were they not equally ready to shout 'Hosanna' and 'Crucify him'?

Yes, Love was condemned in ridicule, in disinterest, in a what-does-it-matter-to-me attitude, in the golden mediocrity which floods the earth and drowns it in nausea.

This is why saints are few and far between.

Our destiny is therefore purgatory, a long one, where we shall have time to consider that our superficial, distracted, tepid lives were intolerable to Someone who loves as God does.

And we shall see written on the door that phrase from Revelation:

> 'I wish you were hot or cold, but since you are neither, but only lukewarm, I will spit you out of my mouth.'
>
> (3:15)

Chapter Seventeen

TRUST AS PRAYER

One of the hardest battles in the spiritual life, perhaps I should say the hardest, is the struggle to see God in our trivial human happenings. How often we have to renew our act of faith! At first we are tempted to see only ourselves, to believe only in ourselves, to value only ourselves. Then gradually we perceive that the thread of life has a rationale, a mysterious unity, and we are led to think that we meet God in its basic stages. Then again, as our religious experience grows, we begin to realize that we meet God not only in the big events of our lives but in all the events, however small and apparently insignificant.

God is never absent from our lives, He cannot be, because 'in Him we live, and move, and exist' (Ac 17:28). But it requires so much effort to turn this truth into a habit!

We need repeated acts of faith before we learn to sail with confidence on the 'immense and endless sea' which is God (St Gregory Nazienzen), knowing that if we founder we do so in Him, the divine eternal ever-present God. How fortunate we are if we can learn to navigate our frail craft on this sea and remain serene even when the storm is raging!

> I love you, Yahweh, my strength.
> Yahweh is my rock and my bastion,
> my deliverer is my God.
>
> (Ps 18:1–2)

The waves of death encircled me,
the torrents of Belial burst on me;
the cords of Sheol girdled me,
the snares of death were before me.

In my distress I called to Yahweh
and to my God I cried;
from his Temple he heard my voice,
my cry came to his ears.

Then the earth quivered and quaked,
the foundations of the mountains trembled.

(Ps 18:4–7)

He sends from on high and takes me,
he draws me from deep waters,
he delivers me from my powerful enemy,
from a foe too strong for me.

(Ps 18:16–17)

David experienced this dramatic rescue by God when he advanced against Goliath, his only weapon weakness, his only support the confidence of youth (1 S 17).

How wonderful this scene is, a stripling striking the Philistine giant dead with a pebble! The youth *lives in his God* and knows that his confidence rests on God the Invincible. The impossible becomes possible, Goliath is struck down, and the memory of it will inspire David for the rest of his life.

Yahweh is my shepherd,
  I lack nothing.

In meadows of green grass he lets me lie.
To the waters of repose he leads me;
there he revives my soul.

(Ps 23:1–3a)

He will celebrate his victory in song long after his youth is over, when his life is harsher and faith more difficult.

Yes, the older we grow the more danger there is of outgrowing our childhood. Faith, great faith, needs the atmosphere of spiritual infancy. And if we lose that, faith is endangered, we find it difficult to *trust* God any more. We grow up, we become 'adult', and our reasoning destroys the substance of our proper sense of dependence on God. We must constantly recall Jesus's warning: 'Unless you change and become like little children you will never enter the kingdom of heaven' (Mt 18:3). We must try and remain very small where life forces us to be big.

The spirit moves in the opposite direction to nature, and the greatest achievement in matters of faith is for a grown person to become small, an adult to return to his childhood, a serpent to change into a dove.

And if, when we are old, full of human experience and wisdom, sharpened by the years and 'cunning as serpents', we are also 'harmless as doves' and 'like little children', we shall be able to lift our hearts up to God and sing with David:

> If you live in the shelter of Elyon
> and make your home in the shadow of Shaddai,
> you can say to Yahweh, 'My refuge, my fortress,
> my God in whom I trust!'
>
> He rescues you from the snares
> of fowlers hoping to destroy you;
> he covers you with his feathers,
> and you find shelter underneath his wings.
>
> You need not fear for the terrors of night,
> the arrow that flies in the daytime,
> the plague that stalks in the dark,
> the scourge that wreaks havoc in broad daylight.

No disaster can overtake you,
no plague come near your tent:
he will put you in his angels' charge
to guard you wherever you go.

They will support you on their hands
in case you hurt your foot against a stone;
you will tread on lion and adder,
trample on savage lions and dragons.

'I rescue all who cling to me,
I protect whoever knows my name,
I answer everyone who invokes me,
I am with them when they are in trouble;
I bring them safety and honour.
I give them life, long and full,
and show them how I can save.'

(Ps 91:1–6, 10–16)

What a longing this psalm inspires! How it makes me want to live a life totally absorbed at last by confidence in God!

How I should love to remain serene in trials, not to fear the terrors of night and the scourge that wreaks havoc at the noon of life!

This is not easy, and we have a lifetime in which to gain this victory and attain this state of peace. Our task is a hard one, a brick-by-brick construction of our spiritual temple, a step-by-step advance towards total faith which only God can give, via acts of faith which depend on us and on our dedication. As in everything else, God looks for our collaboration. He gives us the boat and the oars but asks us to do the rowing, and the more we row the easier it becomes.

Whether we receive gifts in the future depends on our present commitment, just as the athlete's effectiveness depends on constant training.

David was stronger in faith after accepting Goliath's

challenge, Joshua closer to God after attacking Jericho with nothing but trumpets.

Judith was dearer to God after accepting in faith to enter Holofernes' tent, Joseph a 'juster' man after obeying the angel and taking Mary to be his wife.

Acts of faith accustom us to a life of trust in God; trust generates trust and leads to absolute intimacy, perfect unity.

> Yahweh, my heart has no lofty ambitions,
> my eyes do not look too high.
> I am not concerned with great affairs
> or marvels beyond my scope.
> Enough for me to keep my soul tranquil and quiet
> like a child in its mother's arms,
> as content as a child that has been weaned.
> (Ps 131:1–2)

That is the peak of religious life on earth: keeping our soul tranquil and quiet like a child in its mother's arms.

If we wished to sum up the relationship that should exist between man and God, if we wished to give as exact an example as possible of the trust on which the peace of those who live in the mystery of God depends, we could not do better than point to the infant sleeping in the strong arms of its mother, close to the womb of its being, safe under the watchful eye of the person who gave him his existence and who thought of him before he ever was.

Chapter Eighteen

PRAYER AND LIFE

We have all had the experience of going into a sacristy and seeing a good Christian bent over his breviary.

Imagine that it is Friday and that the priest is reciting Lauds, Psalm 143.

> Yahweh, hear my prayer,
> listen to my pleading,
> answer me faithfully, righteously.

He lifts his head as the visitor enters and says, 'Can I help you?'

While waiting for the answer his eye wanders to the next verse:

> Do not put your servant on trial,
> no one is virtuous by your standards.

'I should like to have a mass said, Father.'

> An enemy who hounds me
> to crush me into the dust,
> forces me to dwell in darkness
> like the dead of long ago.

'Would next Friday at eight be OK?'

> My spirit fails me.

'Would you accept this offering please, Father?'

And my heart is full of fear.

'Thank you. Is there anything else?'

I stretch out my hands.

'No, that's all, thank you. Goodbye, Father.'

Like thirsty ground I yearn for you.

This is no joke. All too often we treat prayer like this.

If you are not guilty, thank God, because you have reached a new stage in prayer which is far from easy.

Manzoni was right when he called the human heart a 'jumble'.

And the jumble persists into our most serious activity – talking with God.

How difficult it is to put a bit of order into our minds, to leave the formalism of prayer and turn prayer into something alive, a living union with God!

Too often and for too long prayer and life meet like strangers on the road, live like neighbours not on speaking terms, relate like a mother-in-law and daughter-in-law, grow away from each other like a couple who are no longer in love and who stay together only because they have not the courage to separate.

And that is not the worst of it. Prayer and life can sometimes coexist like two criminals in the same cell or even like two corpses in the same tomb.

How good we are!

And so used to deluding ourselves! Do we never hear mass with hatred for our brother in our hearts?

Could we never bring ourselves to withold mass offerings?

Everything is possible when we leave the straight and narrow.

And when God is tired of our duplicity, He will say such terrible things as Jeremiah or even more Malachi record:

> I will send the curse on you and curse your very blessing. Indeed I have already cursed it, since there is not a single one of you who takes this to heart. Now watch how I am going to paralyse your arm and throw dung in your face – the dung from your very solemnities – and sweep you away with it.
>
> (Ml 2:2b–4)

However, that is not what I wished to talk about – it is too obvious.

I wished to talk about the difficulty of balancing prayer and life even when we are on the right road.

I wished to stress one particular thing: our devotional exercises should not encumber an already overloaded day; the inner spirit must not be stifled by the interminable formulas and actions of a piety which no longer speaks to the heart or mind; action must not eliminate contemplation; contemplation incorrectly understood must not make us eccentric, ill-tempered, disagreeable.

We may begin with a very clear and simple remark. If I find I cannot say the Office because charity makes too many demands on my time, either I ask my superior to dispense me or I dispense myself. Saying the breviary during mass or when I am cooking is not taking it seriously at all. If I do that I am regarding prayer as no more than a *juridical obligation*, a sort of toll to be paid as a price for living. If I say the Office at all, it must be done properly, in peace and quiet, in such a way that it benefits me, nourishes my devotional life in an intelligent and balanced way; above all it must not be a burden.

In the pre-conciliar Church it was not at all unusual to hear a priest intoning his *Iam lucis orto sidere* at eleven o'clock at night. This type of thing possibly helped to develop man's sense of duty, but it definitely created a misunderstanding of prayer as life. The Council, fortunately, made a clean sweep, and even though we shall need patience and courage in applying its spirit and letter, the new times will help to put behind us a type of formalism which to my mind seriously threatened Christianity.

Age quod agis should apply not only to all our human activities in general but to the most serious business of the day, the most radical effort of life, in particular: prayer. Prayer must become a living reality if I am not to complicate still further with external acts an already complicated interior life.

If I wish to attend mass properly on a Sunday, I must make every effort to enter into things. If I wish to get the best out of the liturgical readings, I should close my prayer-book and listen attentively.

If I wish to meditate, I must go somewhere where I can have complete silence. And above all I should not go to a second mass with the idea of taking out a higher heavenly insurance, as many pious – and muddled – people seem to.

And so on.

There is something else, however, which is even more important if we are to eliminate or at least reduce the elements within ourselves which militate against the 'wholeness', the strong, vital integrity, of our lives.

We must eliminate or at least reduce the tensions between action and contemplation, apostolate and prayer, external and internal activity, dedication to others and dedication to self. How can we do this?

People say: 'I'm too busy with work at the moment to find time for prayer.' Or: 'How can I pray with five children to look after?' Or: 'When can I pray with eight hours' office-work and then the housework to do?'

These arguments betray a very serious shortcoming: they radically underestimate the value of human activity.

The impression they give is that professional, social and

family life is totally separate from prayer and the life of the soul.

The advice of pious people serves merely to aggravate the confusion and the depreciation of human activities.

These people say: 'In the morning offer up your day's work and it becomes a prayer', or 'Every so often raise up your heart in prayer', etc.

They talk as if we cannot be united to God unless we leave our work, as if to be a Christian means putting our duties aside!

This betrays a sad confusion and is the product of an age with no proper theology of the laity.

Furthermore it is based on a 'disincarnate' piety, more angelic than human.

Work, study, the household jobs, looking after the children are all such important things!

They are also holy things, because they are human values willed by God to whom I have to devote myself totally in thought and deed.

My work is no easier for making a sign of the cross over it, my day no lighter for offering it up in the morning prayer. On the contrary! But the first thing I must understand and believe is *that my work is of enormous value, that the duties incumbent on me as a human being are holy because they are willed by God and I fulfil them in obedience to His Law.*

And if God allows me a little free time after all the work and chores, I can devote a few minutes to contemplation, enabling my life to achieve its proper balance.

People say: 'I've got too much on in my apostolate, I can't pray.'

Now the contradiction here is so obvious that only Manzoni's word is adequate: our poor hearts are nothing but a 'jumble'.

How can there be any opposition between two ways of expressing love for the same Person?

If prayer is love for God, how can it be excluded from another form of love for God, the apostolate?

Surely the first commandment cannot be said to contradict the second, which 'resembles it' (Mt 22:39)?

How can the charity which takes us out towards our neighbour not take us out towards God at the same time?

Unless, of course, what we call 'apostolate' is not love for our neighbour but agitation, activism, self-seeking, escapism – the 'heresy of action', as the Abbé Chautard called it.

In that case we should have to say not: 'I've got too much on in my apostolate, I can't pray', but: 'I am deluding myself by doing what we call apostolic work, whereas in fact I'm simply wasting my time seeking myself in contact with my neighbour and I've no time to spend with God.'

God is too simple in His relations with us, and He cannot continually thwart us when we are trying to find Him.

But . . . we must really wish to find Him, and this basic desire will unify all our various actions.

We must want to go to Him, to find Him, to look for His will and love; to go to Him with all our being as it left His creative hand and as it has been damaged by our sins.

We must want to go to Him with our spirits and bodies, with our daily effort and the graces we have been given, with our brothers who are with us in the struggle and with the aspirations of the entire universe. Two things are certain in this 'going to God'. The first is that in cases of conflict or doubt charity must be considered the supreme rule, and the second is that as long as we are on earth the bond uniting us with God is the desire to achieve union with Him, and however imperfect that desire it remains the fundamental and vital basis of our religious life.

Chapter Nineteen

PRAYER AS SACRIFICE

It has been said that there are peoples without cities, cities without walls, men without art, but no people, city or men without sacrifice. Sacrifice as a form of prayer, as an expression of religious devotion, was born with man and will die with man.

From the primitive forms found among animists to the organized forms of Hebrewism, from the sacrificed ram of every good Muslim to the sacrifices of the Hindus and Shintoists in the east, sacrifice has shown itself to be a universal form of prayer. If ever we arrived on another planet and there were intelligent beings there, I wager we should find them constructing an altar and sacrificing a victim.

The essential elements of sacrifice – an assembly, an altar, a priest, a victim – are as basic to us as heart, blood and lungs. Urged on by the irrepressible need to express his love for God with presents, man on earth has expressed his subjection to God by offering on altars gifts from his flocks, first-fruits from his harvests.

The Bible offers the most complete and developed casuistry of sacrifice, and one has only to read Leviticus to see this.

'If your offering is a holocaust of an animal out of the herd . . . if your offering is an animal out of the flock . . . if your offering is a holocaust of a bird . . . when you are going to offer an oblation of dough baked in the oven . . .'

If one had to depict in art the essence of religious forms of the ancients, one would unhesitatingly paint a congregation round an altar at the moment when one of them – the priest – was offering sacrifice.

Why the victim, however? Why blood? Why was it not enough to offer peace-offerings as they did at harvest-time?

Peoples universally expressed their subjection to the Creator by offering corn or honey or wool or a candle, and they universally included blood as an element of sacrifice.

Why?

Man felt that something had been snapped, that the balance of things was upset, that peace-offerings were adequate at certain moments but inadequate at others when something more was needed to express one's state of soul. Theologians talk about original sin, St Augustine talked about a disorder. The fact is that man had realized his sinfulness and recognized increasingly that he had to pay, and that blood was the proper price for sin. This thirst for a victim, this urgent need to shed blood and bridge the gap created by sin between God and man is characteristic of world religion.

Humanity seems to be saying, 'Lord, we are nothing but riff-raff, we have done violence, we have killed, robbed, betrayed. We do not deserve your pardon . . . But look at this innocent victim dying on the altar and pardon us by its blood.' Ancient peoples even went so far – totally contrary to God's wishes – as to sacrifice babies and innocent young girls.

They seemed to want to force the hand of justice: O God, look at this! The Hebrews sacrificed millions of victims; rivers of blood were spilt to satisfy the immense thirst for justice in sinful man. When the Temple was inaugurated in Jerusalem, Solomon offered Yahweh 22,000 oxen and 120,000 sheep (1 K 8:62) – a sign of the religious sentiments of ancient peoples.

The most typical summary of the past, however, the finest synthesis of the concept of sacrifice which was to remain as an image and symbol of 'what was to come' was undoubtedly the passover.

> 'Each man must take an animal from the flock, one for each family, and slaughter it between the two evenings. Some of the blood must then be put on the two doorposts and the lintel of the houses where it is eaten. That night the flesh is to be eaten, roasted over the fire. You shall eat it like this: with a girdle round your waist, sandals on your feet, a staff in your hand. It is a passover in honour of Yahweh!
>
> (Ex 12:3–11)

And so they did.

And in memory of that 'passover' the Hebrews celebrated the Pasch annually by sacrificing a lamb. It was the ultimate symbol, from our point of view completely luminous, of what was to happen later: the real, definitive and radical 'passover', *the Pasch of the New Alliance.*

Naturally none of the sacrifices of ancient peoples was anything but symbolic – symbolic of a reality yet to come, of a history yet to mature. That history would be inaugurated by Jesus, the Christ. As a Hebrew and son of His people, He would eat the passover every year with bitter herbs and His loins girt, in memory of the flight from Egypt and the crossing of the Reed Sea.

He would do so with Mary and Joseph as a child, with other relatives and friends during the rest of His short thirty-three years, and with His twelve disciples for that last time in the upper room in Jerusalem.

On that occasion, St Luke tells us, Jesus had told His disciples: 'I have longed to eat this passover with you before I suffer' (22:15).

No longer, however, was it the old passover: the symbol was at an end, the reality of the only authentic sacrifice was about to enter the stage of history.

> As they were eating, Jesus took some bread, and when he had said the blessing he broke it and gave it to his disciples.

'Take it and eat;' he said 'this is my body.' Then he took a cup, and when he had returned thanks he gave it to them. 'Drink all of you from this,' he said 'for this is my blood, the blood of the covenant, which is to be poured out for many for the forgiveness of sins.'

(Mt 26:26–8)

Jesus was to offer himself as innocent victim to the Father on the altar of the world, with all humanity round him, pay the price for all and thus bring the past to a definitive close. That sacrifice, the offertory of which was the Last Supper, which was brought to completion the following day on Calvary and which is repeated at every mass throughout history, was to be the once-for-all, universally valid sacrifice of which the ancient sacrifices were symbols and future masses 'memorials'.

In an eternal present, Jesus, who had accepted in the Incarnation solidarity with all mankind, assumed the role of Eternal Priest and offered Himself as a bloody victim on Calvary, the altar of the world. This sacrifice – foreshadowed in the passover of the old law as a remembrance of the journey from slavery in Egypt to the freedom of the Promised Land, transformed into a reality in the oblation of the Lamb of God at the Last Supper and on Calvary, approved by the Father at Jesus's Resurrection and Ascension into Heaven, and renewed at each mass to the end of time in the strength and will of Christ who foresaw and willed all consecrations when He said, 'Do this as a memorial of me' – is the unique and eternal sacrifice acceptable to God.

No hymn, no poem, expresses this so well as the *Exsultet* of Holy Saturday.

'This is the paschal feast wherein is slain the true Lamb whose blood hallows the doorposts of the faithful. This is the night when, long ago, thou didst cause our forefathers, the sons of Israel, in their passage out of Egypt, to pass dryshod over the Red Sea. This is the night which swept away the blackness of sin by the light of the fiery pillar. This is the night which at this hour throughout the world restores to grace and yokes to holiness those who believe in Christ, detaching them from worldly vice and all the murk of sin. On this night Christ burst the bonds of death and rose victorious from the grave. What good would life have been to us without redemption? How wonderful the pity and care thou hast shown us; how far beyond all reckoning thy loving-kindness! To ransom thy slave, thou gavest up thy Son! O truly necessary sin of Adam, that Christ's death blotted out; and happy fault, that merited so great a Redeemer! Blessed indeed is this, the sole night counted worthy to mark the season and the hour in which Christ rose again from the grave. It is this night of which the scripture says: And the night shall be bright as day. Such is my joy that night itself is light! So holy, this night, it banishes all crimes, washes guilt away, restores lost innocence, brings mourners joy.'

Jesus's offering at the Last Supper (the new passover), the completion of His sacrifice on Calvary and His Resurrection (the Father's reply to the Son's love) form an inseparable whole: the reality of Christianity, the New Covenant, the dawn of the new creation, the centre of the religious universe, the ineffable synthesis of our faith, hope and charity.

When we join with the community of believers at Holy Mass, we are celebrating the Lord's death and Resurrection until He comes again.

The liturgical assembly of the Mass is *the* religious act, the living memorial of Easter, which enables us to accomplish the same 'passover' from death to life, from sin to grace.

When Christ comes to us in the Eucharist and bathes us in His blood, we enter the fulness of God, we come under the Father's forgiving gaze, we are touched by the Spirit's love, and the vital principle of our bodily and spiritual resurrection is instilled into us.

Taking part in the 'Lord's Supper', we make our own Jesus's will to unite all humanity round the Father's Table, building up the Mystical Body which will be completed after the last Mass on earth, when the veil of faith will be torn aside and the Redeemed admitted to the eternal Banquet of Heaven.

Chapter Twenty

THE REVELATION OF GOD

The path of prayer is as long as man's life, neither more nor less. It is now a glorious path through the meadows, now a peaceful country road with no obstacles where we can abandon ourselves to quiet thought, now a rough mule-track winding up the mountains, now a way over the bare rocks on the summit. Sometimes it is like a city street full of noise and distraction, at others it follows the water off the streets into underground drains and so to the river or sea, carrying with it the rubbish and filth of life.

But it is always prayer.

It is still prayer, I believe, even when it is silence and looks to the observer like the dried-up bed of a stream. Surely a blade of grass bent with the heat is still a prayer in Heaven's eyes even though it cannot ask for water?

Surely the pitiable state of someone reduced to running sores by loneliness and evil is a prayer, even though he says nothing but speaks with his life?

It is difficult for a God who is Love not to find a pretext for intervention and assistance in the affairs of His poor creature – man – who prior to sin made the mistake of being in too great a hurry to reach his final end, God, and after sin made the further mistake of no longer being able to believe in such a glorious end for himself.

God, however, hears man's prayer, He hears it whatever its nature.

He hears it when it is expressed in words, He helps it when it becomes thought and meditation, He supports and animates it when it finally becomes life.

That is not enough, however.

Man's destiny goes far beyond this world, beyond the limits of human life. Speech and thought belong to an earth-bound way of life, they are activities which cannot reach beyond death, cannot attain the Transcendence of God.

If our destiny is to meet God and contemplate Him face to face beyond worldly symbols, in His naked reality, we need a prayer more appropriate to God's level, of the same nature as God, in other words, a supernatural form of prayer. We have been given this in infused contemplation.

During man's pilgrimage of faith, God first reveals Himself in symbol, and man can therefore talk to Him as he does to his fellows and think of Him in largely human ways. But even at the very limit of this revelation, man knows that he has seen not God but – how shall I put it? – His garment.

Everything we know about God is not God but a pointer, an image.

And it is here that man discovers his total poverty, the abyss which separates him from his transcendent Lord, his absolute inability to reach and possess God.

In this time of waiting, the only new dimension that can be added to prayer is silence, which transcends all other dimensions and which, to enable man to receive and welcome God in His Word (which is no longer created but, in Christ, uncreated), becomes a painful, dry, crucified silence. God's real self-revelation to man takes place in this framework of man's absolute poverty and powerlessness, the image of which is the aridity of the desert.

We can do nothing beyond that to make progress. Our words turn to lamentation, and even meditation, which was so deep and lively at the beginning, will fall silent in its absolute impotence. At that moment God's true revelation to man begins. Having realized to the point of pain his absolute poverty and dryness, man opens himself to God like a flower in the humidity of night.

Then God reveals Himself to man, 'lifts the veil', makes Himself known, not in human terms, with human images and symbols, but in wordless terms, with images and symbols that go beyond every symbol. It is revelation at God's level, what we call supernatural revelation. Contemplation is in fact defined as the 'rapid, dark and supernatural revelation of God'.

Infused contemplation, which begins here on earth at the exact moment of the soul's maturity in the heat of the divine sun, will continue in eternity and constitute the plenitude of our union with God. If I am asked whether eternal life is just love of God, I reply without hesitation, *'it is, above all, knowledge'*.

There can be no love without knowledge; love is the fruit of knowledge.

Everything therefore begins with knowledge. To make us love Him God must first make us know Him, and if we did not have this real, supernatural if obscure knowledge of God, we could never love and so possess Him.

This is why He reveals Himself to His friends.

Did He never tell us all this?

Of course He did.

At the Last Supper, when He was about to leave His own, Jesus exclaimed:

> 'Anybody who receives my commandments and
> keeps them will be one who loves me;
> and anybody who loves me will be loved by my Father,
> and I shall love him and show myself to him.'
>
> (Jn 14:21)

How can you say you will 'show yourself' to us when you are leaving us, leaving us for ever?

And yet it will be so, because the promised revelation will not require Jesus's physical presence. It will be a new thing not fashioned with words of this world. It will be part of '*a mysterious, personal communication without images, without any mediation between God and the soul*': it will be the Holy Spirit's revelation to man.

It will be a revelation of eternal, supernatural light, disclosing to man the Father's face, the Son's face, the Spirit's face.

It will be the anticipation of Paradise, a proof of the existence of the transcendent God and man's ability to communicate with Him now that he has become a sharer in the divine life, which is eternal life.

Moses had an 'experience' of it in front of the burning bush when God revealed His name: 'I Am who I Am' (Ex 3:14).

Elijah 'felt' it when, after his trial in the wilderness, God revealed Himself on Horeb in the sound of a gentle breeze (1 K 19:12).

The psalmist informs us of God's presence when he exclaims:

> My soul thirsts for God,
> the God of life;
> when shall I go to see
> the face of God?
>
> (Ps 42:2)

and again:

> Yes, with you is the fountain of life,
> by your light we see the light.
>
> (Ps 36:9)

and again, when he is seized by this living Presence and sees his soul's destiny:

> Yahweh, my heart has no lofty ambitions,
> my eyes do not look too high.

I am not concerned with great affairs
or marvels beyond my scope.
Enough for me to keep my soul tranquil and quiet
like a child in its mother's arms,
as content as a child that has been weaned.

(Ps 131:1–2)

The person whose contemplation is his life does not need many words to pray.

He needs one word, at the most two . . . I am not trying to make some sort of joke: his one word of prayer will be enough to sum up everything he wishes to say once his whole life, in its deepest intimacy, has been transformed into prayer.

Let me explain.

Because man's prayer on earth is a tension between God's greatness and man's smallness, between the abyss of the Absolute and the abyss of our nothingness, between the incommunicability of the divine Transcendence and the possessed irrationality of sin, man feels the need to cast his prayer up like a flaming arrow towards the divine Mystery or down into the abyss of sin, the expression of his deepest wretchedness.

He therefore feels urged both to cry his thirst for the Almighty with a word which is the name of God and to remind himself of the state of his soul which is 'sin'.

He needs only these two words which he forges into steel darts that seek to pierce the Cloud of God's Unknowing, thereby expressing all the insatiability of his prayer.

God,

Sin, the English mystics used to say.

Kyrie eleison, pomiliu Gospodi, say the Greeks and Russians in the long litanies so typical of their liturgy.

The Latins more often express this drama of love in other ways:

Jesus, I love You,
have mercy on me.

And it is certainly magnificent to remain there, one's whole soul poised between those two phrases, with no other wish than to throw oneself towards the Cloud of Unknowing and pierce it with the sheer force of one's love; than to throw oneself towards the Cloud which conceals God in His naked Being and which the soul seeks in the darkness of faith without considering itself and without distractions from external things.

Nothing can be more profitable than this loving effort on the soul's part sharpened to one word of prayer.

Nothing is more useful for the person concerned and his loved ones, for the living and dead, for the whole Church.

Nothing is more definitive for people during their earthly pilgrimage, nothing better sums up their 'contemplation on the road'.

The person who has reached this position needs only continue without deviating to right or left. He knows that 'what is to come must come thence'.

When St Thomas, at the completion of his work on the *Summa*, had a momentary experience in prayer of God's Transcendence concealed in the Cloud of Unknowing, he cried out in ecstasy: 'Everything I have written is but straw.'

Not that straw is useless, and well he knew it!

Without it, without the long stem, how can the ear on top reach up to open itself to the action of God's sun?

Theology, culture, philosophy, science are the human stem slowly bearing the ear of our soul towards the warmth of the divine sun.

But once the ear lies in the sun and begins to open with the approach of autumn, the stem becomes straw because its work is finished and the soul needs nothing but sun before being harvested into God's eternal granary.

Chapter Twenty-One

GOD'S LOVE IN US

When someone on earth has reached the state of contemplation, lives contemplation, he is finally at peace, like a child on its mother's breast: 'My soul is tranquil and quiet like a child in its mother's arms' (Ps 131:2).

Magnetized by God's love, the rocket of his soul, like an astronaut's space-craft, has broken the sound-barrier (no longer needs a lot of words to explain itself), snapped the thread of gravity which held it down to itself (no longer needs meditation) and gone into orbit like a tiny planet round God's sun.

He can say with the psalmist: 'I am as content as a child that has been weaned' (Ps 131:2).

The first proof that someone has gone into orbit round God is that he no longer feels he himself is the *centre of the universe* – which is the real nature of sin – but feels and vividly understands that God is the centre of everything. This might seem easy, but . . . how much effort goes into reaching this understanding!

Now at last God bears him, leads him by 'ways which are not our ways', draws him into the whirlpool of charity, prepares him for an ever deeper union with Himself, for that eternal possession of Himself which is the goal of our human-divine destiny.

The soul in orbit round God begins to realize that there is another stability than the kind known and experienced on earth, another fulness, another dimension. Above all, another 'peace'.

The peace promised by Jesus:

'my own peace I give you,
a peace the world cannot give.'

(Jn 14:27)

And this peace communicates to the soul such a sense of 'new life', such a 'chaste joy' despite the tremendous trials of the spatial flight round God, such a richness of hope in 'what is to come' despite the crosses of every day, that the soul can exclaim with St Francis:

So great is the good that even pain is a delight.

That is quite something!

At bottom, what is the real difficulty in living on earth?

Is it not surmounting pain, fear, illness, old age, death? Well, if we have found something which enables us to overcome these negative aspects of our earthly pilgrimage, which helps us to smile through our tears, to hope even as we slowly decline, to be certain of life even in death, we have experienced in ourselves the victory brought by Christ.

'I have conquered the world.'

(Jn 16:33)

Christ's victory is love bestowed on us in its divine dimension which is called 'charity'. If we are in charity God is in us, and charity is the fruit of contemplation as love is the fruit of knowledge.

Revealing Himself to us in contemplation, God communicates charity, that is, His love, and by living this love of His we live in Him and share in His 'victory' during our struggle on earth, just as we shall share in the beatific possession of Him 'above', when every struggle will be at an end.

It is said that 'love conquers everything' – *omnia vincit amor*. And it is true.

Yes, love conquers everything, always.

It conquers even the most horrible things.

Like Jesus's life.

Is it not horrible to be born in a stable a few hours after the citizens of Bethlehem had refused to give lodging to His mother who was near her time and was looking for a minimum of warmth because otherwise she ran the risk of seeing her child die with cold in the night?

Well, Mary's and Joseph's love and willingness to put up with these horrible things gave the world the 'Christmas Story' which has made the hardest hearts dissolve in tears and which is the irreplaceable masterpiece and the authentic account of God's infinity and omnipotence enclosed in the tiny body of a baby at the mercy of history.

Is it not horrible, men's treatment of Jesus during His life and in His death? Is Calvary not horrible?

Well, Jesus's love transformed the horror of it into sublimity. His acceptance, His humility, His meekness changed the aspect of things, and the most obscene chapter in history becomes the most beautiful, the most tender, the most grandiose, the most exemplary, the most alluring, in which a dying God smiles on man who is killing Him and pardons him.

Only love, of all things in heaven and on earth, has such transforming, sublimating, redeeming, enriching, life-giving power!

Love is superior to everything else, can substitute for everything else, by touching what man on earth cannot attain: *perfection*. As St Paul says: 'Charity is the bond which makes us perfect' (Col 3:14, Knox).

Having convinced myself of the primacy of charity, having become aware that in touching charity I am touching God, that in living charity I am living God in me, I must this evening, before finishing my meditation, look at tomorrow to subject it to this light and live it out under the inspiration of this synthesis of love. Basically I must do what Jesus – who brought God's love to earth and communicated it to us – would do in my position. I must remember that the opportunities I shall have to suffer, to pardon, to accept are treasures not to be lost through distraction and values that I must make my own as a worthy response to God's plan in creation.

My life is worth living if I can learn to transform everything that happens to me into love, in imitation of Jesus: because *love is for living.*

When I meet a brother of mine who has caused me great pain in the past by viciously calumniating me, I shall love him, and in loving him I shall transform the evil done to me into good: because *love is for living.*

When I have to live with people who do not see things the way I see them, who say they are enemies of my faith, I shall love them, and in loving them I shall sow the seeds of future dialogue in my heart and theirs: because *love is for living.*

When I go into a shop to buy something for myself – clothes, food, or whatever it may be – I shall think of my brothers who are poorer than I am, of the hungry and the naked, and I shall use this thought to govern my purchases, trying out of love to be tight with myself and generous with them: because *love is for living.*

When I see time's destructive traces in my body and the approach of old age, I shall try to love even more in order to transform the coldest season of life into a total gift of myself in preparation for the imminent holocaust: because *love is for living.*

When I see the evening of my life, or, on the tarmac in a car accident, in the agony of a fatal illness, in the ward of a geriatric hospital, feel the end coming, I shall reach out again for love, striving to accept in joy whatever fate God has had in store for me: because *love is for living.*

Yes, love is God in me, and if I am in love I am in God, that is, in life, in grace: a sharer in God's being.

No one has seen this so clearly and expressed it so forcibly as St Paul:

> If I have all the eloquence of men or of angels, but speak without love, I am simply a gong booming or a cymbal clashing. If I have the gift of prophecy, understanding all the mysteries there are, and knowing everything, and if I have faith in all its fulness, to move mountains, but without love, then I am nothing at all. If I give away all that I possess, piece by piece, and if I even let them take my body to burn it, but am without love, it will do me no good whatever.
>
> Love is always patient and kind; it is never jealous; love is never boastful or conceited; it is never rude or selfish; it does not take offence, and is not resentful. Love takes no pleasure in other people's sins but delights in the truth; it is always ready to excuse, to trust, to hope, and to endure whatever comes.
>
> (1 Co 13:1–7)

Could any words be clearer?

If charity is God in me, why look for God any further than myself?

And if He is in me as love, why do I change or disfigure His face with acts or values which are not love?

PART IV

We are now approaching the end of our road.

We have meditated on the various degrees of human love and the mysterious way in which charity, which is the divine dimension of love, takes hold of us.

We are left with three meditations which, though very simple, are vitally important because they concern Jesus's deepest desire, which He Himself defined as '*His commandment*'.

Chapter Twenty-Two

THE NEW COMMANDMENT

The ancients were right when they said that there was nothing new under the sun, because they had as yet no knowledge of the only new thing that could happen, the only Person capable of producing something new: Jesus.

Jesus contradicted the old adage because He was something new under the sun, the only new thing there could be.

There was even something new in love!

In olden times it was said: 'You shall love your neighbour as yourself', and that was perfectly logical. Love being the proper response to a value and men being of equal value, it was right to love others as oneself, even at great cost to oneself.

Theoretically it is obvious. Your skin is as important as mine, I must love the two equally; your hunger is as important as mine, I must satisfy it with the same bread; your nakedness is as regrettable as mine, I must prevent it with the same degree of concern. And so on.

To get this far is no mean feat, and the difficulty in putting it into practice betrays the imbalance and disorder of sin in us; it is the proof that we are ill, that our priorities are fundamentally wrong, because otherwise the equation 'love for you = love for myself' would be almost automatically put into practice.

The person who loves himself and not others, who feeds himself and not others, who clothes himself and not others is a 'mistake', an 'aberration', and he must correct himself if he wishes to enter the Kingdom, which is a Kingdom of Truth. It is impossible to gain entrance to the Kingdom of God, which means equality, with inequality in one's mind, heart or will.

We have a lifetime in which to correct the error – with the help of grace – and if we have not managed it here we shall continue to try hereafter. One way or another, the books must be in order before the Master arrives to inspect them.

And this particular Master is not easily satisfied in matters of love!

He seems to be in such a hurry!

Jesus reveals to the people of the old Law, the fulfilment of which was already very difficult because of sin, another type of love which He jealously defines as 'His commandment'. This new commandment is not human but divine, and it expresses in all its splendour the height of perfection to which Jesus wishes to lead us:

'You also must love one another just as I have loved you.'
(Jn 13:34)

It was already difficult to establish equality; Jesus went further.

'Love as I have loved, that is, to the ultimate sacrifice, to the total gift of yourself.'

The past had spent all its time establishing justice in human relationships: one for me and one for you, a slap in the face for me and a slap in the face for you, an eye for an eye and a tooth for a tooth. Jesus comes on the scene and shouts: 'But *I* tell you!'

What does He tell us?

> 'Love your enemies, do good to those who hate you, bless those who curse you, pray for those who treat you badly. To the man who slaps you on the cheek, present the other cheek too; to the man who takes your cloak from you, do not refuse your tunic. Give to everyone who asks you, and do not ask for your property back from the man who robs you.'
> (Lk 6:27–30)

No, humanity did not have to wait for Gandhi to discover non-violence! But perhaps the human race – mitred gorillas, as Merton called them – was not ready for it.

Today Jesus would have been condemned as a proponent of man's right to conscientious objection.

It is always too early for a prophet to say certain things; always too late at death to put Jesus's teaching into practice if, out of laziness or cowardice, we have not done so already.

The Gospel should be prohibited: it should be a banned book in civilized countries, especially those of established bourgeois culture. It is an uncomfortable book for pagans and an even more uncomfortable one for Christians. It denounces us continually, its tremendous words pronounce judgement on the centuries. Theologians will expatiate on the justice of war, saints will preach crusades, Christians will bear arms as readily as they bear the cross and will fight as if it were cardboard puppets they were running through.

Mystery of contradiction! Undisputed sign of our littleness! Evident testimony of the infinite superiority of the Gospel over poor human history! Astronomical distance between the word of God and man's morality! But . . . wait a moment: I have the impression there is something new under the sun . . .

Giovanni Papini made a sort of prophecy in his old age. He suggested that each year of Jesus's life corresponded to a century of Church history. This would mean that we have entered our twenty-first year, the year of our majority.

Perhaps we have; the Second Vatican Council is a sign of it.

And perhaps a few Christians are beginning to accept proper responsibility and take Jesus's words seriously:

> 'To the man who slaps you on one cheek, present the other cheek too; to the man who takes your cloak from you, do not refuse your tunic.'
>
> (Lk 6:29)

Now that is not child's play! Who is really capable of taking

Jesus's words seriously? Who really believes this kind of teaching? It is too easy to think: 'Well, what He really meant by this was . . .' or 'taken metaphorically this would mean . . .' And because we cannot take Jesus literally, we have managed in the space of thirty years two world wars that have bled Europe with weapons blessed by the various religions!

Perhaps we needed the discovery of atomic energy and the apocalypse that would ensue if nuclear war broke out before we began to wonder whether, after all . . . *even a war of defence would be unjustifiable because of the frightful consequences even of defence.*

In other words, Jesus was right.

But Jesus's teaching applies equally in such relatively minor incidents as a blow in the face and a stolen cloak! Is the peace which results from yielding to violence on the part of a brother not worth more than the cloak?

Do the advantages that accrue from pardoning his use of violence and doing without law-courts and lawyers not outweigh the value of the tunic? I know that it is difficult to talk like this because we suffer from a surfeit not of 'love' but of 'justice', while Jesus suffers from love and wishes to win the battle of justice with love.

We are trying to reconcile two different positions, and this is probably why, after centuries of disquisitions on morality, we have forged a moral theology which leaves us bewildered and in which few people still really believe.

It is probably why there is a shindy whenever conscientious objection makes the news. The sad thing is that young men who refuse to bear arms are imprisoned. I confess that I fail to follow the reasoning here, and in this specific case I should merely repeat the Council's wise words:

> It seems right that laws make humane provisions for the case of those who for reasons of conscience refuse to bear arms.
> (*Gaudium et Spes* 79)

We should lose nothing by forming young conscientious objectors into 'peace corps' to reconstruct villages destroyed in earthquakes, give schooling to illiterate people, bring assistance to lepers or the starving. In peace-time there is no problem. But in war? It is better to say nothing here for fear of infuriating the 'moderates', the defenders of established order, nationalist fanatics. But one tiny plea I shall make. Members of government, think twice before declaring war. That is all I ask: think twice!

It could be that *not* declaring war is the better solution. Take extreme care.

You might entrust an atomic bomb to a pilot who drops it in the middle of the sea without a detonator; or you might give bayonets to youngsters who use them to cut flowers to welcome the arriving enemy: 'please come in, won't you? there's coffee ready.'

You will no doubt call me a defeatist.

I suppose it is a question of deciding whether the young Austrian who preferred to be condemned to death by a military tribunal rather than take up arms with Hitler was a martyr or a traitor.

It is a question of deciding whether the few voices raised against Mussolini in protest at his invasion of Ethiopia were more Christian than the screams of the masses intoxicated by an undiscriminating nationalism and blinded by colossal historical ignorance.

It is a question of deciding whether those who in Algeria refused to obey orders to torture prisoners in the service of victory at any price were defeatists or Christians.

In short, it is a question of deciding whether someone has the right to trample on my conscience merely because he is in charge, whether the State can force me to take part in its schemes . . . when they are evil.

Perhaps as never before the moment has come in which we shall see blossoming in a soil ploughed by the atrocious suffering of thousands of wars the flower of man's conscience able to stand firm not only in defence of belief in Christ, as in times past, but – and this would be new – in defence of belief in man.

I am wasting time, however, talking about things that will never happen: there will not be any real wars again.

I must talk instead to those who believe in Jesus, who look for the happiness of peace – 'happy the peacemakers: they shall be called sons of God' (Mt 5:9) – who have no need to puff their chests out and strike their neighbour in the face, who know they are small and weak, in short, to the poor, and I have something very important to say.

Do you want to know the secret of true happiness? of deep and genuine peace?

Do you want to solve at a blow all your difficulties in relations with your neighbour, bring all polemic to an end, avoid all dissension?

Well, decide here and now to love things and men as Jesus loved them, that is, to the point of self-sacrifice.

Don't bother with the book-keeping of love; love without keeping accounts.

If you know someone who is decent and likeable, love him, but if someone else is very *un*likeable, love him just the same.

If someone greets you and smiles, greet him and smile back, but if someone else treads on your feet, smile just the same. If someone does you a good turn, thank the Lord for it, but if someone else slanders you, persecutes you, curses you, strikes you, thank him and carry on.

Do not say: 'I'm right, he's wrong.' Say: 'I must love him as myself.' This is the kind of love Jesus taught: a love which transforms, vivifies, enriches, brings peace.

Love is not an easy thing, and I should like to say to those who decide to tread this path of love: 'take courage and stand firm; be well prepared and go with the help of grace, because the journey is long and you will have shed blood before the end of it. You'll be lucky to get there the minute before you die.'

Every day I beg the Lord to grant me one grace in particular: to love and learn to love as He has done!

To love as Jesus did at Bethlehem when He fled into exile rather than use His divine omnipotence to kill Herod.

To love as Jesus did at Nazareth, where He lived as the last of men without appealing to His incarnate and hidden divinity.

To love as Jesus did at the sight of the hungry, shepherdless crowd, with a greater determination to solve the problem with sacrifice than with miracles and glory.

To love as Jesus did in Gethsemane when for our sake He endured the frightful agony of His loneliness and the Father's condemnation.

To love as Jesus did before the Sanhedrin when, with His silence and His acceptance of condemnation and rejection, He gave us the exact measure of His power of love.

To love as Jesus did on Calvary, when, at the height of His passion and already in the last throes of death, He prayed His last prayer to Heaven: 'Father, forgive them.'

This is the supreme life, and Jesus lived it in all His splendour and superhuman power.

He loved without setting a limit.

And He invites us to do the same; nothing else matters so much as this.

Why do we wrap ourselves up in a juridical and narrow Christianity, occupy our minds with an exasperating casuistry which no longer convinces anyone, instead of throwing ourselves down towards men with only love in our hearts?

Why, after Jesus's mission on earth, do we insist on the defence of justice when justice alone is not able to save us?

We have the *right* but not the *duty* to defend ourselves, and we can very well waive it as an offering to love, pardon, peace, dialogue with men.

No?

Oh, how I wish the Church born from the Council will be a

Church concerned less with the length of girls' skirts and more with the problems posed by love in the world; a Church capable of giving more than of receiving, a Church which, for love of men, can renounce its own rights and privileges, a Church which dispenses with self-defence and travels the road of its exile as small and poor as Jesus's family on their flight to Egypt.

Chapter Twenty-Three

THE FIRE OF PURGATORY

If the Master should knock on my door tonight and tell me that my earthly pilgrimage is at an end, I feel that on balance I should not be consigned to hell.

Why?

Because neither God nor myself wishes it, He for love of me, I for love of Him. Despite immense evil in me, I feel, in the strength of His love, the desire to be with Him, and this seems to me to be quite normal between friends. I know sin as ignorance and even more so as weakness, but I have never felt 'opposed' to God. I cannot even visualize – thanks to His grace – the 'sin against the Holy Spirit'; I cannot imagine how someone could impugn the known truth. Theologians discuss it at length, but their subtleties do not impress me.

I was saying, then, that if I died today, I should not on balance be condemned to an eternity of torment. But then neither should I be admitted to Heaven! I am not ready for it. I felt that very, very keenly under the rock when I had denied Kadà my blanket, and I still feel it today, Good Friday, as I meditate on our Lord's passion. Yes, I am afraid to suffer for others, I tremble before the cold blade of charity.

And so? If I am not to go to hell and Heaven is too good for me, where shall I go?

I must stay here, I cannot pass beyond, and purgatory is certainly this side of the eternal watershed.

I am not a theologian, but even theologians know little about purgatory. It is a passing place or state or condition in which those not yet ready for the Kingdom of Perfect Love pray and suffer and so prepare themselves for the day when they will be admitted to the eternal banquet.

I imagine purgatory to be like the large cupboard where my grandmother put medlars to ripen. Please forgive this curious comparison. When I was young, I occasionally stayed at my grandmother's house, which was a farm in the Langhe hills of Piedmont, and I remember my grandmother putting the medlars which were still not ripe by the autumn into this cupboard, amongst the straw. 'Everything comes to him who waits.' A spiritual fruit that has failed to ripen under the sun of God's charity will ripen in the cupboard.

The comparison is perhaps a good one because the cupboard is part of the house.

I should not like to offend anyone's sensibilities, and so I say this from a purely personal point of view, but I think of purgatory as being this side of eternity and therefore still tied to my home. I think of the souls of the dead completing their period of expiation near where they lived, perhaps even in their homes themselves. If I can make a request at the moment of death, I know what I shall ask: 'Send me to the stretch of desert between Tit and Silet', where I had the deepest insight into the need for perfect love at the earliest possible moment.

And the fire? Ah, I thought that question would come.

Well, I think there is fire but not of a material kind. Many times as a boy, especially in the sacristies of mountain churches, I have seen the souls in purgatory wrapped in flames – real flames – with fiery tongues higher than the highest heads there. It is natural for artists to think and paint in this way: how else could one depict the spiritual fire of purgatory? In the Middle Ages, and since, the flames are always shown as real ones, simply because it is easier that way.

Everyone, however, knows that real fire would damage the body . . . and the body is not in purgatory but in the cemetery, like a piece of cast-off clothing.

To touch my soul another type of fire is necessary: charity, which I rejected on earth, or at least did not fully accept. Now that I have my back to the wall, I cannot escape it any longer, I must accept it. I cannot put it off any more.

The fire of charity, that is, this supernatural kind of love, will attack my soul as flames attack wood. My soul will writhe, sizzle and smoke like green wood, but it will burn in the end. Not a single fibre shall escape, all must be consumed by that divine love.

How long will this take? It will go on until the work is done. Some people will need no more than a few days, others thousands of years; the important thing is that the purification must be completed. All this will take place while a sort of film of our lives is screened before our eyes.

There is more than enough there. When I think that I shall have to relive in slow motion certain episodes in my life which I did not subject to the flames of love but constructed on egoism, falsehood, cowardice and pride, and all the time with the fire of charity in my veins, I can assure you that it comes home to me what a serious, deadly serious, business it will be. Imagine me arriving in purgatory wearing a mask put together with years of patience and skill which I have never dared or been able to remove for fear of revealing myself as I really am to God and men.

When the fire of love licks up at it, gets beneath it and burns it off my soul, it will, I have no doubt, prove an agonizing experience. And what will happen when the fire starts to burn the property to which I was clinging so firmly: a blanket perhaps, or a piece of meat I took first from the plate when Jesus would have wanted me to be last?

No, there is no need for a coal fire to burn my soul: the fire of failed responsibility, of injustices, of thefts, of lies, of help denied to someone who needed me, of love not lived with those who were my brothers, is more than sufficient.

Not very much, you say? Well, that is only a part of it, the part we can imagine by the standards of earthly justice. True justice, measured on God's justice, on the Transcendence of the Absolute, appalled St John of the Cross when he was undergoing the terrors of the dark night of the soul.

Yes, the fire of purgatory is charity, that is, the highest degree of love in its supernatural state.

It is the fire which consumed Jesus's sacrifice on Calvary, the fire which burned the saints with inextinguishable love, the fire which led the martyrs to martyrdom and baptized them if they were not already baptized, giving them access to the Kingdom. We shall not escape this fire, nothing we do can avert it.

On the other hand I should not wish to escape it. I know it will hurt, but I also know that I have to go through it.

I have no desire to continue for all eternity the ups and downs of my sensibility, the perennial resistance to the fire of love. I am green wood, and I do not wish to enter Paradise still green. I want to burn in purgatory and then be finished with it.

I want to go where Jesus went, to feel what He felt in His divine heart. I shall suffer, I know, but there is no other way, and in any case God's power will be there beside me to bring me assistance.

Here and now I accept that fire which will smelt from me and my earthly slag the hidden metal of my person, willed by God but obscured by sin.

I shall be given a new face, the face that God saw when He drew me from the primeval chaos and that Satan sullied with his slaver.

I shall emerge a child, God's child for ever.

And since purgatory is this side of the eternal watershed, the only appropriate course for me is to combine it with my life on earth, pretend I am already there, apply the fire of charity to myself a little at a time but courageously, start to burn out the clinkers, at least the biggest and most obvious ones.

What I do here I shall not need to do hereafter: I have

therefore gained. I must accept the asceticism my life imposes on me, the sufferings and trials I experience on the road, the tedium and troubles of human society, the inconveniences and inevitable illnesses as precious and providential opportunities for advance payment.

I say 'opportunities', because there is more to paying than suffering. One must suffer with love, with patience, otherwise it is useless. We were saved not by the scourges on Jesus's flesh but by the love with which He accepted them.

We were redeemed not by His road to Calvary but by the patience, mercy, obedience with which He trod it.

In short, the Redemption renewed the world by Jesus's charity. Charity is the essence of Christianity. Yes, we can state with absolute certainty that *love is for living*.

And if we can transform every moment of our existence into an act of love, all our problems will be resolved. The fire of purgatory is love, and if we wish to avoid purgatory, we must accept its fire on earth.

Chapter Twenty-Four

COME, LORD!

The only course open to us now is to wait.

Whatever can or will happen belongs not to us but to Christ.

And we have one great hope, which should sustain us beyond all our poor human efforts. On Calvary Jesus uttered this astounding phrase in reply to the Good Thief: 'Indeed I promise you, today you will be with me in paradise' (Lk 23:43).

Today . . . today . . . today . . . today!

This word echoes in my soul's ear like a message of hope, a shout of joy.

Today!

What about all our own calculations?

And I talked about thousands of years to be spent in purgatory!

It is possible – indeed certain – that the Good Thief was more prepared than I am to enter the Kingdom of Perfect Love, because of my incurable egoism, but . . .

No, weighing the pros and cons is an earthly not a heavenly activity, it belongs to justice not to the gratuity of love.

No, eternity is not the sum of all possible centuries, infinity is not a succession of spatial units, and grace is not the fruit or reward of a sufficient amount of effort on man's part. Eternity is eternity, infinity infinity, and grace grace, that is, gratuitous, absolutely gratuitous.

It is a mystery, and we must accept it in its totality if we do not wish to lose our way in the darkness of the human mind.

There have been saints who felt the fire of hell at their feet all their lives and could talk of nothing else; others preferred not to emphasize it because they could think of nothing but the resplendent fire of the divine mercy.

In His divine teaching Jesus Himself seems to have taken care not to be too precise, limiting Himself to stressing the essential, what we need to know and should not forget.

There is nothing to be done, therefore. We must not ask too many questions on the how and how much of purgatory, otherwise we shall oblige the Divine Master to answer us as He answered the over-curious apostles: 'As for that day and hour, nobody knows it, neither the angels in heaven, nor the Son, no one but the Father only' (Mt 24:36).

What we *do* know from Jesus's clear teaching is this: 'Stay awake and stand ready' (Mt 24:42, 44); 'be like men waiting for their master to return from the wedding feast, ready to open the door as soon as he comes and knocks' (Lk 12:36).

In the Gospel and in the thought of St John and St Paul who were Jesus's most passionate and accurate interpreters in the first Christian communities, there was a typical feature: the profound and dramatic sense of 'expectation', the expectation of an extraordinary event which would renew the face of the earth: 'Now I am making the whole of creation new' (Rv 21:5), and a surprise even for the most vigilant: 'I shall come to you like a thief' (Rv 3:3), like 'lightning flashing from one part of heaven to the other' (Lk 17:24).

Apart from the exaggeration of a number of early Christians who interpreted 'the expectation' as Christ's imminent return, a 'parousia' soon to take place, because of the impatience of their love, such a deeply evangelical attitude seems to me to be the most appropriate and the truest for all who wish to enter into the spirit of the things of God and live on this earth as a preparation for the eternal season of heaven.

The Christian life is an expectation, a waiting for something, a continual movement from one point to another.

When we pray, we are waiting for something. When we act, we are waiting for something.

What is perfect if not a tireless and endless motion from the limited to the Infinite, from man to God?

It is expectation.

And expectation is primarily an awareness that things do not depend on us.

This is vital because it gives us access to true humility, to truth. Things do not depend on us, the result does not depend on us, salvation does not depend on us.

'When I open, nobody can close, and when I close, nobody can open', says Christ in the Apocalypse (Rv 3:7).

It was the most dramatic element in the conversion of St Paul, who was deeply Hebrew and a profound believer in the Law.

Salvation comes not from the law and efforts to observe it but from God's gratuitous love.

We are justified not by our works but by faith and the promise.

This affects the balance of the entire God-man relationship, and we have to be very small and helpless in the Father's arms if we do not wish to suffer from giddiness.

Salvation, then, is not my doing.

Just as something dramatic had to happen if the Israelites were to cross the Reed Sea dryshod, so some new event which does not depend on me must take place in my soul as I strain towards love. I shall not be the one to stand on my grave and shout, 'Rise up': Christ will, no one else.

This, I think, brings me to the end of this book, and in order to conclude these meditations with a modicum of order I should like to invoke the help of our Lady, who of all creatures saw things clearly because of all creatures she was the smallest and the humblest.

You will remember that it all began one day in a small piece of desert in the solitude of the Sahara, when I dreamt I was being crushed by a great mass of granite under which I had gone to sleep.

I stood condemned at God's judgement-seat, and I was condemned for lack of love: nothing else.

A blanket withheld from a poor man sent me on my way to purgatory, and there I realized that to leave purgatory I should have to perform some act of perfect love, that is, an act of the same kind as Jesus's love.

I felt it was beyond me.

Many years have passed since then, and yesterday, Good Friday, meditating on Jesus's passion, I found myself in the same position as that time beneath the rock.

I cannot love perfectly, I have not the strength to follow Jesus to Calvary.

Should I ever feel I could?

If I thought I had the strength to, should I not be even worse than I am?

That is the truth I have finally discovered in my long and hard religious experience.

If my salvation depended on me, I should never be saved!

Something must happen first: a flash of lightning, a visit from someone, an event.

And I shall never be able to discover it, anticipate it, foresee it!

I must wait, praying, loving, weeping, beseeching.

This is all man can do on earth and in purgatory.

God, who is God of the impossible, will come unexpectedly and touching my soul will make me capable of following Him wherever He has decided to lead me like the Good Thief on that first Good Friday.

And by the time I discover I am capable, I shall already be beyond death and I shall have no time to admire myself like Narcissus and therefore destroy in pride the gratuity of the grace which has produced in me the power to love as Jesus loved.

In *The Dialogue of the Carmelites*, Bernanos depicts two very different nuns. One represents tenacity, strength, will-power; the other smallness and weakness.

In death it is the latter who wins through, managing to sing as she mounts the guillotine.

The other will always be afraid of death – even in her bed.

On the other hand, if we accept the thesis of victorious weakness, of the thief who gains Paradise at the last moment, of the person whose whole life is prayer and in some sense inactivity, do we not run the risk of quietism, of the lack of human commitment, of idleness and inaction?

If we accept the thesis that it is faith which justifies and not our effort and apostolate, are we not raking up the age-old dispute that has so painfully divided Christians?

No, not at all, if we give this approach its proper value, which the Church in its divine balance has always done, supported as it is by the Spirit of God.

Jesus's words are always normative in the search for truth:

> 'See that you are dressed for action and have your lamps lit. Be like men waiting for their master to return from the wedding feast, ready to open the door as soon as he comes and knocks. Happy those servants whom the master finds awake when he comes.'
>
> (Lk 12:35–7a)

Attentive, dynamic, virile and passionate vigilance is all here.

To be quite ready the servant does not even sit down for fear of dozing off.

Matthew records the same words:

> 'What sort of servant, then, is faithful and wise enough for the master to place him over his household to give them their food at the proper time? Happy that servant if his master's arrival finds him at this employment.'
>
> (Mt 24:45–6)

That is the real significance of waiting: 'the master will find him at this employment'.

Criticism of the mystical life, of prayer, of contemplation is shown to be totally unfounded where Matthew 24:46 is verified:

> 'the master will find him at this employment.'

Teilhard de Chardin says that God's will is on the point of my effort, on the point of my pencil, on the point of my plough – powerful imagery to express the fact that man must act, that the Christian must exert himself to the full.

God gives Himself to the person who acts and acts as if he were immobile. God communicates Himself to the person who looks for Him knowing that the search would be in vain if God were not looking for him at the same time. St Ignatius, who was a great contemplative, summed up the problem as follows:

> 'Act as if everything depended on you and wait as if everything depended on God.'

And Don Bosco, who combined authentic mysticism and action to a remarkable degree, displayed his supernatural equilibrium when, tired of running about after ministers, he went to sleep in their antechambers. This response to the difficulties of conversation with the important ones of the world seems to me to be the clearest sign of Don Bosco's contemplative soul totally surrendered to the Father. And it also seems to me to be the clearest indication for us Christians today that having to live in the spirit of the Council which God's infinite Providence bestowed on His ever youthful, fresh and fertile Church we run the risk – as Paul VI put it so aptly – of losing our sense of balance in the interplay of opposing forces.

Action or thought?
Prayer or evangelization?
Speech or witness?
I think we have already given the answer.

May the strong wind of the Spirit, which blew so vigorously through the Church at the Council, bring us the divine power, and may God guide us with sweetness and strength on the roads of the modern world.